STARK COUNTY'S SPORTS

ICONS

& HIGH SCHOOL GREATS

FOREWORD BY
JIM TRESSEL

ICONS

ICONS

STARK COUNTY'S SPORTS

ICONS

& HIGH SCHOOL GREATS

ICONS

ICONS

THE CANTON
REPOSITORY

Printed and bound in the United States of America.

ISBN: 978-0-692-72895-6

10 9 8 7 6 5 4 3 2 1

THE CANTON REPOSITORY
CantonRep.com

THE CANTON REPOSITORY | GATEHOUSE OHIO MEDIA
500 MARKET AVENUE S, CANTON, OHIO 44702
(330) 580-8300 | CANTONREP.COM

COVER DESIGN: JESS BENNETT
BOOK DESIGN: JESS BENNETT, KELSEY REINHART & MURPHY REDMOND

CONTRIBUTORS:
MICHAEL BALASH, CHRIS BEAVEN, JULIE BOTOS, STEVE DOERSCHUK, SCOTT HECKEL, CLIFF HICKMAN, MIKE POPOVICH, TODD PORTER, BOB ROSSITER, JOE SCALZO, RAY STEWART, JIM THOMAS, JOSH WEIR

CONTENTS

FOREWORD

By Jim Tressel

I WAS ONLY 3 YEARS OLD WHEN I CAME TO STARK COUNTY. I WAS 5 WHEN WE LEFT. THOSE AREN'T EXACTLY THE FORMATIVE YEARS FOR A YOUNG FELLOW. I WOULD, HOWEVER, SPEND A CAREER COMING TO STARK COUNTY AND GETTING TO KNOW SOME OF THE BEST OF THE BEST HIGH SCHOOL FOOTBALL PLAYERS TO EVER COME OUT OF THERE.

My dad, Lee Tressel, was Massillon's football coach in 1956 and 1957. He went 16-3 in those two seasons, and Dad always spoke highly of Massillon as I grew up. I remember going back to Massillon when my dad was the head coach at Baldwin-Wallace and he would recruit there. We'd go back to see old friends of ours, the Baslers (Maury and Katie were always kind people). Then I recruited there when I was a coach. My college roommate was Tom Cardinal. When my dad would get a kid from Massillon, he knew he was getting someone who would make a difference. My dad took great pride in having been at Massillon.

As I look at these Stark County icons, I know all of the names. I coached some of them (Mike Doss and Chris Spielman), I coached against others (Todd Blackledge tore us up one Saturday when I was at Syracuse).

Football was important to this whole region. If you look at everything from Western Pennsylvania to Northeast Ohio, this region was the epicenter of the Industrial Revolution, and all that immigration to this area really spurred growth. My take on why football was so important here is you take all those different ethnic groups that came to this region, and they're thousands of miles from home. They didn't have anybody here so they created these tight-knit communities. They had to have competition to build communities, and that became football. It started with high school football, and then it became college football, semi-pro ball and then professional football. It became part of the culture from Pennsylvania to Ohio.

Now take a look at the 150-mile stretch from Pittsburgh to Cleveland. Draw a circle around that area and you've got Akron, Canton, Massillon, Cleveland, Youngstown. Professionally, you have the Browns and Steelers, the Canton Bulldogs were in there, Akron had a team, Buffalo isn't that far away, neither is Detroit. Sports became a huge part of the American culture. You had a lot of big, strong people who immigrated here. Guys like Jim Houston and Larry Csonka were the mold for a lot of people. I'm sure in other parts of the country, you had big, strong people who took to other things. I guess it would be like hockey in Canada.

You become what you're around. Like I said, those people came here and created tight-knit communities because they didn't have family and friends around here. They stayed in their communities, and they took pride in their community. How do you take pride in it? No one measures one community against another by comparing restaurants. If you're from Massillon, you don't tell someone from Canton that you have a better restaurant than they do.

You measure it with high school football. It came down to how did your high school football team do?

So it is fitting that Paul Brown is at the top of this list. I do not think I ever had the opportunity to meet Paul Brown. I know Mike Brown pretty well. Paul Brown recruited my dad to Ohio State. He played spring football there in 1943. My dad graduated early from high school and enlisted in the U.S. Navy V-12 program, which assigned him to Baldwin-Wallace.

Dad had a real affinity for Paul Brown. He made the game a science. I call him the Thomas Edison of football. If there was a better way to do something, he would find it. He was constantly experimenting. When I was at Ohio State, I got copies of a lot of his old letters back to his players at Ohio State and even Massillon. He was meticulous.

You take guys like Chris Spielman and Mike Doss. Those two are cut from the same cloth. Any Stark County kid I ever coached, the game meant a lot to them. Stark County kids were highly competitive and they attached an importance to the game of football that helped raise your level. When I coached at Youngstown State, we had guys from Stark County who brought an edge to the team. That is something you can't really coach. When you brought a Stark County kid into your program, you knew their expectations were to be darn good, win and be the best.

My second year at Ohio State was Mike Doss' last season. His years at Ohio State had not been, team-wise, what he was used to. Doss was not going to leave Ohio State without being on a great team. He was an All-American twice. He could have left early, or he could have big-timed us in his final season. Mike was a team guy. He had the attitude that, "I don't care if this new coaching staff is any good or not, we're going to be good." That group of seniors were 6-6, 8-4 and 7-5 before the year we won the national title.

Those records are not why you come to Ohio State.

Mike decided in his heart that the 2002 team was going to be a championship team. We were going to be better than we were in 2001 simply because of an influx in talent from recruiting, but Mike decided we were going to be great. That's the trademark of a Stark County kid from Massillon or McKinley or Perry or North Canton, or wherever. Their legacy in the world was how did they do in the game of football? I don't know if it is quite as deep today. Stark County kids have it branded on their brain that their legacy is how they do as a team.

I was an assistant on Earle Bruce's staff when we were recruiting Chris Spielman. We were good in 1983, but Chris had an expectation that we were going to be better. On that team, we had Chris coming from the north, Cris Carter coming from the south, Tom Tupa was from Cleveland and William White from the northwest. All of those guys were freshman starters on the Rose Bowl team. Chris brought that Stark County expectation. He brought a seriousness. He was a relentless trainer. Our weight room is a piece of what it is now. Chris took that to a whole new level.

In practice the year Chris was a freshman, I remember the coaches having discussions about him. And it was, "This guy doesn't appear to be that fast or that strong, but he's going to make every tackle." Earle did a great job with Bob Tucker of figuring out that Chris Spielman just had a certain "something" that made him special. Of course, he made 20 tackles in the second half of his first game, and the rest is history.

Larry Kehres is another guy on this list. He put an exclamation point on excellence. A lot of times when you're so good for a period of time, jealousy or complacency sets in. Larry Kehres was great at Mount Union for 30 years. Again, that's a Stark County expectation.

I didn't know a lot of the guys who weren't football players, but I knew of them. I knew of Dave Wottle, the great runner. When I played baseball, I was a catcher, and everyone loved Thurman Munson. Stark County has produced a lot of very special players, athletes and coaches in many sports. But, really, everything you need to know about Stark County you can see by looking at the Pro Football Hall of Fame. How many other counties in the country can say they have five players in the Hall of Fame, built right in their backyard?

It would be neat to get about 10 or 20 people between the ages of 60 and 70 years old together to look at this list of icons, debate it and have them all vote. It would be neat to hear from the people who saw these people and hear the stories they have about them. A book like this makes those discussions all the more interesting because everyone has a memory or a story about these great athletes.

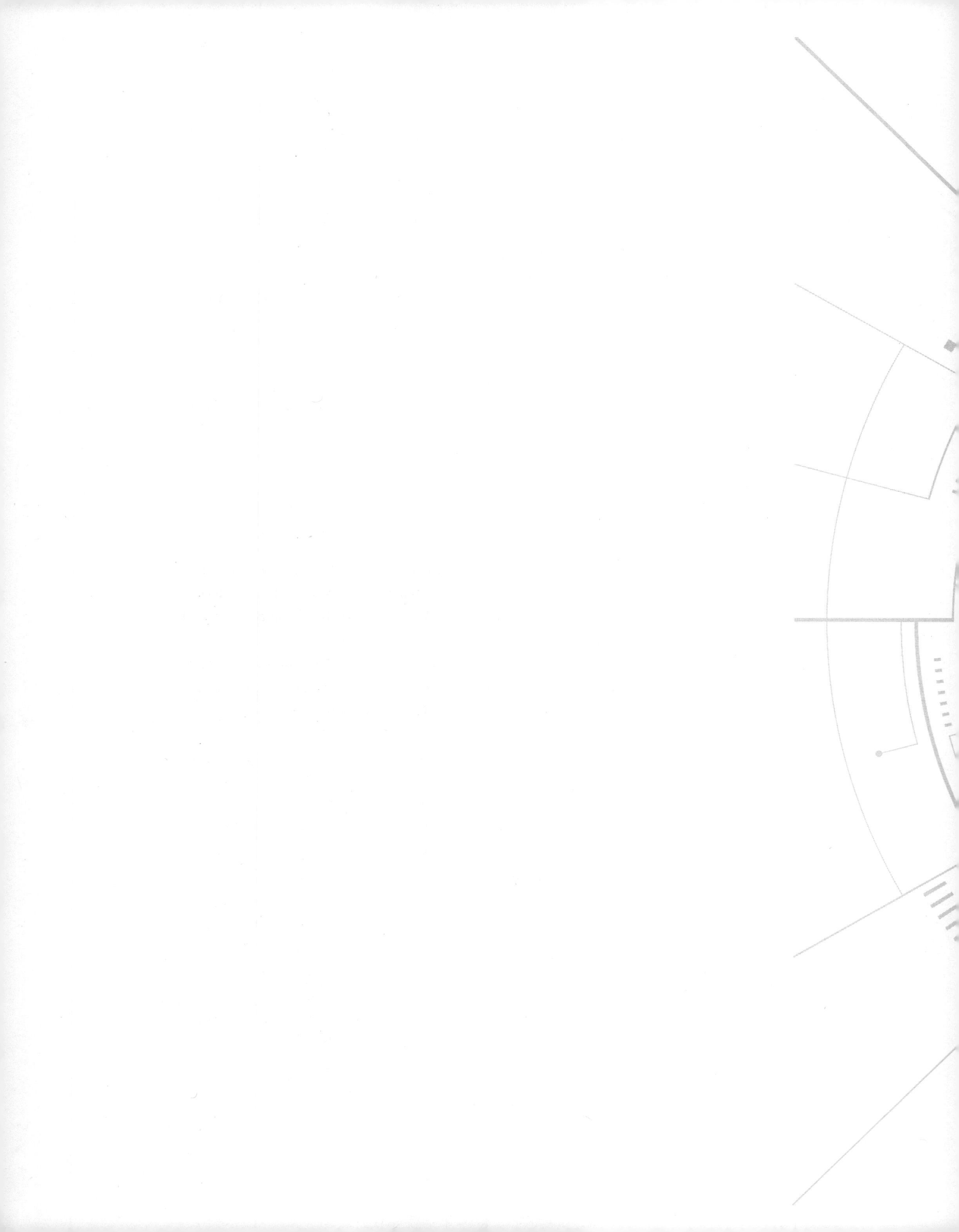

INTRODUCTION

By Chris Beaven

SOON AFTER ARRIVING AT THE REPOSITORY 25 YEARS AGO, ONE THING QUICKLY BECAME APPARENT: FOR A YOUNG SPORTS WRITER WITH A LOVE OF HISTORY, THIS WAS THE PLACE TO BE.

Not only because Stark County is the birthplace of the National Football League and the home of the Pro Football Hall of Fame, but also because the county is home to some of our country's greatest and most inspiring athletes and coaches.

Gold medalists, Hall of Famers, World Series heroes, sports pioneers and many, many other athletic greats all called Stark County home at one time. Many, of course, starred in football, baseball and basketball. But the greatness of the Stark County sports scene is that it's never been limited to those sports. Spending any amount of time here talking to the people who cherish their memories of such a vast array of athletes and coaches makes that apparent.

That's why Olympic gold has been won by Stark athletes in wrestling, boxing and track. It's why a kid from Canton was regarded as the "fastest swimmer in the world" (Marty Mull) for a time in the 1960s and a half-century later, the "fastest man in rugby" (Carlin Isles) hails from Jackson Township. And it's why today anyone visiting the county can find state-ranked and nationally ranked high school teams and athletes in cross country, golf, lacrosse, softball, swimming, tennis, track and field, volleyball and wrestling, in addition to football, basketball and baseball. And, oh yeah, the nation's premier small-college football powerhouse resides here, too, at the University of Mount Union.

Talk to those who created this legacy, and pride in where they came from often is an overriding emotion. It is for Ron Blackledge, a longtime college football and NFL coach—and a Timken High School icon. He grew up in Canton in the 1940s and '50s, returned to the county throughout his coaching journey and retired here two decades ago.

It's with pure pride that he likes to tell all of his friends and colleagues not from Stark County that this community, to him, "is God's country" because of the bond people share here.

A gathering of his college alma mater's athletic hall of fame brought Blackledge back to Bowling Green a couple years ago. It might as well have returned him to Canton and Stark County.

All around him was his hometown's deep impact on just this one university in northwest Ohio.

"We're having a big weekend celebration," Blackledge recalled, "... and it was being hosted by the athletes that were there playing at the time and (basketball player) Jehvon Clarke was the kid seating us, and he was from Canton Timken, and I thought that was neat. ... And then they start announcing the Hall of Famers."

With the introductions being done alphabetically, Blackledge was near the start of the list of Hall of Famers who attended. "In the first five, four of us were from Timken High School," he said. "It was kind of amazing. I thought, 'Are you kidding me?' It's Angie Bonner and the two Colaner boys (Jerry and Tom) after me. ... And down the line, you had David Greer from Canton McKinley, a couple other kids from Canton. I thought, 'Wow, that's pretty neat.' Again, God's country."

In celebrating our own 200th anniversary as a newspaper throughout 2015-16, we took a look at Stark County's rich sports history. That legacy, stretching back more than a century, resulted in the creation of our Sports Icons projects.

We started it in the summer of 2015 with a release of our ranking of the 20 greatest Stark County Sports Icons. We continued it in the spring of 2016 by releasing our lists of the 10 greatest sports icons for the county's high schools.

Those collections are found here in the first book produced by the award-winning sports staff of The Repository and our award-winning magazine division of GateHouse Ohio Media.

And since this is Stark County—and there are so many great stories still to tell—our Icons projects will continue regularly in The Canton Repository in the years to come and will perhaps again be showcased at a local book store.

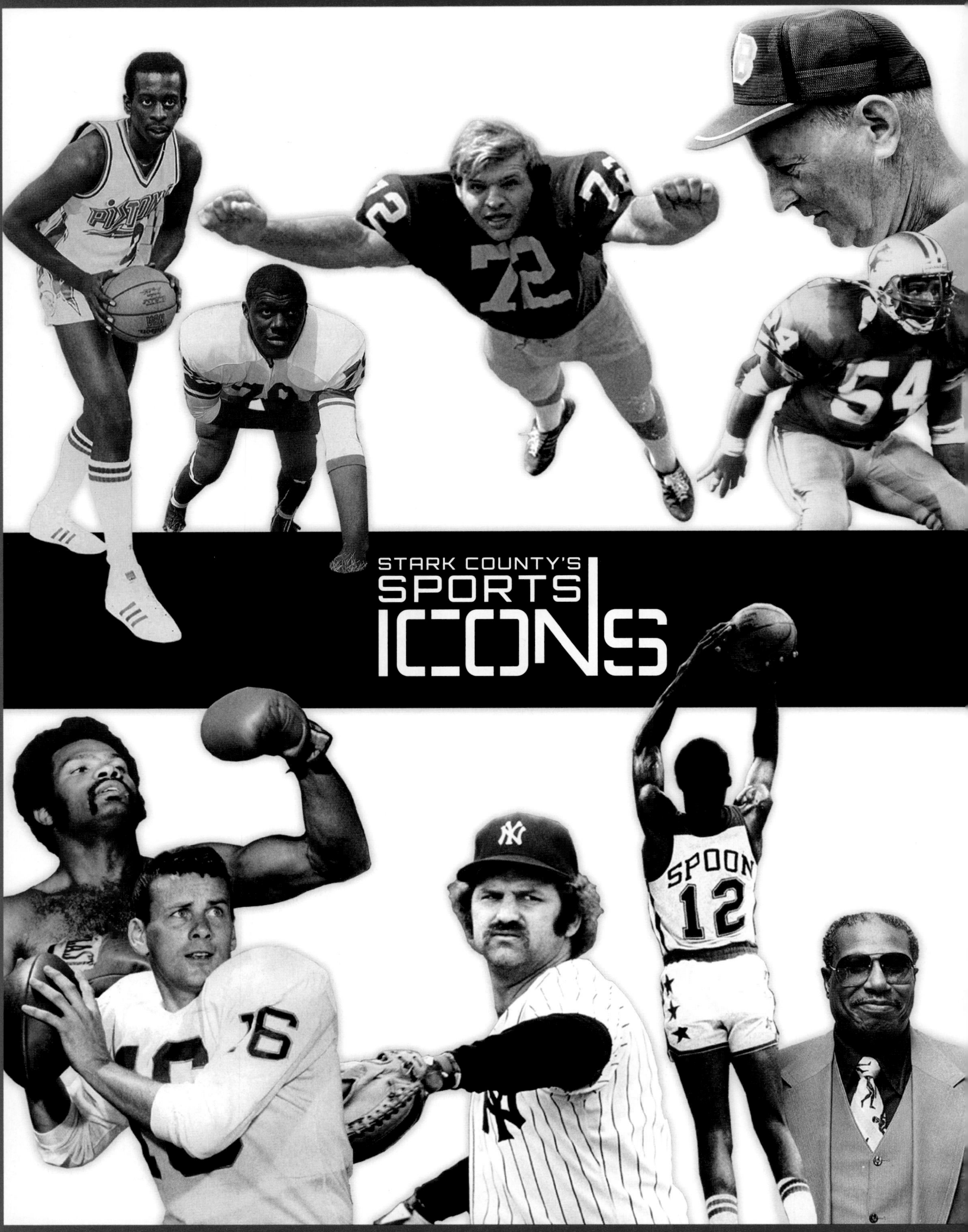

STARK COUNTY'S SPORTS ICONS

STARK COUNTY'S

TOP 20 ALL-TIME SPORTS ICONS

STARK COUNTY'S IMPACT ON SPORTS HAS BEEN FELT ACROSS THE NATION AND AROUND THE WORLD FOR THE BETTER PART OF A CENTURY. From the formation of the NFL in Canton nearly 100 years ago, to our athletes competing at the highest levels around the globe, the sports world has been influenced by our county's athletes and coaches.

The following pages rank Stark County's greatest all-time sports icons for their contributions and impact on sports within the county and around the world.

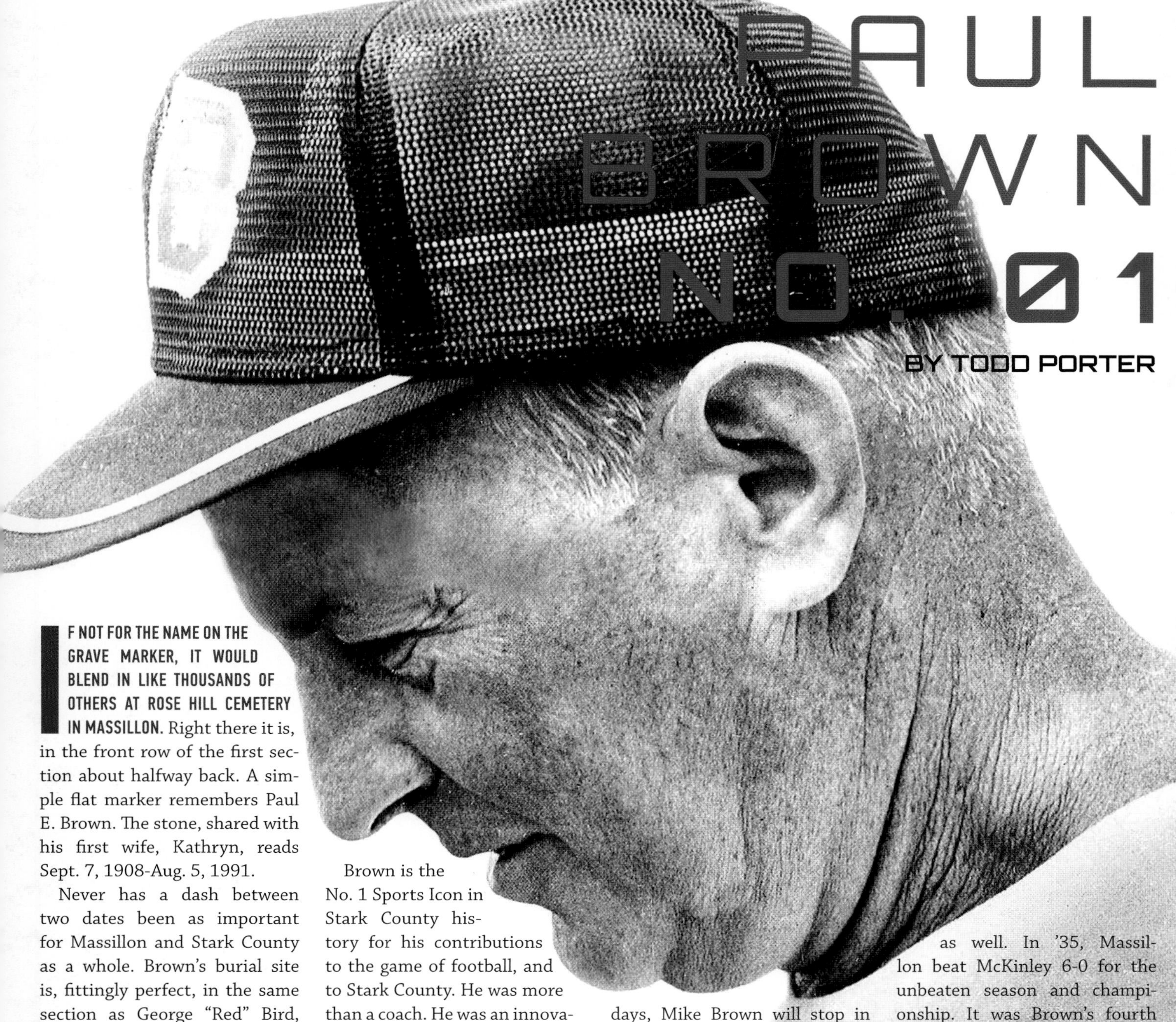

PAUL BROWN NO. 01

BY TODD PORTER

IF NOT FOR THE NAME ON THE GRAVE MARKER, IT WOULD BLEND IN LIKE THOUSANDS OF OTHERS AT ROSE HILL CEMETERY IN MASSILLON. Right there it is, in the front row of the first section about halfway back. A simple flat marker remembers Paul E. Brown. The stone, shared with his first wife, Kathryn, reads Sept. 7, 1908-Aug. 5, 1991.

Never has a dash between two dates been as important for Massillon and Stark County as a whole. Brown's burial site is, fittingly perfect, in the same section as George "Red" Bird, the band director at Washington High School when Brown was putting the school on the map across the country by dominating teams in the state and winning national and state titles. A short field goal away is the marker of Tommy James. He played for Brown at Massillon, Ohio State and the Cleveland Browns and won championships at each level.

Brown is the No. 1 Sports Icon in Stark County history for his contributions to the game of football, and to Stark County. He was more than a coach. He was an innovator, a league executive, founder of the Cincinnati Bengals. Above all, Paul Brown was a winner.

He has been dead for nearly 25 years. His son, Michael, took over operation of the Bengals. Mike Brown was born in Massillon in 1935, the year of his father's first 10-0 season in Massillon and his first state and national title there. On quiet days, Mike Brown will stop in Massillon unannounced and pay his respects at his father's grave. Every holiday season, the Massillon Tiger Booster Club places a Christmas wreath at Brown's burial site.

That 1935 season was important to Brown. It was the first undefeated season in Massillon since 1922 and gave the Tigers their first state title in 13 years as well. In '35, Massillon beat McKinley 6-0 for the unbeaten season and championship. It was Brown's fourth season. In the three previous seasons, his Tigers finished 22-7-1 and lost to McKinley all three years. Hardly the stuff legends are built on.

Two weeks before the 1935 season started, Kathryn Brown gave birth to Mike, who would grow to revere his father. To this day, despite being one of the NFL's longest-tenured owners,

Mike Brown still asks himself what his father would do before making key decisions.

"On occasion I do," Mike Brown said from his office in Cincinnati. "After he died, I would still find myself picking up the phone to talk to him, and, of course, he was gone. My initial reaction was to think in those terms, 'Oh geez, I should talk this over with him ... what does he have to say?' That was just something that was built into me. I had that thinking for some time even after he died. It wasn't just days, a week or a month. It was a few years, I would do that.

"Just the other day, I had a discussion with myself about something the NFL was doing and I took exception to it and said so. I asked myself how I thought he would have handled this. It's curious to me that even all these years later, the thought of judging myself in that way is still a part of me."

During his tenure in Massillon, and at the height of his popularity, Brown convinced local leaders to build a new football stadium through the Works Progress Administration. It opened in 1939, and Brown's 1940 team—regarded by some historians as the best team in Ohio history—filled the stadium and dominated opponents.

Massillon wouldn't be what it is today without Paul Brown, and Brown wouldn't have become who he did without Massillon. In 1930, Brown, a pre-law graduate at Miami University, could have studied history on a Rhodes Scholarship. He already was married to Kathryn, his high school sweetheart. However, the Great Depression forced him into working, and he took a job as coach.

Football was about to change forever.

"After Dave Stewart left as head coach, Massillon was in a down period," former Massillon Booster Club President William Dorman said. "It was the beginning stages of the Great Depression. Things didn't look very good. When Massillon went to look for a coach, they asked Dave Stewart. Paul Brown was coaching Severn Prep in Maryland, and Dave Stewart was his mentor. Dave recommended Paul Brown for the job.

"Is Massillon the same without Paul Brown? I don't think so. During the '30s, coming off the Great Depression, it was pitiful around here. A lot of people don't realize this, but the largest venue in most communities is the football stadium. Paul Brown realized that back then. He was instrumental in the design and construction of the stadium. You never get as many people together as you do in a football stadium. It's the epicenter of the community."

Filling Paul Brown's shoes was a monumental task at every level. By the time Brown left Massillon after the 1940 season, his Tigers won six straight national titles and had a 33-game winning streak. He jumped from the hotbed of Massillon to the frying pan of Ohio State in 1941 and won the Buckeyes' first national title in 1942. A year later, World War II enlistments decimated Ohio State's roster. Brown was commissioned as a lieutenant in the Navy in 1944 and was stationed at the Great Lakes Naval Training Station outside of Chicago. He coached the football team there.

Paul Brown (center) with two of his stars from Massillon—Horace Gillom (left) and Ray Getz.

Meanwhile, the All-American Football Conference was proposed as an alternative to the NFL. Brown was hired to coach the Cleveland franchise in 1946 for $17,500 a year. He was the highest-paid coach in the country.

According to author George Cantor in his book, "Paul Brown: The Man Who Invented Modern Football," Brown set out to build a dynasty in Cleveland. "I want to be what the New York Yankees are in baseball, or what Ben Hogan is in golf," Brown said at the time.

It was in Cleveland when Brown began to change the game. He was the first to hire a dedicated coaching staff, use a playbook and teach players in a classroom setting, and he developed the "taxi squad." The latter was a group of developmental players who were not on the active roster, but were on team owner Mickey McBride's taxi car company's payroll even though they didn't drive cabs.

Brown was the first coach to embrace racially integrated teams, but he never made mention of it.

"Paul Brown integrated pro football without uttering a single word about integration. He just went out, signed a bunch of great black athletes and started kicking butt," Hall of Famer Jim Brown said, according to "Browns Town 1964: Cleveland Browns and the 1964 Championship."

"That's how you do it. You don't talk about it. Paul never said one word about race. But this was a time in sports when you'd play in some cities and the white players could stay at the nice hotel, but the blacks had to stay in the homes of some black families in town. But not with Paul. We always stayed in hotels that took the entire team. Again, he never said a word. But in his own way, the man integrated football the right way—and no one was going to stop him."

Brown was demanding of his players. He won four straight AAFC championships. In 1950, Cleveland joined the NFL, and Brown won the championship in 1950, '54 and '55. By the time Art Modell bought the Browns in 1961—the same year the NFL with Brown's blessing decided to build the Pro Football Hall of Fame in Canton—Brown's relationship with players was spoiling. In 1963, Modell fired Brown in one of the most controversial and debated firings in sports history.

"It was something my father never got over. I mean never," Mike Brown said. "Modell reached out to my father over the years, and my father did not accept that. There was always a rift between them. I know (Modell) made statements publicly over the years that it had been bridged, but I don't think it was

> "I watched him his whole life. He was my role model. ... I was blessed to have him as a father."
> —Mike Brown

ever bridged. My father never said much about it publicly, but privately, I knew how he felt. What happened never changed with him. That's just how he was.

"There was no need for my father and Modell to sit and talk. It wasn't something that was going to change with further discussion."

Modell had to continue to pay Brown's $82,500 a year salary. He spent the next five years out of coaching and became an avid golfer. In 1966, Brown invested in a new AFL team, the Cincinnati Bengals and was the third-largest shareholder of the franchise. He would be the team's head coach and general manager and represent the franchise at all league meetings. Having complete control was something Brown wanted after losing it in Cleveland.

Mike Brown observed his dad and learned from him.

"I had complete respect for my father," Mike Brown said. "We didn't interact probably as much as fathers do with their sons today, but I knew where the line was. I never crossed it. If he told me to do something, I literally would find myself in the air out of my chair en route to do what it was before I could totally contemplate what it was I was about to do.

"I watched him his whole life. I watched how he did things. I would discuss with myself why he did things. He was my role model. I followed how he went about things closely, and probably judged them too harshly. You hold your parents to a high standard. I was blessed to have him as a father."

In meetings with the Bengals, Mike Brown learned not to question his father. He laughed when talking about whether he ever asked his father why he made a move with the team.

"It didn't really work like that," Mike Brown said. "He would do what he wanted to do. I could say my piece, but he was going to go do what he decided to do. Over time, I absorbed how and why he went about things. They became the way I did them without thinking why. I adopted how he did it without questioning."

After the AFL-NFL merger in 1970, the Bengals and Browns were in the same division. Brown and assistant Bill Walsh devised a new offense, which would become known as the West Coast Offense.

Perhaps Brown's greatest legacy to Stark County is the Pro Football Hall of Fame. It was Brown who went to Repository sports writers in 1959 to pitch the idea of the Hall of Fame when he was Cleveland's coach. Brown was so influential as a coach, he knew the league was talking about creating a shrine. In 1961, Brown, Bears owner George Halas and Edwin Anderson, general manager of the Detroit Lions, were chosen as the committee that would pick the site of the Hall of Fame from among Canton, Detroit and Pittsburgh. Halas, who was at the 1920 meeting in Canton that organized the league that became the NFL, was with Brown, decidedly in Canton's corner.

In 1960, when the NFL wanted to award the Hall of Fame to a city, Brown got the decision tabled for a year until Canton was better organized and had money to present to the NFL to build it.

"I know that to be a fact," Mike Brown said. "He was proud to have the Hall of Fame in Canton. That's where he thought it should be. There were different contenders, but none of the others made sense. In Detroit, they were going to put it in an airport. You tell me why."

In 1967, Brown was inducted in the Hall of Fame. In 1969, Kathryn died. Brown purchased a double burial plot at Rose Hill. Four years later, Brown married Mary Rightsell. In 1975, Brown retired from coaching and turned his attention toward running the Bengals as president and owner. He was shrewd with players' contracts. He was hands-on in league matters. Paul Brown remained well respected until his death in 1991. He told Mike he wished to be buried in Massillon next to Kathryn, the first love of his life.

"He was a Massillon guy. Those were his people," Mike Brown said. "That's where his roots are. He never lost the feeling for home. He is buried there because that's where he wanted to be buried. Those were his people in Massillon. He felt an allegiance to them all his life."

IN THEIR WORDS

BY LEE OWENS

IF I WERE IN THE CAR BUSINESS, I WOULD DREAM OF MEETING HENRY FORD. BUT I'M A FOOTBALL COACH, AND AS THE FOOTBALL COACH AT MASSILLON WASHINGTON HIGH SCHOOL, I HAD THE OPPORTUNITY TO MEET "THE MAN" OR THE "OLD MAN" AS PAUL DAVID REVERENTLY CALLED HIS FRIEND PAUL BROWN.

I've coached in Paul Brown Tiger Stadium. I grew up a Buckeye and a Browns fan. I've read all the Paul Brown books, and I've heard all Junie Studers' PB stories. But after spending an afternoon with Paul Brown at Washington High School and after spending a game with him in the Bengals press box, this was my impression of the legendary Hall of Fame coach.

His demeanor was intimidating, but respectful. When he asked me a question, his penetrating eyes seemed to patiently search for the honesty of my answers. His focus was so intense that it kept me from being distracted. During the Bengals game, I watched as he filled out several pages of a legal pad with game notes that he planned to share with his coach later that evening.

Paul Brown always will be responsible for the foundations of coaching the modern game of football. He is the father of the game I've dedicated my life to coaching, although the only personal insight Paul Brown ever shared with me was during a phone call concerning the Massillon Tiger head coaching position. I was a relatively new head coach at Lancaster High School and I was considering the Massillon job. Here was Paul Brown on the phone with me. He simply stated that football was a very competitive sport and for the team to win, it must be important to the community. He concluded by assuring me that football always will be important in Massillon, Ohio.

Lee Owens is the head football coach at Ashland University. He is the former head coach at Massillon, an assistant coach at Ohio State and head coach at the University of Akron. He won a state title at Galion High School.

MARION MOTLEY NO. 02

BY STEVE DOERSCHUK

MARION MOTLEY, WHO WORE NO. 76, AND LOU GROZA, WHO WORE IT LATER, BECAME ACQUAINTED AT BOWLING GREEN STATE UNIVERSITY.

They met there in a collision in the Cleveland Browns' first training camp.

"I saw a big flash of light," Groza said.

Motley's is a story of light and shade.

He and Groza are the only two Cleveland Browns to have worn 76. Yet, the number is retired by the franchise solely in Groza's honor. The address of Browns headquarters in Berea is 76 Lou Groza Blvd.

Groza's legacy is marvelous as a tackle, kicker and a man about town in Berea prior to his death in 2000. It can be argued that Motley's legacy is greater.

Between his youth in Canton and death in 1999 in Cleveland, Motley in a sense was Jackie Robinson before Jackie Robinson. In addition to breaking pro football's "color barrier," he was a big back for the ages who doubled as a linebacker during the greatest pro sports run in Ohio history.

Historian Paul Zimmerman—a New Yorker known to his large reading audience as Dr. Z—regarded Motley as "the greatest player I've ever seen," both in a 1971 book and in conversations during ensuing decades.

Paul Brown, the czar who developed Motley and drafted Jim Brown, called Motley the best back he coached.

It is odd in a way that Jackie Robinson's No. 42 is retired in all of Major League Baseball, while in the very city where Motley played, No. 76 belongs only to "Lou the Toe."

Motley wore the number first, from 1946-51, while he helped the Browns win five league championships in six years. He and Groza were teammates the whole time.

Motley was a 6-foot-1, 240-pound running, blocking and tackling machine on teams that won All-American Conference championships in 1946, '47, '48 and '49. His per-carry average in postseason play during that run was an astounding 8.1.

In the 1948 title game, Motley ran 14 times for 133 yards and three touchdowns against the Buffalo Bills.

In 1950, the Browns jumped leagues and won the NFL title, with Motley leading the league in rushing. A film clip of a 1950 blowout of Pittsburgh covers a play on which Motley:

Marion Motley (standing) with actor Greg Morris during a Civic Enshrinees Dinner.

- *Turns up the left sideline and sheds leaping middle linebacker Frank Sinkovitz, who gets his arms on Motley's shoulders.*
- *Doesn't slow down as a second Steeler lodges his helmet in Motley's right ribcage.*
- *Runs through linebacker Jerry Shipkey, whose right arm rakes the front of Motley's body and tears off his helmet.*
- *Stays inbounds with a dancer's feet while making a fourth defender whiff.*
- *Finishes a long touchdown run after defender George Hayes jumps on his back and flies away.*

The next season in which the Browns went 11-1, was the last in which Motley wore No. 76. In 1952, the NFL adopted a system restricting numbers according to position groups. Quarterback Otto Graham switched from 60 to 14. Motley gave up 76 and became 36. Groza, who had worn 46 for six years, was the new 76.

Groza wound up wearing 76 longer than Motley did. Motley wore it first and relinquished it only because he had to.

Credit former Browns owner Art Modell with two all-time snubs of Stark County icons.

After the 1962 season, Modell fired the great Massillon icon, Brown. In 1968, the team retired No. 76 as a tribute to Groza, ignoring Motley.

The year 1968 would have been just the year for a co-tribute to No. 76, in that Groza had just retired, while Motley was inducted into the Pro Football Hall of Fame, in the shadow of the stadium that opened when he was a Canton McKinley High School senior 30 years earlier.

Ironically, Blanton Collier, the coach Modell hired to replace Brown, called Motley "the greatest all-around football player I ever saw."

Motley was 2 when his family moved from Alabama to Canton. He grew to be very big and very fast.

As a varsity starter in 1936, when he was a McKinley sophomore, he played guard. He moved to the backfield in 1937, scored four touchdowns in the first two games, and in a game against Collinwood ran for 239 yards while also throwing two touchdown passes.

Late in the '37 season, coach John Reed moved Motley back to guard, ostensibly to make room for a back who was returning from an injury. The Bulldogs' only loss, 19-6 to Paul Brown's Massillon Tigers, came in the 10th game with Motley playing guard.

Reed was fired after going 0-5 against Brown's Tigers. It made for a good punch line in future Brown dinner speeches: "Anyone who would play Motley at guard deserved to be fired."

In terms of racism Motley dealt with throughout his career, the most incendiary example was a death threat that led to his withdrawal from a 1946 game against the Miami Seahawks.

Those who knew Motley best say he occasionally talked in vivid detail about his struggles against prejudice. He preferred, they say, to dwell on family, friends and living a decent life. It was impossible to escape the racial component. He was inducted into the Hall of Fame four months after the assassination of Dr. Martin Luther King, which triggered nationwide "disturbances," two years after the Hough race riots in Cleveland.

The theme of racial pioneering was avoided during the 1968 ceremony in Canton.

Mayor Stanley Cmich gave a welcome. WHBC's Jim Muzzy took particular pride in being a McKinley High School graduate, as master of ceremonies.

"During his days with the Browns," Muzzy told a crowd packed around the front steps of the museum, "Bill Willis was the fastest-charging lineman in all of football. Here he is to present Canton's own Marion Motley."

Jackie Robinson broke Major League Baseball's "color barrier" on April 15, 1947. Motley and Willis were the only black men in the newly created All-American Football Conference in 1946. That same year, Woody Strode and Kenny Washington became the only blacks in the NFL, as players on the Los Angeles Rams team that had been the Cleveland Rams after winning the 1945 NFL championship. They were four Jackie Robinsons, and as a star ball carrier, Motley was the most conspicuous.

In Willis' three-minute introduction, he called Motley "the greatest all-around player in professional history." Motley's acceptance speech lasted less than two minutes. There is little doubt he said much less than was on his mind.

Nine years later, at Willis' own induction, he elaborated.

"Marion did prove to be the best the pro football game has ever seen, in my opinion," Willis said. "Marion and I became fast friends because we had to be fast friends. We had to go through a lot together, and we had to depend on each other."

Motley was 79 when he died in 1999. Dave Robinson, who was among the few black players in Green Bay in the 1960s, was a pall bearer at the funeral in Cleveland.

Robinson grew up in New Jersey revering Jackie Robinson. After football, he settled in Ohio, getting to know Motley and ex-Cleveland Indian Larry Doby, the first black player in the American League.

"Marion Motley and Larry Doby taught me so much about what it was like for African-Americans in pro sports years before I got there," Robinson said. "I went through a lot in the '60s, but ...

"My mother always wanted to meet Marion. She told me that was the guy who made it possible for me to play pro ball."

Robinson became a Pro Football Hall of Fame trustee and is in the Hall as a player. Motley and Robinson became good friends who traveled to charity golf outings, some in Stark County. Robinson laughs when he thinks of Motley stepping to the tee while smoking a big cigar, then smashing drives with his unique, homemade swing.

"People don't realize how much it costs to be involved in some of those outings, traveling to Chicago, or wherever," Robinson said. "Marion would tell me, 'Boy, you've got to pay back. You had a good life in football.'

"Marion Motley was the man."

Hall of Famer Lenny Moore played college ball at Penn State. One time he was in Pittsburgh to take on Pitt during a weekend the Browns were facing the Steelers.

"Marion Motley invited me up to his room," Moore said. "And he sat down and talked to me. I mean, he really talked to me."

When Moore gave his Hall of Fame acceptance speech in Canton about 20 years later, he addressed Motley and Ollie Matson, fellow black pioneers. His induction speech became a personal thank you to them. By the time he was finished, all three were wiping tears.

Moore said Motley taught him to live with humility and determination.

"You wouldn't know that he was Marion Motley," Moore said, "because he wasn't a guy who talked about himself. He knew who he was, and everybody kind of revered him.

MARION MOTLEY'S PRO FOOTBALL HALL OF FAME INDUCTION SPEECH

MARION MOTLEY'S ACCEPTANCE SPEECH AT HIS 1968 PRO FOOTBALL HALL OF FAME INDUCTION WAS SHORTER THAN THAT OF HIS PRESENTER, BILL WILLIS.

Here's what Motley said:

"Thank you, Bill, and I'd like to thank the many friends that have come to pay tribute to seven of us today. I look out over this crowd and see many faces that I know that I've gone to school with. And it makes a person being inducted into the Hall of Fame in the hometown ... it's a wonderful feeling.

"I've been asked many times the last two or three days as to how you feel, or will be feeling. Well, trying to express or say how you feel about this, going into the Hall of Fame, it's rather hard.

"I'd like to thank the many teammates that I've played with that helped me be the so-called player that I was. Fellows like Bill Willis, Lin Houston, Cliff Lewis, Dante Lavelli and many others that I could go on and name, but it would take quite awhile.

"But I'd just like to thank everyone for coming and thank the people that inducted me into the Hall of Fame. Thank you very much."

THURMAN MUNSON NO. 03

BY TODD PORTER

MORE THAN 13,000 DAYS HAVE PASSED SINCE THE DAY THAT CHANGED EVERYTHING FOR DIANA MUNSON AND HER THREE CHILDREN. Not a single one of them has been easy. Those days—more than 36 years worth of them now—have been easier, but not easy. Because easy is relative.

Thurman Munson wasn't just Diana Munson's husband. He wasn't just the father of their three young children when he tragically died Aug. 2, 1979 practicing touch-and-go landings in his new private jet. Thurman was her best friend.

"They say time heals, which it does, thank God," Diana said. "But you never lose the hurt. It's always there. You don't know if it will be a song or a smell, or something that takes you back to that moment."

Their love story does not start in the minor leagues or college. It does not even start at Lehman High School. Their love story starts at Worley Elementary School. Diana was in the fifth grade. Thurman was in the seventh grade. He was hitting home runs on the playground.

"I was amazed because I was a tomboy. We hit it off right away. I admired his cocky attitude because he backed it up," Diana said, remembering more than 50 years ago as if it was a few days ago. "He was one of those kids who said, 'I'm going to do this,' and he went out and did it. He had confidence. I didn't have confidence. I was attracted to that.

"He always teased me and said he was more attracted to my wallet."

Diana laughs now.

Thurman Munson came from humble beginnings, the son of an absentee father who traveled much and paid his son few compliments. Thurman would wait for Diana to finish junior patrol duty, where she would help younger kids cross the street on their way to school.

"We would go to Schaffner's drug store on Cleveland Avenue and 22nd Street. That was the big hang out for after-school walkers," Diana said. "We'd go there and get a Coke and chips. He never had money, I did. Out of the goodness of my heart, I would buy for him. He always said that investment paid off for me."

Diana laughs at the memory.

"That's the cocky attitude that intrigued me about him," Diana said.

They would deliver newspapers together. Right about the time Diana started at Lehman, Thurman started dating her. It was Diana's family where Thurman learned what it felt like to be a family.

"He felt protected with my family," Diana said. "Thurman had some insecurities, and he covered those up with his cockiness. ... We loved each other as friends first. We were best friends."

And that is one of the last things Diana remembers Thurman telling her. They had a phone conversation before he went to the Akron-Canton Airport to get more flight time in his new twin-jet Cessna Citation with friend Jerry Anderson and flight instructor Dave Hall.

"He told me how amazed he was to still be married to his best friend," Diana said. "I think that says everything about our relationship."

Don McLean coined the phrase "The day the music died" in his song "American Pie." It was a reference to the 1959 plane crash that killed Buddy Holly, Ritchie Valens and "The Big Bopper." If that's the day the music died, Aug. 2, 1979 is the day Stark County lost a chunk of its innocence.

"That's the effect it had on many people," Diana said. "You don't expect to lose a sports icon, the captain of the New York Yankees, in his prime so tragically, especially during the season. You almost think those kind of people will never pass in a tragic way. You expect their careers will go on. He was the father of three little children.

"You don't expect that to happen to a young athlete in his prime. He still had so much to offer, not only in sports, but to Canton, Ohio. He loved and breathed Canton. He owned New York, and he could've done anything in New York. He chose to stay in Canton. It's where his heart belonged."

The world knows how Munson died. After a few passes of the runway, Munson flew the Cessna too low. It hit a tree stump. He suffered a broken neck. Anderson and Hall escaped with burns and injuries. Munson was pinned in the cockpit. The Cessna burst into flames after hitting the tree stump.

Thurman Munson was one of baseball's best players when he died. He is the only Yankee to win both the Rookie of the Year

(1970) and the MVP (1976) awards. He hit .302 with 17 home runs and 105 RBIs in that MVP season, the first of three consecutive World Series appearances for the Yankees. Munson played biggest and grittiest in the postseason. He hit .357 with 22 RBIs and three home runs in his 30 postseason games. Munson was so important to New York that owner George Steinbrenner named him the Yankee team captain in 1976, the first since Lou Gehrig in 1939.

The captain of the Yankees was gone at 32 years old. Munson was so beloved in New York that grown men still break down when they meet Diana and tell her how much they admired her husband. He played the game tough. When New York star Reggie Jackson needed checked, Munson checked him. Reggie didn't ask questions.

"Thurman was blue collar," said Joe Gilhousen, Munson's high school teammate at Lehman and then later at Kent State. "He wasn't afraid to stick his nose in there and mix it up. He'd get bumps and bruises and play with those. His reputation was such that even after he was gone, later day Yankee players still respected him as a player, and his memory."

In the summer of 2015, Diana headed to Yankee Stadium with her grandchildren to make sure they gain an understanding for who their grandfather was. More than context is lost when one generation passes along the stories to a second, and now a third. Diana wants to make sure her grandkids understand exactly who their grandfather was.

"The kids have very little concept who their grandpa was as far as baseball is concerned," Diana said before the trip. "This is a great time for them to see how beloved he is in New York. They've only been to Yankee Stadium when they were little. I don't think they remember it. There will be a ceremony on the field."

The Thurman Munson the world doesn't know is the one who once pulled into a full-service gas station wearing a stocking cap and pumped his own gas, and when another car pulled into the station, not recognizing the Yankee catcher, told Munson to fill his tank up, too. Munson pumped the stranger's gas, collected the money and paid the attendant without ever letting anyone know who he was.

Or how Munson thought he was a great singer. Diana and Thurman would sing to each other in the car. There would be Thurman bellowing out the lyrics of "You've Made Me So Very Happy."

"The one we both thought we were really good at is 'Sloop John B' by the Beach Boys," Diana said. "We used to have so much fun. The one that still makes me sad when I hear it is 'Rainy Night in Georgia.' Every year, we would drive to spring training and take the kids. This one year, the kids stayed back with my parents, and this time we were alone for the whole trip. We usually drove straight through, but we stayed in Georgia this time. 'Rainy Night in Georgia' came on the radio several times. It's a painful memory because I remember how much fun we had. I'm a person who memorizes moments. Your mind is like a steel trap, which is good and bad."

All of Diana's children—Tracy, Kelly and Michael—are all now parents themselves with their own careers. Tracy works for Mitchell Piping in Hartville. Michael is a partner and owner of Danny Boy's Italian Eatery in North Canton. Kelly is a high-ranking executive with a health care company in Kentucky.

"They're wonderful people," Diana said. "I don't know how you teach it, but by golly they learned it."

Some believe Thurman Munson is a Hall of Famer. Others say if he had played a few more years, he'd be in Cooperstown. His career numbers make a strong argument for induction. What if Munson were still alive?

There is no doubt in Diana Munson's mind what he'd be doing.

"I'm sure he would have been hired and fired by George Steinbrenner many times," Diana said. "George was grooming Thurman to become his manager. He used to tell him that. I'm sure he would have been in baseball most of his life. He had so many loves and interests. Flying was one, real estate was another. He loved the art of the deal. I know he would have loved watching his children and grandchildren grow up. He would be amazed that 36 years later, they're having bobblehead Thurman Munson day at Yankee Stadium. I think he would be astonished at how beloved he is, even today, in New York. Thurman's family life was not so great growing up, so I know he would have loved his family time."

IN THEIR WORDS

BY TRACY EVANS

MANY PEOPLE ARE FAMILIAR WITH THE STORY OF MY DAD. HOWEVER, STATISTICS AND COMMON KNOWLEDGE DO NOT ALWAYS GIVE YOU THE MEASURE OF A MAN.

People knew him as a baseball player, a businessman or a philanthropist.

Only three of us knew him as dad.

His gentleness was best illustrated when he dried our hair at night. My dad was gentle, fun-loving and had a wonderful sense of humor. Dad would use the lowest heat setting and really take his time with the brush to get it nice and straight. We always wanted him to do it before watching "Wild Kingdom" on TV.

My mom used the highest heat and was not exactly gentle with the brush. Our mom is loving and kind, and she made her children her priority. I had to become a mom myself to realize that by that time of night, moms are tired and want to just finish the job!

Dad never wasted a minute of family time when he was home. I think the fact that he spent so much time on the road helped him to really make the most of his time with us.

He would drive us to school every morning in the offseason. He had a terrible sense of style, though, so I was usually pretty embarrassed. He would wear an awful striped robe with green fishing boots and a lavender Arctic Cat snowmobile hat to take me to school.

The best way to describe him: He was a big kid. He always took us to get our Halloween costumes, and the entire neighborhood would pile in the back of his black truck to hit as many houses as possible.

We ate dinner once a week at Lucia's. He only had one rule: No autographs during dinner. He would respectfully tell them that this was his family's time and he would be happy to sign in the lobby as soon as we were done.

Even if he was hurt or tired, he always signed autographs for his fans. I knew it was hard for him to set that boundary, but I really appreciated it. It was the one time in public that we didn't have to share him.

Tracy Evans is Thurman and Diana Munson's daughter, the oldest of their three children. Her sister is Kelly, and her brother is Michael.

CHRIS SPIELMAN'S FOOTBALL LIFE BEGAN IN A QUIET DREAMLAND. EVEN THEN THE BACKDROP WAS A ROAR.

"I remember going to the McKinley-Massillon game when we were little," said Rick Spielman, Chris' older brother. "My dad was coaching at McKinley. I was in the stands watching the game with my mom. Chris was sleeping on her lap."

By 1981, Rick was a senior quarterback at Massillon for the season opener against Perry.

"Chris was a sophomore," said Mike Currence, who was in his sixth year as head coach of the Tigers then. "We had 90 players who were juniors or seniors, and we just didn't dress sophomores.

"Chris was the first sophomore to dress for me. To keep him happy, I put him on the kickoff team.

"Earle Bruce was up from Ohio State to watch the game, and we scored a lot, and therefore, we kicked off a lot.

"The first four times we kicked off, Chris went down and got the tackle. Walt Bronczek, the stadium announcer, started saying, 'Well, there's Spielman again.

"Earle said, 'Who is that kid?' I said, 'He's only a sophomore, Earle.' "

By his senior year, before signing with Bruce at Ohio State, Charles Christopher Spielman was on the cover of Wheaties boxes from California to Kalamazoo.

Long after Spielman's career as a Pro Bowl linebacker in the NFL ended, a Columbus TV station running a feature on the greatest Ohio State players opened a description of Spielman with this:

"A legend even before he wore the scarlet and gray ..."

The legend just wanted in the game. He lived his first nine years with his parents, Charles (better known as "Sonny") and Nancy and big brother Rick on 36th Street just north of the Canton city limits.

"The landmark was the Milk and Honey ice cream store," Chris recalls. "Our street was a dead end with a field at the end. There was always a game. There was a kid named Joe who had a basketball court, and we played other games in the field.

"There were always games and always kids. It wasn't AAU or leagues. It was neighborhood kids making up rules, resolving disputes, competing. And it was very competitive."

For Rick, it's organized to the hilt these days. He is general manager of the Minnesota Vikings. The road to the NFL began on 36th Street.

Rick was born Dec. 2, 1962. Chris arrived Oct. 11, 1965, and is his only sibling.

"We would play tackle football on that field on the dead end," Rick says. "Even when he was real young, Chris always wanted to play. Some of the older kids didn't want him to.

"After he played one or two times, you could see he was better than half the older guys who were there."

Sonny Spielman had coached at Central Catholic and later McKinley. His boys started hanging out with him at work.

"I remember being at old McKinley High School in downtown Canton," Chris said. "Dad would have Rick and me there with him. A highlight was getting a cold pop out of an old machine.

"One night, somebody came to the house and talked to my dad. Dad told us he was going to be the head coach at Timken. I was maybe 5 years old."

The address remained 36th Street for a while. Chris soon imagined playing for the Cleveland Browns, as he actually did in his last stand as a pro, during the 1999 preseason.

"I thought everybody could grow up to be a pro football player if they wanted," he said.

Sonny Spielman, since deceased, used to laugh about knowing Chris was on the aggressive side from seeing him "beat the crap out of his G.I. Joes."

"I would get mad at the G.I. Joe guys for getting hurt, or their plastic leg would fall off, and I'd yell at them, and I'd start crying because they couldn't play any more," Chris said. "From being the head coach at Timken, dad would be coach, slash counselor, slash father figure, slash trainer, slash ankle taper.

"He would be my counselor with the G.I. Joes. He would say, 'I'll just tape 'em up like one of my football guys, and they'll be good to go.' "

Chris turned 9 the year Sonny's Timken Trojans went 8-0-1. They knocked off Oakwood 18-2, Glenwood 33-0, Orrville 20-14, Canton Lincoln 22-14 and Canton Lehman 52-6. They tied St. Thomas Aquinas, 20-all.

He loved the rhythm of those Timken autumns no matter the record.

"Those times were always really special," Chris says. "I remember sitting at Edgefield on Friday afternoons watching the clock. I'd be counting the hours until it was time to go to Fawcett Stadium that night, or to ride on the bus to wherever the team was going.

"We would go and help with the equipment or whatever was needed and just be a part of it."

CHRIS SPIELMAN NO. 04

BY STEVE DOERSCHUK

Chris' first organized team was the Lions, coached by Ron Grasse. They went 8-0 and beat the Bears in a Plain Local Midget Football League championship game.

"We were the maroon team. The Bears were blue," Chris said, surprised by how much he remembers.

His reputation grew as he played for C. Wright Crawford and James Vance in the Greater Canton

Midget Football League.

"I was running back, and a quarterback and a linebacker," he said. "When I was 12, they wouldn't let me play linebacker. People were mad at me because I was hitting pretty hard. There was something about a petition about not letting me play.

"When I wasn't allowed to play linebacker, I got in a three-point stance 4 yards off the ball and stood up when the ball was snapped and played linebacker.

"I didn't feel like I was cheating. I felt like I was getting an edge."

In junior high, he suited up for Jim Lowe's eighth-grade team at Lehman, which played at the old stadium by the cement steps.

"I was going to go against the grain and play high school ball at Timken," Chris said. "With my dad being at Timken, I don't know how he would have approached that, but ..."

He never found out.

Sonny took a job in Massillon, and Chris played ninth-grade ball for Tom Jarvis at Longfellow Junior High in 1980. Rick was a junior linebacker on a Massillon team that reached a state title game against Cincinnati Moeller.

"The aura in Massillon on Friday nights was unique," Chris says. "On my first Friday in ninth grade there, I was the only kid in the school that didn't have on a Massillon shirt. Not just the only kid ... the only person.

"I was like ... somebody's got to tell me the rules over here."

Rick was Massillon's senior quarterback. Chris became a varsity linebacker.

"Their story starts with Sonny," said the Massillon coach of that era, Currence. "Both were raised to be tough players who could withstand a little bit of pain."

Chris' sophomore year ended with the pain of a 9-6 loss to eventual state champion McKinley.

As a junior, he helped the Tigers finish a 10-0 regular season with a 7-0 win over McKinley, en route to a loss in the state finals to Moeller.

As a senior, Spielman was a force at linebacker and running back on a team that went 9-1. A fluky loss to Akron Garfield cost the Tigers a spot in the playoffs.

"I really thought that team could have won it all," Currence said. "I thought we were good enough to beat Moeller."

A town campaign landed Spielman on the cover of the Wheaties box.

"It was a great contest, and it did get Chris the publicity, but it wasn't something he really needed," Currence said. "It almost made him look superhuman. He was not. Earle Bruce really questioned his size. As a senior, Chris only weighed a couple hundred pounds."

Spielman struggled with the hype that followed him around.

"Kids today wouldn't think it would be all that much, with social media being what it is," Spielman said. "For me, it was a lot, but it was fine. I was pretty focused. I never got a big head from it.

"At times, it was uncomfortable because I was embarrassed for being singled out."

Thom McDaniels, who coached against Spielman as a McKinley assistant in 1981 and as McKinley's head coach in 1982 and '83, does not remember Spielman for the hype.

"He played the game better than anybody I ever coached against," McDaniels said. "I thought that then, and a whole lot of years later, I still believe that to be true.

"You can be the best player or you can play the game better. I'm not sure. Chris may be both of those. But he's absolutely the guy that played the game better than any other kid I ever coached against."

IN THEIR WORDS

BY EARLE BRUCE

I KNEW I HAD TO RECRUIT CHRIS SPIELMAN. HOW COULD I—AS HEAD COACH AT OHIO STATE—LET THE KID ON THE COVER OF WHEATIES GET OUT OF STATE? IT WAS OHIO STATE OR MICHIGAN, AND I'LL NEVER FORGET HOW IT CAME DOWN.

During Chris' senior season, I went to see him play in Massillon in back-to-back weeks. So I'm at his first game, and I see this kid playing tailback and he ran the ball 25 times, he played linebacker and made most of the tackles, he kicked off, he returned kicks and punts. What the hell else could he do?

The next week, I drive up to Massillon and I see the same things. He's running the ball. He's making all the tackles. He's kicking off. He's returning kicks. Hell, I went out to get popcorn at halftime and he was selling popcorn. I tell you that because that's how important Chris Spielman was to his team.

Football season ends and I drive to Massillon to see Chris play a basketball game. Glen Mason, one of my assistant coaches, was responsible for recruiting Chris, and Glen told me Chris may commit to Ohio State after the game, but he might not. I talked to Chris after the game, and he said he wanted to talk to his mom and dad one more time and he'd call me. I drive back to Columbus and I don't get in until late.

It's 2:30 in the morning and my phone rings. It's Chris, and here's how it goes: He said to me, "Coach, I made my decision."

Then there's nothing. There's nothing. There's nothing. It's dead silence on the line, and I think, "Oh my god, he's going to Michigan and he can't tell me." Finally, he breaks the silence and says, "I'm gonna be a Buckeye." I said to him, "That's great you son of a gun, but you just put me through three minutes of hell waiting for that, I'm going to pay you back when you get down here."

Chris Spielman was one hell of a player. In a hundred years from now, they will still be talking about Chris Spielman at Ohio State. I know they will still be talking about him in Massillon, I know that. Chris Spielman was a champion.

Earle Bruce was Ohio State's head football coach from 1979-87 and was an assistant under Woody Hayes before that. Bruce, who coached 1964-65 at Massillon, lives in Columbus and still stays in contact with Chris Spielman.

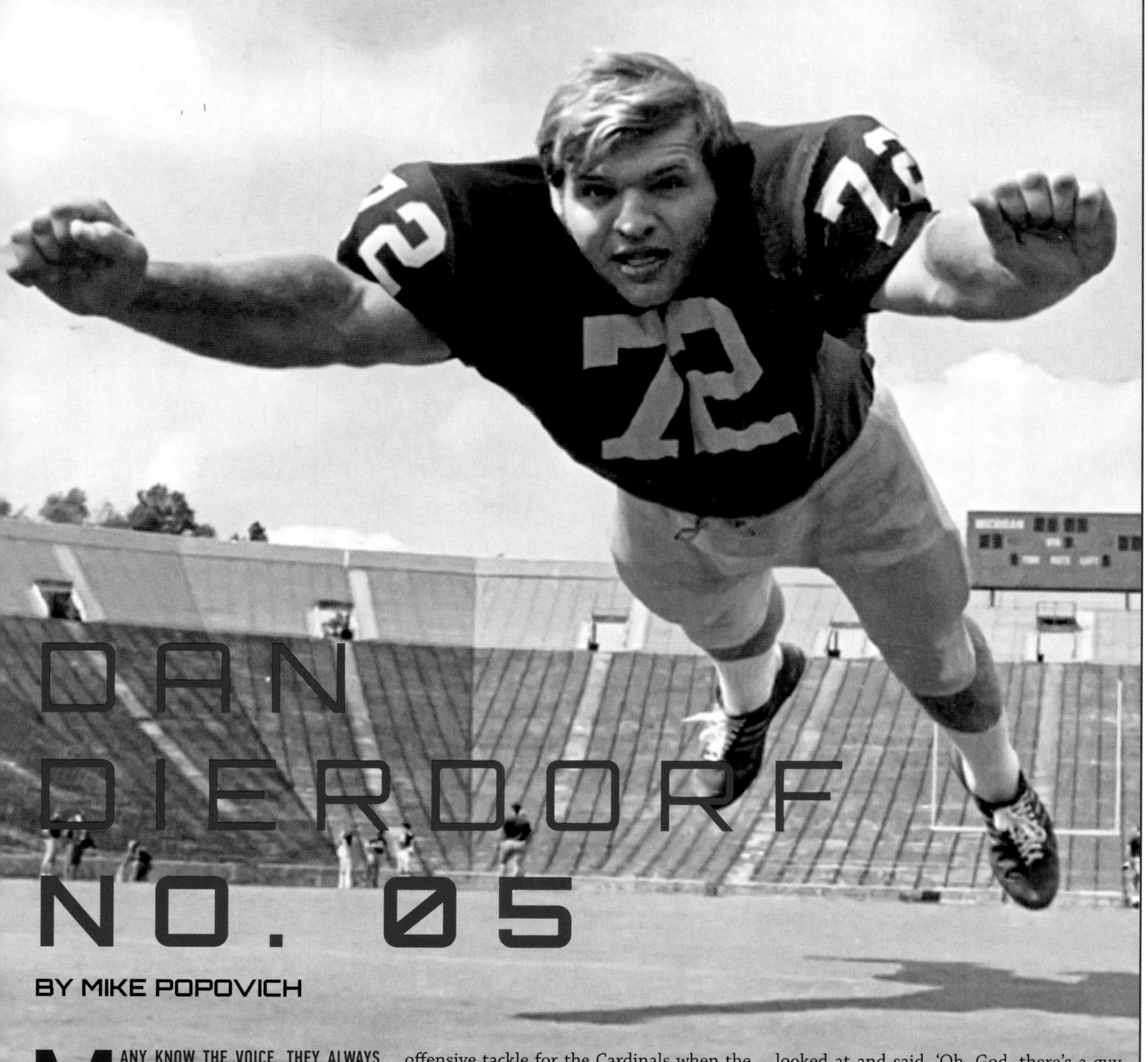

DAN DIERDORF NO. 05

BY MIKE POPOVICH

MANY KNOW THE VOICE. THEY ALWAYS WILL RECOGNIZE THE FACE.

Dan Dierdorf spent more than three decades as a National Football League analyst, including a 12-year run on "Monday Night Football." After retiring from television, he became the University of Michigan radio network's football analyst.

Older generations also remember Dierdorf the football player. He was an All-Pro offensive tackle for the Cardinals when the team was based in St. Louis. In 1996, he joined Alan Page as the only Canton natives to be inducted into the Pro Football Hall of Fame.

Dierdorf wouldn't have predicted a Hall of Fame career in the 1960s when he learned the game. He did not play football until he was a seventh-grader at Taft Middle School. He once described himself as a late bloomer.

"I wasn't one of those guys who people looked at and said, 'Oh, God, there's a guy who's going to end up in the Pro Football Hall of Fame,' " Dierdorf said prior to his induction into the Stark County High School Football Hall of Fame. "... I was not as coordinated as I ultimately became. Mentally, I was not as aggressive as I ultimately became. I was kind of the original glad-to-be-here guy."

He turned out to be more than that.

Dierdorf lettered as a two-way tackle at

> "Some kids, even the good ones, look like they would rather not be practicing during two-a-days in August. Dan always seemed to enjoy every minute he was on the football field, even the tough practices. He demonstrated a lot of leadership because of that attitude."
>
> —Jim Reichenbach in 2002

Glenwood High School in 1965 and 1966. He helped lead the Eagles to a 9-1 record and the Federal League title his senior year.

The late Jim Reichenbach coached Dierdorf at Glenwood. In an interview with The Repository in 2002, he clearly recalled Dierdorf's dedication and passion for football.

"Some kids, even the good ones, look like they would rather not be practicing during two-a-days in August," Reichenbach said. "Dan always seemed to enjoy every minute he was on the football field, even the tough practices. He demonstrated a lot of leadership because of that attitude.

"Dan didn't have to do much talking. He just demonstrated. When the kids saw how much he enjoyed practice and the effort he put into practice, it made him a tremendous asset as far as getting them in the right frame of mind."

Dierdorf also wrestled and was a thrower on Glenwood's track and field team. He set the Stark County boys shot put record with a throw of 60 feet, 8 inches. The record stood for 32 years.

Football, though, would offer opportunities to last a lifetime.

Dierdorf became a consensus All-American at Michigan and helped lead the Wolverines to a 25-6 record in his three years as a starter. His 1969 team beat Ohio State to win the Big Ten title and end the Buckeyes' hope of repeating as national champions.

The Cardinals selected Dierdorf in the second round of the 1971 NFL Draft. He played guard and tackle in his first two seasons before he settled in at right tackle for the remainder of his 13-year career. He was named All-Pro five times and selected to play in six Pro Bowls.

Playing in the shadow of the Dallas Cowboys in the NFC East, Dierdorf's St. Louis teams struggled. The Cardinals made just three playoff appearances during his career and lost in the first round all three times. They finished under .500 seven times.

Dierdorf is one of a handful of players to be elected to the Hall of Fame without winning a playoff game. He had no complaints prior to his enshrinement in 1996.

"What kind of pompous ass would I have to be to complain about my life," he said then. "I mean, how full does your plate have to be?

"I got to play professional football. I got in the Hall of Fame in my hometown without ever playing for a championship team, and I got hired as an announcer on 'Monday Night Football' without being a marquee player."

Dierdorf was added to ABC's "Monday Night Football" lineup in 1987. He worked with Frank Gifford and Al Michaels and remained with the series in 1998 when Boomer Esiason replaced Gifford. After leaving "Monday Night Football," he joined CBS as an NFL analyst and worked mostly Sunday afternoon games.

Citing travel becoming tough on his artificial knees, hips and bad back, Dierdorf announced his retirement in 2013. His absence from the broadcast booth would not be permanent. In 2014, he joined Jim Brandstatter as a member of Michigan's radio broadcast team. Brandstatter was Dierdorf's backup at Michigan in 1969 and 1970.

"I'm so excited to be able to come back to my alma mater and contribute in this manner," Dierdorf said. "This is the only broadcasting job that I would have considered after retiring from network television.

"I was always jealous of Jim calling games at Michigan and often said that one of my goals was to come back and call a couple of series with him. To work with one of my best friends, someone that I've known my entire adult life, is really special."

ALAN PAGE NO. 06

BY JIM THOMAS

HAVING A SUCCESSFUL CAREER OF YOUR CHOICE IS THE ADULT DREAM. TO HAVE PURSUED TWO HIGH-PROFILE AND DISTINCTLY DIFFERENT CAREERS AND ACHIEVED CELEBRITY IN EACH IS ATYPICAL. Alan Cedric Page has been, is and always will be different. Pro Football Hall of Famer. Union activist. Marathon runner in a behemoth's body. Supporter of people of color. Philanthropist. Trial lawyer. Author. State Supreme Court Associate Justice.

Page has been all those things and more in his 70 years. You can not say any one of them defined him, because of his constant evolution. He would be the first to say he is more proud of becoming the first African-American member of the Minnesota Supreme Court than being the NFL's first defensive player to earn the MVP award.

"I'll have 22 years, 8 months, just shy of 23 years, in the legal system when I retire (in August 2015)," Page said via phone from his chamber in May 2015. "I had an extremely long football career (23 years from high school through NFL). Most people aren't that fortunate.

"It is so important for those that can play and do play to recognize that there is a life beyond the athletic fields."

Belden Brick President and CEO Bob Belden was a teammate of Page's at both Central Catholic High School and the University of Notre Dame. He is not surprised at Page's excellence outside the lines.

"I would say he has a passion for education," Belden said of Page. "Particularly through his foundation for minority students. Obviously, the law is important to him given his career.

"He is very much a guy who played his own tune. He does what he thinks is best."

"Isn't that what you should do?" mused Page. "Do what you think is right, and continue to assess (it)."

The early years were an amalgamation of all things Page. He endured racism growing up in East Canton, learned the importance of education from his parents while attending Central Catholic and discovered his athleticism.

From his teenage adolescence to the unveiling of his bust in the Pro Football Hall of Fame in 1988, Page was recognized first as a great football player. He starred at Central Catholic under legendary coach John McVay and, as a senior, for Joe Eaglowski.

"He was a tough, fast-moving, hard-hitting lineman," Eaglowski told The Repository in 2002. "But a gentleman all the way. Add to that being a good student."

Those contrasting characteristics were the foundation of Page's football career. Page went to Notre Dame in 1963 and helped the Fighting Irish win the 1966 National Championship as an All-American defensive end. But he also was in tune with the racial and political issues of the times and graduated with a bachelor's in political science.

A first-round draft pick by the Minnesota Vikings in 1967, Page was switched to tackle upon his first training camp. As quickly as he moved his feet, he became an immediate star. The now 6-foot-4, 245-pounder was named NFC Rookie of the Year to begin a string of honors.

All-Pro. All-NFL. Two-time NFL Defensive Player of the Year. And NFL MVP in 1971, the first defensive player to have been accorded the honor.

Page was at the center of the nationally known 'Purple People Eaters' defensive line, along with Carl Eller, Jim Marshall and Gary Larsen. Page spent 11-plus years in the trenches in frigid Minnesota, and his Vikings won four NFC championships. Despite a great defense, Minnesota lost all four of its Super Bowl appearances with Page.

By his 12th season in Minnesota, Page had become a dedicated distance runner. He began while helping his wife, Diane, kick the smoking habit, and running soon became a habit of his. Page became the first NFL player to run a marathon. Training dropped 20 pounds off his frame and allegedly became a reason the Vikings waived him in 1978. Though Page latched on with Chicago and played three-plus years as a Bear—giving him a 234-game streak where he didn't miss a game in 15 years—his life's course had been plotted long ago.

Early in his years in Minnesota, Page became the team's player representative for the NFL Players Association. He fought for better pay, better benefits and, eventually, the league's version of free agency. That whetted his appetite to further his education, but his interest in the legal system pre-dated football.

"When I was 9 or 10, I had a young child's interest in the law," Page said. "It was about fairness and helping people.

"I didn't find an interest in football until ninth grade ..."

He attended the University of Minnesota's Law School as a full-time student while with the Vikings and graduated with his Juris Doctorate in 1978. That accelerated Page's lifetime crusade for education and justice involving youth, people of color, the underprivileged. He became a high school principal, then an assistant state attorney general. He and Diane set up the Page Education Foundation in 1988 to offer financial and mentoring assistance to those students who committed to volunteer service in their communities. The foundation has since distributed more than $12 million in grants.

In 1992, Page forced his name onto the Minnesota Supreme Court ballot. Not surprisingly, he was elected. When he ran again in 2004, he garnered the state's highest voting percentage in history. Page turned 70 in August 2015, and was forced from the court by Minnesota's mandatory retirement age.

It simply opened another door for Page.

At his Hall of Fame induction speech in Canton in 1988, Page said, "On this occasion, I ask myself, 'What contribution can I still make that would be truly worthy of the outpouring of warmth and good feelings as I have received today?'

"And the answer for me is clear: To help give other children the chance to achieve their dreams."

"I had an extremely long football career (23 years from high school through NFL). Most people aren't that fortunate. It is so important for those that can play and do play to recognize that there is a life beyond the athletic fields." —Alan Page

DON'T GIVE UP. IF YOU GIVE UP, YOUR CAREER IS OVER. ALL YOU CAN ASK FOR IS AN OPPORTUNITY." —LEN DAWSON

LEN DAWSON NO. 07

BY JIM THOMAS

BACK IN THE SPRING OF 2012, LEN DAWSON MADE AN APPEARANCE AT HIS OLD HIGH SCHOOL AS PART OF THE PRO FOOTBALL HALL OF FAME'S HOMETOWN HEROES.

"I used to deliver The Repository growing up," he said. "I remember one time I didn't get paid. You ask them what happened."

Dawson has come a long way since pocketing a penny per paper.

He went from delivering newspapers, to starring in The Repository sports pages at Alliance High to eventually becoming Super Bowl IV Most Valuable Player for Kansas City. That led to enshrinement in the Pro Football Hall of Fame in 1987. After his playing days were done, Dawson became a pioneer in cable sports as host of HBO's award-winning "Inside the NFL" program for 23 seasons.

By the time his football and broadcast careers were over, everybody in America knew the name of Len Dawson, the first Stark County native to be inducted into the Hall of Fame.

It wasn't an easy road for Dawson, however. Few worked as hard or endured as much neglect in the ranks of the NFL as Dawson did.

The fifth overall pick by Pittsburgh out of Purdue University in 1957, Dawson fizzled rather than sizzled upon his entry into the professional ranks. He was with the Steelers for three years and then with Paul Brown's Cleveland Browns for two.

"I started two games in five years," Dawson told that Alliance crowd in 2012. "Basically the only thing I did was hold on extra points."

What he didn't do was pout or pack his bags. Not the seventh son of a seventh son. Not with 10 brothers and sisters and supportive parents who stuck with him.

The message he had learned, Dawson said, was "Don't give up. If you give up, your career is over. All you can ask for is an opportunity."

Dawson's opportunity came in 1962 in the form of an old benefactor and a new league. Hank Stram was watching over Dawson. He had been for years, first at Purdue as an assistant football and baseball coach and then as the head coach of the Dallas Texans of the upstart American Football League.

Dawson took advantage of his opportunity after being released by the Browns. At age 27, Dawson enjoyed a monstrous first season with the Texans in 1962, throwing a league-high 29 touchdown passes. He led the Texans to the AFL championship with a 20-17 double-overtime win over the rival Houston Oilers.

"This acquisition was really the turning point for our team," Stram said at Dawson's induction.

Due to low attendance and the existence of a Houston team, Dallas owner Lamar Hunt moved the team to Kansas City the next season. If not for Dawson's arrival in Dallas, Stram said, there might not be a Chiefs team in Kansas City or even a Super Bowl.

"If Leonard doesn't come to Dallas, we don't win the (AFL) Championship," Stram said in a phone interview prior to his own HOF induction in 2003. "If we don't move to Kansas City, maybe we don't have a merger (between the AFL-NFL)."

Hunt called Dawson, "The heart and soul of the Chiefs."

Dawson's crowning moment came in the 1969 season. After losing the first AFL-NFL World Championship (later to become the Super Bowl) to Green Bay in 1966, Dawson led Kansas City to a 23-7 win over Minnesota in what was the last AFL-NFL World Championship Game.

Sitting the bench his first five years might have helped Dawson's career as much as it slowed it. The slender 6-foot-1, 190-pounder wound up with a 19-year pro career, the final 14 in the Chiefs' red, gold and white.

During his early days in Kansas City, Dawson accepted an offer to work on local television, which down the road led to his time with HBO.

Dawson said, for him, it all began growing up in Stark County. The sandlot fields were plentiful here in the 1940s. With six older brothers, teammates were plentiful. All a young Lenny Dawson needed was a ball, and he was ready to play.

He was all-state in basketball as well as football, and a dandy baseball player, too. Throwing the football was his thing, though, and that was because of coach Mel Knowlton.

"He wasn't afraid to throw the ball back then," Dawson said during his enshrinement speech in 1987. "He was an innovator, because he didn't have as much talent as some of the other teams, like McKinley and Massillon."

Dawson was innovative, and confident flipping a football. At Dawson's enshrinement, Stram recalled when a Purdue coach wished Dawson luck before his first start. "Dawson replied, 'Thank you, coach, but you don't need luck. All you need is ability,' " Stram said.

Dawson then backed up his words with four touchdown passes in a 30-0 win over Missouri. He fired four more the next week to defeat vaunted Notre Dame 28-14. Dawson went on to lead the Big Ten in passing for three straight years, which sparked Pittsburgh to draft him.

He always had the ability. When Dawson finally got his chance in the pros five years later, he stepped up, grabbed it by the horns and rode it to become an icon.

NICK WEATHERSPOON NO. 08

BY CHRIS BEAVEN

EVERY GENERATION HAS ITS DEFINING ATHLETE. FOR MANY GROWING UP IN STARK COUNTY IN THE LATE 1960S, THAT ATHLETE SIMPLY WAS KNOWN AS 'SPOON. Starring in basketball at McKinley High School, Nick Weatherspoon was in many ways a player well ahead of the times.

At 6-foot-7, he had the size of a big man who could dominate in the paint in the '60s. Weatherspoon was a presence and a force around the rim. But what made him such a defining athlete to so many was what he could do at that size.

He could run the floor. He could handle the ball. And he could shoot. Boy, could he shoot.

Adding to his legend, 'Spoon had a jump shot that was all his own. Great lift. The ball leaving his hands from behind his head. His body naturally fading away. From the baseline, he seemed to never miss.

Defend it? Good luck.

"I don't have any recollection of anyone coming close to blocking one of his shots," said area attorney Sam Rubin in May 2014, a McKinley teammate of Weatherspoon's during the 1968-69 season. "It was a deadly shot. And he had range, too, for a big guy. At that time, it wasn't usual for a big guy to go away from the basket and score. But he had that ability. Plus, he could put the ball on the floor."

In the NBA of today, 6-foot-7 players gliding up and down the floor, dropping in jumpers from all over the floor are the norm. That was not the case on the playgrounds or in the gyms of the 1960s. That's why crowds flocked to see him play, and why so many still look back fondly on the high-scoring, but humble, Weatherspoon.

"I think 'Spoon was the first guy at McKinley and the first guy around here that you had above 6-5 who could basically do everything on the basketball court," Larry Hackenberg said in 2014 before the late Weatherspoon was inducted into the Ohio Basketball Hall of Fame.

Hackenberg starred in the '60s at Canton South. He later enjoyed a lengthy coaching career in the county. He also is quite the Stark sports historian.

In Hackenberg's opinion, Weatherspoon "might have defined the more modern basketball a little bit."

And that's what made him so special in the eyes of those who watched him, such as R.C. Hill, who played at McKinley a few years after Weatherspoon. Hill later became an assistant coach at McKinley for a number of years. He's well versed on all of the great McKinley basketball players over the years. But he has no problem naming the best he saw.

"Inside, outside, (Weatherspoon) was the man," Hill told The Repository in 2003. "He can shoot it and he can do it all. And what most guys don't understand was Nick was a great defensive player."

His unique blend of talents allowed Weatherspoon to set scoring records at McKinley and the University of Illinois before becoming the 13th pick of the 1973 NBA Draft by the Capital Bullets.

"He was the prototype kid from Canton that could play basketball and go to the next level," longtime area official Henry Armstead said when Weatherspoon died in October 2008. "He set a precedent for the young men around here, to go to school and to advance in life."

Weatherspoon started a streak of 35 years of at least one McKinley graduate playing in the NBA. Phil Hubbard, Gary Grant, Eric Snow, Michael Hawkins and Keith McLeod all followed Weatherspoon's path to the NBA.

"He was always good to me both in life and in basketball," Hubbard said in May 2014. "A lot of things that happened to me were because of him, because I think I followed his pattern. I wanted to be just like him.

"Knowing him and being able to associate with him gives you motivation. But those steps are hard to follow. He scored a lot of points and grabbed a lot of rebounds."

His 1,431 career points at McKinley stood as a Bulldogs record for 37 years. His 684 points as a senior are still the single-season record at the school.

At Illinois, he graduated as the school's career scoring leader and become an All-American. He still holds the Illinois record for career scoring average (20.9) and rebounding average (11.4). That's why his No. 12 jersey hangs in Assembly Hall.

He earned a spot on the NBA All-Rookie first team in 1973-74 with the Bullets and helped them reach the NBA Finals a year later. His seven-year NBA career also included stops with the Seattle SuperSonics, Chicago Bulls and San Diego Clippers. He averaged a career-high 13.8 points in the 1978-79 season with the Clippers, but retired a season later because of nagging injuries.

Weatherspoon, who was born in Mississippi and moved to Canton with his family as a child, operated his own insurance agency in his post-basketball career. He made Canton his home.

"He loved living in Canton," said his brother, Charlie Weatherspoon, prior to the Hall of Fame induction. "That gives you a good indication of the type of person he was."

Weatherspoon battled health problems in his later years. A degenerative disc disease caused debilitating pain. It ultimately led to an eating disorder, which caused his death at age 58.

His death touched many, including a longtime opponent who also was a friend.

Luke Witte, a former Marlington star, played against Weatherspoon in high school, college and the pros. When Weatherspoon died, Witte told The Repository how much he "appreciated" and "really cared" for him.

"We are linked," Witte said then. "We've been linked since the middle '60s together. It's something I hold dear to my heart."

Hubbard remembers Weatherspoon as someone who always was approachable by anyone.

"He was just Nick," Armstead said. "A quiet, soft-spoken guy. He never bragged about anything. He was a very humble guy."

> Knowing him and being able to associate with him gives you motivation. But those steps are hard to follow. He scored a lot of points and grabbed a lot of rebounds."
>
> —Phil Hubbard

IN THEIR WORDS

BY PHIL HUBBARD

AS A PLAYER, HE WAS AHEAD OF ME, SO I GOT A CHANCE TO WATCH HIM. ... THEN TO BE ABLE TO SEE HIM AND TALK TO HIM WHEN HE CAME HOME (FROM THE NBA) WAS BIG.

It was a very special part of my life, just him being a leader and being a guy that gave you that good advice. He had gone through the same things I was going through. Things like picking an agent, getting ready for the pro game, he gave me a lot of good advice since we were leading the same path.

"It was an easy connection, and he was always like my idol. Not even knowing the basketball part, knowing I was going to follow him in the basketball part, but just knowing him. ... I'd been following him for a long time. And the advice he gave me on and off the court was great.

"He was a good man. That's what made him so easy to talk with, to approach him. He was very humble and very approachable, and not just by me but by anyone. And you learn to try to treat people right (from that example) because you want them to treat you the same way."

Hubbard, like Weatherspoon, was a record-setting player at McKinley High School before following in his footsteps as a college star at a Big Ten school and then enjoying a long NBA career. Like Weatherspoon, Hubbard, too, is a Stark County Sports Icon.

RONNIE HARRIS NO. 09

BY STEVE DOERSCHUK

THE GUY MAYBE SHOULD HAVE BEEN FIRED OVER SAYING WHAT HE DID, BUT AT THE SAME TIME HE DID RONNIE HARRIS A FAVOR.

Harris was a skinny kid with this fat dream of pigskin glory in a town that was just then building the Pro Football Hall of Fame.

He showed up for a football tryout, his first step as a future star for the Canton McKinley Bulldogs.

"The coach looked at me and said, 'What are you doing here?' " Harris recalls. "I said, 'I'm here to play football.'

"He said, 'Man, you don't stand a chance to play football here.' I said, 'What?' "

Skinny Ronnie was disgusted to have flunked some guy's eyeball test.

"So I said, 'OK, don't you worry about it,' " Harris said. " 'You take your football and stick it. You'll read about me one day.' "

He won an Olympic gold medal in boxing in 1968, in Mexico City.

The road to gold was hard and sometimes cold. It began in the Harris home at 1817 Penn Place NE, between roads now named after The O'Jays and Marion Motley, a mile east of the Palace Theatre.

"It was a rough neighborhood," Harris recalls. "The kids were a year or two older than me. We would run home from school because they were looking for somebody to beat up."

There were eight siblings, mostly sisters, who looked out for each other. One time, a tough guy in his early 20s grabbed one of his sisters inappropriately.

"I said, 'You can't be doing that,' " Harris said. "The guy wanted to jump on me. My sister stepped in between me and him. She was going to fight him, but he went away."

His parents pointed him to the Canton Police Boys Club on Navarre Road, where boxing was taught. The four-mile walk from the northeast side to the southwest side became a habit.

To get into his first Golden Gloves boxing tournament in the Canton Auditorium, he lied about his age. On his first try, he won the novice division at 112 pounds. He was novice champ at 118 a year later.

He moved to the open division and never slowed down. He finally was "legal," 16 years old. He was beating 20-something tough guys. People recognized him. Some would stop their cars and drive him to the Boys Club. Ronnie's father wasn't into free rides.

Willie "Red" Harris devised a running route that began at the intersection of Harrisburg Road and U.S. Route 62. He would make Ronnie run on the grassy median of the divided four-lane highway while carrying a brick in each hand and wearing combat boots.

"We would go before he went to work on a day shift," Ronnie said. "It might be 4:30 a.m.

"In the winter, I would heat the bricks on the register. I would have ice all over my face and my eyebrows and under my nose, but my hands were warm.

"Sometimes the snow would come up to my knees. I'd be stepping through the snow for five miles, up and down hills. I was 14 or 15 years old."

Ronnie was laughing as if he could feel the bricks in his hands.

"I couldn't quit," he said. "My dad wouldn't pick me up until I was done.

"He would follow me in his car. Sometimes the state Highway Patrol would stop him. He said, 'Look over here, officer. I got my boy. I'm training him to be a prizefighter.' They said, 'OK. Be careful.' "

Harris became a smart, tough, relentless boxer. His hands and mind were lightning quick. He could take a punch on the off chance you could hit him.

His Golden Gloves reputation spread to the state level. He went national, winning AAU lightweight championships in 1966, '67 and '68. When he lost a decision to a Cuban fighter at the Pan-Am Games, it only made him mad.

He settled on a purpose. His mission became winning an Olympic gold medal for his mother, Geraldine.

When he went to Mexico City, his dad was his "road buddy" and trainer. His mom was back in Canton.

"Dad knew what I was trying to do," Harris said, "which was to win for my mother.

"She was a wonderful lady who had her hands full with eight children. She would walk with us to school and walk home by herself ... an oppressed individual with eight children living in the ghetto.

"I know her heart wanted us to have more. All of us graduated from college, and it started with her."

Winning the gold got complicated.

"Two days after I got to Mexico City, I was sick with dysentery," Harris said. "I was watching the food and the water, but they didn't tell me the plates and the silverware got washed in that water, so I got sick anyway.

"I was boxing in the 132-pound division at 5-foot-10, fighting my fights at 115. The communist countries brought 29- and 30-year-old men in who were professionals.

"You had to become a victor over that situation. It was very frightening. You had to take it second by second in the fight, and then you had to hope that you got the proper judging. I was not a knockout artist.

"It was a thing where you had to be blessed by God, then you had to be in great shape, you had to be tough, you had to have all the skills possible to beat these ... (laughs) these men."

Turbulence rocked the months leading into the Olympics. In the United States, assassins gunned down Martin Luther King and Robert F. Kennedy. Protests over racial in-

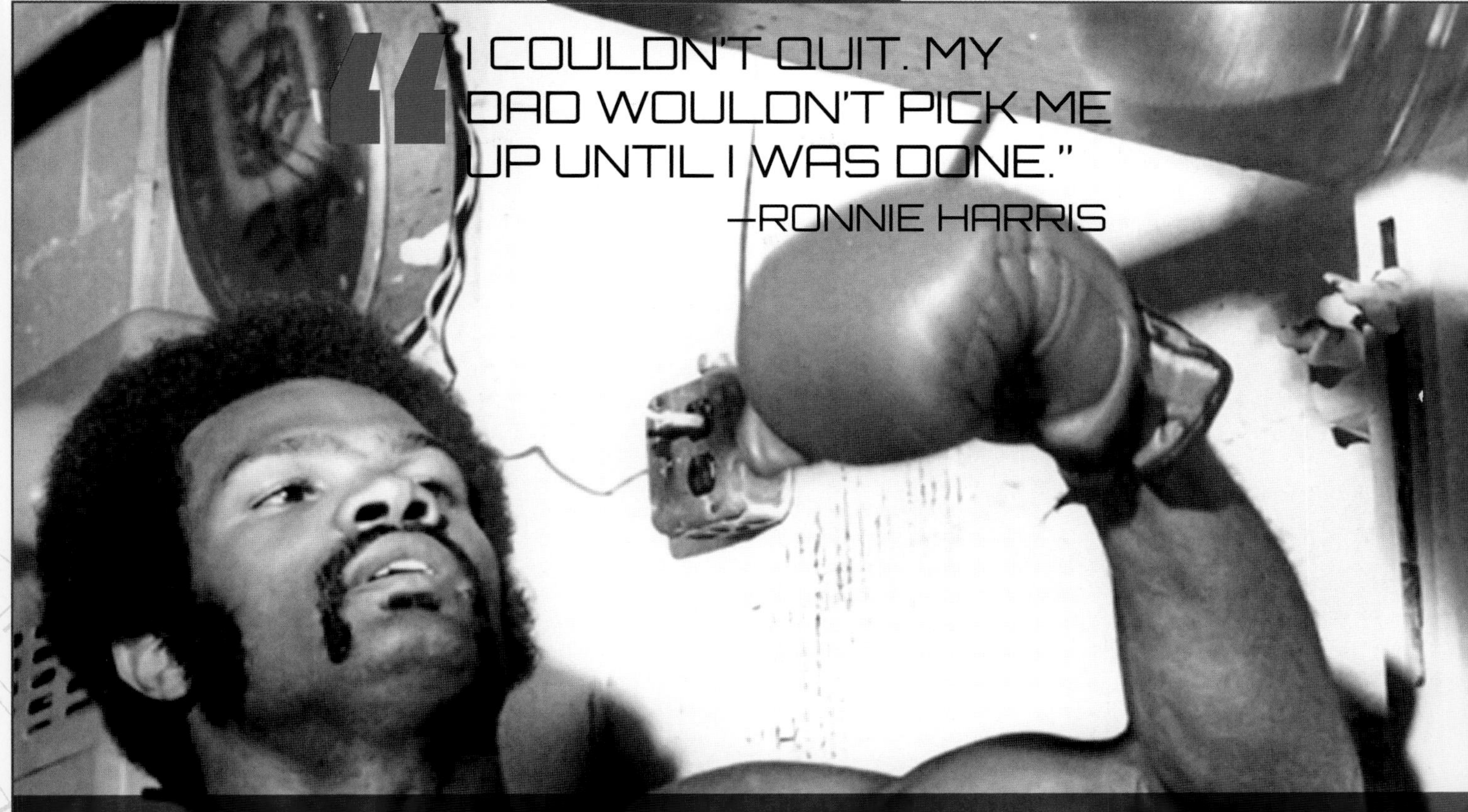

"I COULDN'T QUIT. MY DAD WOULDN'T PICK ME UP UNTIL I WAS DONE."
—RONNIE HARRIS

IN THEIR WORDS

BY GEORGE FOREMAN

I T WAS 1968 AND I WAS IN PRE-TRAINING FOR THE OLYMPIC GAMES IN MEXICO CITY LATER THAT YEAR. THAT'S WHEN I FIRST MET RONNIE HARRIS.

Our friendship grew from there. Ron always has been a little smarter than me. He had his dad, Red, with him all the time. Red was a great man. They had this way about them. They used their minds to figure things out. They were really the first people that I learned boxing was more about the mind than about brute strength. They made boxing a brain game. You could look at them and watch them and you knew, these dudes know some things the rest of us don't. Ronnie was about delivering punches, moving his feet and not getting caught in awkward positions. I was just about knockouts. I could close my eyes, swing wildly, and do just as good. Ronnie was smart.

Think back to 1968. It was a very different time. Martin Luther King Jr. was assassinated in April. It was in one world we qualified for the Olympics and in another when we left Mexico City. The world changed when Martin Luther King was killed.

My friendship with Ronnie was a smooth transition. We were so nervous about boxing matches, we didn't get too much into what was happening socially.

That Olympic team, boy, we were clean-cut Americans. We were true Americans. I remember winning the gold medal like it was yesterday, too. We were in the dressing room and we were nervous and we were scared. Ronnie, though, he carried himself like he knew something no one else did.

To this day, we still talk a few times a week. We're both grandpas now, so we talk about grandchildren and business. Ronnie is in business. I'm in business. Boxing sneaks in occasionally, but usually it's business. Ronnie Harris is one of my true friends in this world.

George Foreman won a gold medal along with Ronnie Harris in the 1968 Olympics. He knocked out Joe Frazier to win the heavyweight championship in 1973.

equality and the Vietnam War raged. In Mexico City, social unrest led to massive marches that left dozens dead within weeks of the Olympics. Activists pressured Harris and other black Olympians either to boycott the games or to politicize any successes.

On Oct. 16, after Americans Tommie Smith and John Carlos won medals in the 200-meter dash, both put on black gloves and raised them with bowed heads on the awards stand while the National Anthem played.

Harris recalls being pressured by "two or three demonstrators" who wanted him to be a protest symbol on the awards stand.

"I was told, 'You're going to have to choose sides.' ... It was a very, very, very awkward situation," Harris said. "I just said I was going to take care of my business. I was most concerned about my mother, because I made her a promise."

He outboxed all three of his opponents, scoring 5-0 decisions in each bout to win the lightweight gold medal. As a pro, Harris' record was 35-2. He got as far as a world middleweight title bout against Hugo Corro 10 years after Mexico City. On Corro's home turf, Argentina, Harris lost a split decision.

He said a year ago he would love to fight undefeated Floyd Mayweather, 30 years his junior, and would stand a good chance to win. He was completely serious.

EVEN 40-SOME YEARS LATER, THE MEMORIES REMAIN STRONG FOR PHIL HUBBARD. HE'S BACK IN THE CANTON YMCA GYM WITH A DREAM AND A PLAN.

The dream? It seemed lofty to secure a big-time college basketball scholarship like his idol, Nick Weatherspoon. The plan? That was easy; just go to work on becoming a better basketball player.

So the summer before his senior year—aside from four hours cutting grass each morning for his city job—Hubbard spent endless hours in the gym. He shot by himself, played one-on-one against others in the gym, jumped into games with guys from the men's league and lifted weights.

"I stayed there and shot and worked on my game all day," Hubbard said. "I'd go home and do it again the next day, just working and staying in the gym."

Day after day, the routine never changed. Cut grass, play ball, eat and get some sleep. The job cutting grass didn't last the entire summer. Eventually, it was just work on his game, eat and sleep.

Basketball fans know the rest. The plan worked, and dreams beyond his initial imagination were achieved.

The 6-foot-8 Hubbard became one of the nation's top high school basketball players his senior year at McKinley. The next summer, he was honing his game at the University of Michigan. The summer after that, he was winning an Olympic gold medal on the United States men's team with Dean Smith as his coach. A couple summers later, he was an NBA first-round draft pick by the Detroit Pistons, on his way to 10 years in the league.

"I didn't have any expectations," Hubbard said as he looked back on his career. "I just wanted to be a pretty good player."

Growing up watching Weatherspoon in person and on TV, from his days at McKinley to his NBA career, set the standard for Hubbard and other McKinley players from the early 1970s. But to Hubbard, as a teenager, coming close to Weatherspoon's success didn't even seem realistic.

Hubbard took things one step at a time. So when asked now to look back, the first thing he recalls is just being a Bulldog.

"That was one of the things I always wanted to do as young kid, play at McKinley High School," he said. "To have a chance to play varsity basketball was a big thrill. ... The uniform, the whole thing. The first chance I got to wear that varsity uniform was my junior year, and I'll always remember that."

There were no dreams of being a gold medalist, an All-American or making money as an NBA player.

As a junior on a talented, senior-laden McKinley team, Hubbard's lone goal was just "trying to fit in."

"I didn't get a whole lot of shots as junior, so I decided to rebound and do what I could do," Hubbard said. "I think it helped me because I had to learn how to play and accept a role. And I was just happy to have a role on McKinley's team."

The Bulldogs reached the state tournament that season, losing in the 1974 title game. The lanky junior forward started getting noticed throughout the season.

"I started getting a few letters from colleges, things like that," Hubbard said. "I wanted to work hard and see what happened. That's when I thought I started changing. I just worked really hard over the summer.

"They gave us a membership to the downtown Y, and I went every day. I was cutting grass for four hours on the morning shift and then go to the Y. ... I had to work on stuff."

Hubbard saw improvements in his game throughout the summer, but still kept his goals on the short-term side.

"I never thought about the pros," he said. "I was thinking about college. I wanted to see if we could get back to the state tournament and win it. ... I was never thinking about more than that."

PHIL HUBBARD NO. 10

BY CHRIS BEAVEN

His senior season, Hubbard led McKinley back to the state tournament, where he broke some of Weatherspoon's records along the way. His 25.8 points per game in 1974-75 remains a McKinley record. He also grabbed 15 rebounds a game.

And he got better as the season went on, averaging 31.9 points over the final 10 games—highlighted by a 42-point game against Timken to claim the city championship. He scored 70 points in two regional games.

"He is the finest player I have ever coached," McKinley head coach Bob Rupert told The Repository that year. "He is better at this stage than Weatherspoon was when he was in high school."

Prep basketball hype was in its infancy, with no full-on offseason AAU circuit nor social media to create dozens of teenage superstars every year.

Still, word about McKinley's latest basketball sensation spread beyond Stark County. Coach & Athlete Magazine selected him as one of its "Super Ten" from the list of 100 prep basketball All-Americans. He joined a group that included Darryl Dawkins and Bill Willoughby, who each went directly from high school to the NBA.

Hubbard also played in three national all-star games, and earned MVP honors in the Dapper Dan Classic in Pittsburgh—a precursor to the McDonald's All-American Game.

Once at Michigan, he helped the Wolverines reach the NCAA Tournament Championship Game as a freshman in 1976, where they lost to the undefeated Indiana Hoosiers. Hubbard grabbed a game-high 11 rebounds in the title game to go with 10 points. He averaged 16.1 points and 11.0 rebounds for the season.

His strong play as a freshman earned him an invitation to try out for the U.S. Olympic team coached by Dean Smith.

"Once I got the tryout letter, I just assumed I was going to try out and maybe next time I'd make the team," Hubbard said.

He made that team and Hubbard was headed to the Summer Olympics in Montreal.

"That was a great experience because we were such a tight-knit team," he said. "The thing was, they were trying to get us ready in that short period of time, and we were college players trying to get ready to play pros, and it was a very intense situation. We were trying to avenge the Russians that beat us before (in 1972)."

Hubbard and the Americans never got a crack at the Soviet Union team in '76 (Yugoslavia upset the Soviets), but they won Olympic gold nonetheless.

"It was pretty exciting," said Hubbard, who keeps his gold medal in a safe deposit box.

Hubbard was a consensus second team All-American as a sophomore in 1977 for the 26-4 Wolverines, who won the Big Ten. He scored 19.5 points per game and set a single-season rebound record by grabbing 389. He also set an NCAA Tournament record with 26 rebounds in a regional semifinal win over Detroit. A knee injury during the World University Games cost him his junior season. He returned as a senior and finished out his career as Michigan's fourth all-time leading rebounder (979, 11.1 average).

Headed to the NBA, as the 15th pick in the 1979 draft by the Pistons, he set a new goal.

"Once I got to the NBA, I said to myself I wanted stay around 10 years or more," Hubbard said.

He achieved that goal, too, playing exactly 10 seasons—the final seven-plus with the Cleveland Cavaliers. He was never a star, but learned to play his role. He was looked to for rebounds and defense, though, he did average 10.9 points over his career.

"I found out everybody couldn't be a star," Hubbard said. "Once you got to the pros, there were a number of players that were at the same level as you. ... You had to figure out how you could be effective and how you could help the team.

"At some point, you realize it's good to show leadership and show the right way you can win and be a part of something. Everybody has to accept a role. Other guys might get more shots or more minutes than you, but you've got to find out how you fit in, finding a way to be as consistent a player as you can be to contribute to the team every night."

That's a mindset Hubbard often sold to players as a coach. He spent 12 seasons as an NBA assistant, coached overseas and worked for five years in the NBA D-League, where he was the head coach of the Los Angeles D-Fenders for the 2014-15 season.

"I always want to coach," said Hubbard, who calls Virginia home in the offseason. "Something always comes up. ... I never know what level that's going to be, but I always enjoy it. I guess I'm a lifer. Basketball has been a big part of my life, and I guess it always will be."

DAVE WOTTLE NO. 11

BY JIM THOMAS

RELATIVELY UNKNOWN. NOT HIS BEST EVENT. AND MOSTLY UNTESTED IN INTERNATIONAL COMPETITION. HARDLY THE STUFF OF LEGENDS.

Canton's Dave Wottle was made of sterner material. That he turned the running world upside down in 1972 is still unbelievable some 44 years later. The instant the 22-year-old from Lincoln High School claimed Olympic gold in Munich, Germany, in the 800 meters, he became a Stark County icon.

"I tell people, there aren't many days I don't think about that, and the impact it had on my life," Wottle said in 2015 from his home in Tennessee. "It changed my life. I wouldn't be the same person today if I hadn't won."

But against the odds, he did. When Wottle had the temerity to tell U.S. Olympic coach Bill Bowerman that he was getting married before the Olympics despite Bowerman's request to wait, it showed what kind of a fighter he was.

Before ABC's Chris Schenkle offered Wottle congratulations "on behalf of all the skinny guys in America," Wottle indeed did not look like a man capable of tracking down a field of the world's elite 800 runners.

In fact, the ABC announcer on Wottle's race wondered whether the recent Bowling Green State University graduate was "seriously injured or just laying back to stay out of trouble," so badly did he trail early on. Wottle was 25-30 meters off the pace at one point in the first of two laps.

Yet he was so strong that Wottle ran down all seven finalists on the gun lap. That included outkicking Kenyans' Mike Boit and Robert Ouko and the Ukraine's Evani Arzhanov, the favorite, over the final 50 meters. The hard-driving Wottle edged a diving Arzhanov in a photo finish to win in a time of 1:45.9.

Wottle was stunned enough that forgot he was wearing his hallmark golf hat during the playing of the national anthem. On the podium, Wottle—who had served in ROTC in college—put his hand over his heart while singing. Unfortunately, he had covered his USA emblem, in addition to wearing his hat.

That slight uproar from fans back home only added to his legend.

"I was worried that people thought I was covering up the patch," Wottle said. "I apologized to Jim McKay and Howard Cosell (of ABC Sports), and they accepted it (because) I was in ROTC."

Despite everything, Wottle did have the credentials to run in Munich.

He was Ohio's mile champion his senior year in high school. He was second at the NCAA Championships in the mile in 1970 at Bowling Green, and won it in both '72 and '73 after missing a season with an injury.

The mile, not the half, was Wottle's specialty. After the Olympics, he ran a 3:53.3 that was the second-fastest ever, behind Jim Ryan's 3:51.1. Wottle qualified for Munich in both but it was in the 800 at Eugene, Ore., at the Olympic Trials where Wottle shined brightest. Using the legendary Ryan as his rabbit, Wottle stayed back and then outkicked the leaders to tie the world record of 1:44.3.

He married his wife, Jan, six days later. "I don't think I could have told her we weren't getting married," Wottle said.

So determined was Wottle to "prove (Bowerman) wrong" that he overtrained after honeymooning at Salt Fork and developed tendinitis in his knees.

"Five weeks before the Olympics, I was running zero miles," Wottle said. "I wasn't in real good shape."

Good enough, it turned out, to run down the best Munich had to offer.

Wottle turned professional after that but went into coaching and education a year later. Wottle came back home and coached at Walsh University, then Bethany College before becoming an administrator at Rhodes College in Tennessee for 29 years.

Forty-four years later, Wottle still has the gold, and is still happily married to Jan. Iconic stuff, indeed.

TOMMY HENRICH NO. 12

BY CHRIS BEAVEN

EVERYONE KNOWS PRO FOOTBALL'S HISTORY LIVES YEAR ROUND IN STARK COUNTY.

Baseball history?

Massillon's Tommy Henrich lived and breathed it as part of perhaps the greatest dynasty in American sports: the New York Yankees of the 1930s and '40s. His 11 Major League seasons, all with the Yankees, saw him help the Bronx Bombers win seven World Series championships, while he made five American League All-Star teams.

Henrich was the "ultimate Yankee" in the eyes of former teammate Bobby Brown. He played alongside the Iron Horse, Joltin' Joe and The Scooter, but had a pretty good nickname of his own—Old Reliable, courtesy of legendary Yankees announcer Mel Allen.

No Yankee nickname might have been more perfect than his. Henrich was a Mr. October of sorts in the Golden Age of Baseball.

- *He hit the first walk-off home run in World Series history in Game 1 in 1949 against the Brooklyn Dodgers—long before anyone thought of the term.*
- *A decade earlier, in 1939, he homered in the decisive game of a four-game sweep of the Chicago Cubs.*
- *He played a key role in a pivotal 1941 World Series game by improbably reaching base on a dropped third strike. That triggered a game-winning rally in Game 4 to give Yankees a 3-1 series lead on their way to another title over the Dodgers.*
- *In Game 7 of the 1947 series, he drove in the series-winning run with a go-ahead hit in the fourth to break a 2-2 tie with the Dodgers. He hit .323 that series with five RBIs.*

He was called "The Clutch" on the back of a Bowman baseball card.

"If we were ahead 10-1 or 10-2, he was just average," Brown told the Los Angeles Times when Henrich died in 2009. "If we were behind 10-1 or 10-2, same thing. But get him in a big game and he was terrific."

Henrich, who played little organized baseball growing up in Massillon, could almost be his own category in Trivial Pursuit.

Henrich was the last living teammate to have played with Lou Gehrig and the oldest living Yankee, at age 96, at the time of his death. Henrich hit in front of Joe DiMaggio throughout his record-setting 56-game hitting streak in 1941. He was the Yankee who played the longest with DiMaggio. They spent the bulk of their 11-year run in pinstripes together with DiMaggio in center and Henrich in right. DiMaggio called Henrich, "the smartest player in the big leagues," in a 1971 New York Times story on Old Reliable.

Henrich also became Major League Baseball's first free agent in 1937, leaving the Indians for the Yankees. After starring on area semipro teams in the early 1930s while working as a typist at Republic Steel, Henrich hit well over .300 during three seasons in the minors for the Indians. They looked to stash him in the minors in the spring of '37. This angered Henrich. He wrote Commissioner Kenesaw Mountain Landis saying he was not being treated fairly. Landis agreed, declared Henrich free to sign elsewhere, and 11 teams pursued him.

Henrich had grown up a fan of Babe Ruth and the Yankees. His decision was easy. He hit .320 as a rookie and over time established himself in the heart of the Yankee lineup. Hall of Fame pitcher Bob Feller often called Henrich his toughest opponent. "That guy can hit me in the middle of the night, blindfolded and with two broken feet to boot."

Henrich's career spanned from 1937-42 and 1946-50, serving in a Coast Guard training center during World War II. His Yankee teams won eight AL pennants, averaging 97.5 wins a regular season.

Henrich loved being a Yankee. He played with no ego, but with self-confidence. He was a family man who didn't swear or party after hours. He sang and played piano. To his fellow Yankees, he was the consummate teammate.

"Being around Tommy made you feel good, whether playing cards or listening to him sing with that great voice," Hall of Famer Yogi Berra said.

Famed sports writer Red Smith once wrote that Henrich "got more pure joy out of baseball than any player I ever knew."

Henrich hit .282 for his career, with 183 home runs, 795 RBIs and 901 runs. He scored 100 or more runs in a season four times, leading the league with 138 in 1948. He led the AL in triples twice, and tied a league record by hitting four grand slams in '48. A year later, he was third in the AL in slugging percentage (.526) and homers (24) despite being limited to 115 games with a broken vertebrae in his back and a broken toe.

Even at age 36, he always found his way back to the field, and the '49 season is perhaps his most impressive. With DiMaggio injured early on, Henrich batted cleanup and hit 16 homers in his first 65 games, including 12 game-winners. The Yankees were in an epic battle for the AL pennant with the Red Sox. On the last day of the season, they were tied for first and played each other in Yankee Stadium.

Old Reliable delivered.

Henrich drove in the game's first two runs, including crushing a solo home run 10 rows deep into right field in the eighth inning of a 5-3 win.

"My first year with him was in 1949, and it seemed like every home run he hit won the game," former teammate Jerry Coleman said. " ... When he hit, it counted."

BY MIKE POPOVICH

> "I was blessed and gifted athletically. My personal challenge was to go above and beyond what was required." –MIKE DOSS

MIKE DOSS' FOOTBALL CAREER ENDED BEFORE HE TURNED 30.

It was short, but it was very successful—as he earned a championship ring at each level.

A dominant runner and a hard-hitting safety, Doss helped lead McKinley to a Division I state championship in 1997 and 1998. He went to Ohio State and won a BCS national title in his final game with the Buckeyes. He was drafted by the Indianapolis Colts and was a member of their Super Bowl winning team.

He hit every opponent head on from start to finish.

A Doss interception on the first play of the 1997 state championship game put McKinley on a fast track to a 31-16 win over Cincinnati Moeller. When Cleveland St. Ignatius threatened to derail the Bulldogs' bid for back-to-back titles a year later, Doss responded again. He drove a St. Ignatius receiver out of bounds at the 1 on the final play of McKinley's 31-24 state semifinal victory.

Those plays just scratch the surface.

Doss finished his McKinley career with a school-record 15 interceptions. He made 111 tackles, 12 tackles for loss, caused two fumbles and recovered two fumbles his senior year.

He also was a force at running back in his final high school season. Doss ran for 210 yards in a playoff win over Jackson, scored four touchdowns in the state championship game against Cincinnati St. Xavier and ended the year with 1,454 yards rushing.

"I was blessed and gifted athletically," Doss said in 2010 before he was inducted into the Stark County High School Football Hall of Fame. "My personal challenge was to go above and beyond what was required."

To no one's surprise, he also did that throughout his Ohio State career.

Doss became just the Buckeyes' seventh three-time All-American after receiving first team honors as a sophomore, junior and senior. He was voted the Big Ten Defensive Player of the Year in 2002 when he made a collegiate-best 107 tackles and helped lead the Buckeyes to the BCS championship game against Miami.

A first-quarter interception by Doss helped Ohio State tie the game at 7-7. He went on to deliver nine tackles and earn defensive MVP honors as the Buckeyes defeated the Hurricanes 31-24 in double overtime.

The Colts selected Doss in the second round of the 2003 draft. He made 42 starts in four seasons with Indianapolis, but played in just 11 games with Minnesota and Cincinnati over the final two years of his career.

A short NFL career does not accurately portray Doss' impact as a football player.

"I always wanted to help raise the team's level of play, to raise my level of play, to be respected for that," he once said. "I always wanted to be the best of the best."

LARRY KEHRES NO. 14

BY JIM THOMAS

SMALL COLLEGE COACHES HAVE TO FIGHT THEIR WAY TO THE TOP OF THEIR PROFESSION TO EARN PROMOTIONS, PAY HIKES, BETTER RECRUITS AND RESPECT AMONG THEIR PEERS.

It's hard to imagine a Division III coach who accomplished more and gained greater respect, in any sport, anywhere, than Mount Union's Larry Kehres.

That he was the president of the American Football Coaches Association and Ohio State's Jim Tressel was the organization's vice president at one point, spoke volumes about Kehres' place in the game.

To many, Kehres is Mount Union. And for good reason. Kehres starred there as a quarterback under coach Ken Wable and except for a brief interlude has served as a coach and administrator since 1974.

What they remember most is how he turned a solid NCAA Division III football program into the nation's best, perhaps at any level.

In 27 seasons as head coach, Kehres' teams lost a total of 24 games. His 332 victories produced a .929 winning percentage that was unmatched when he retired after Mount Union won the 2012 national championship.

His Purple Raiders became more than just a team; they turned into The Machine. Kehres' Mount Union teams didn't just dominate, they destroyed the competition and put together the two (55 and 54 games) longest winning streaks in college football history.

But there's more than just sheer numbers to Kehres' magic.

Kehres recruited not just in Stark County and Ohio, but Florida and California. Recruits flocked to Alliance to the point hundreds wanted to play there each fall.

"When I think of coach, I think of his passion for the game and coaching and Mount Union football," former Mount Union running back great Nate Kmic said when Kehres resigned in 2012. "If you were ever in Alliance, Ohio, on a Saturday afternoon in the fall, there was one guy (Kehres) on the field who was most passionate about winning."

Nobody won more consistently than Kehres. Beginning in 1993, Mount Union won 11 Division III national championships in a 19-year span under Kehres. In 16 of 20 seasons, the Purple Raiders played for the title. Ten of those years they went undefeated.

After retiring as football coach, Kehres has stayed on as director of athletics, a title he has held for the last 30 years. That only adds to his legacy, said Mount Union President Richard Giese.

"Coach Kehres has been an incredible success, not only in winning football games and national championships at an unprecedented level, but also in positively shaping the lives of countless student-athletes," Giese said in the school's release following Kehres' retirement.

IN THEIR WORDS

BY JIM TRESSEL

LARRY KEHRES IS A GIANT IN THE WORLD OF COLLEGE FOOTBALL, BUT SOMETIMES LEFT OUT OF SAID DISCUSSION IS HIS INFLUENCE ON THE YOUNG PEOPLE HE HAS IMPACTED, ALONG WITH THE TRANSFORMATION THAT HE WAS THE CATALYST FOR AT THE UNIVERSITY OF MOUNT UNION.

Larry took over the head coaching duties and later the director of athletics duties at his alma mater, and at that moment began an extraordinary transformation of the small, liberal arts college in Alliance. Larry Kehres raises the expectations of everyone around him. He is intelligent, tough, compassionate and fully aware of what it takes to exceed one's grandest dreams.

He will not settle for anything less than greatness, and that spirit permeated the entire institution. In my 55 years being in and around higher education, I have never witnessed a greater impact for "the good of the whole" than what Larry Kehres demonstrated at Mount Union.

In large part because of Larry Kehres, Mount Union has reached heights as an entire university, that most people never would have conceived. Our region, state and nation is better due to Coach Kehres and all of the Purple Raiders who believed.

Jim Tressel is the president of Youngstown State University. He is the former head football coach at Ohio State and a national championship coach for the Buckeyes. He is a member of the College Football Hall of Fame.

ERIC SNOW NO. 15

BY MIKE POPOVICH

ERIC SNOW IS PROUD TO BE A PART OF MCKINLEY HIGH SCHOOL'S STORIED TRADITION. HE EXPERIENCED IT AT A YOUNG AGE WHEN HIS OLDER BROTHER PERCY PLAYED FOOTBALL. He attended the basketball camps run by Phil Hubbard and Gary Grant. He always will remember going to Memorial Field House to see other Bulldogs greats such as David Greer, Ron Stokes and Troy Taylor.

"I just felt like it was a privilege to do it and to be a part of a tradition and history," Snow said. "When I had an opportunity to do it, it felt great. It felt like it was something you want to be a part of. It's long gone, but I still take pride in being a McKinley Bulldog and a Canton Ohioan forever."

Snow was a two-time first team All-Ohio guard for the Bulldogs in the early 1990s and followed Hubbard and Grant to the NBA, where he played 13 seasons. The last four were spent with the hometown Cleveland Cavaliers. Snow had an opportunity to play with LeBron James and was a member of the Cavs' team that reached the NBA Finals in 2007. He also played in the finals with the Seattle SuperSonics and Philadelphia 76ers.

"That was a great way to finish my career, to play with the team I grew up watching," Snow said. "It made it easier for my parents to come to the majority of my games. I could be home, and my kids could be around my parents a little more.

"At the same time, being a part of the changing of the culture with the Cavs. They're doing terrific now, but I think the time I was there kind of set the tone for the changing expectations. That wasn't happening in Cleveland when I was in the NBA. ... You didn't have that kind of excitement you have now."

Snow was an extension of a long continuous history of McKinley ties to the NBA. Beginning in 1973 when Nick Weatherspoon was an all-rookie selection with the then-Capital Bullets until Snow's retirement, there was at least one former McKinley player in the league.

A defensive-minded player known for his leadership, Snow's impact also was felt off the court.

Snow won the NBA's J. Walter Kennedy Citizenship Award when he played in Philadelphia. The award is presented to a player, coach or team staff member who shows outstanding service and dedication to the community.

Retirement has not slowed Snow's efforts to help others. He donated $1 million to the new downtown Canton YMCA that bears his name. The building opened in 2013.

"The YMCA did a lot of things to help me when I was younger," Snow said. "I had a good friend of mine who brought it to my attention. He was just trying to find different ways to provide something that could be a resource for so many people, and this was a way I felt it could happen.

"We have different programs, and it's just starting back and building. We're looking to continue to grow and make it bigger so its reach can be as big as possible for a lot of people, youths and adults."

Snow remains involved with basketball. He spent two seasons working under Larry Brown at Southern Methodist University as the Mustangs' director of player development. In 2014, he moved to Florida Atlantic, where he is an assistant coach.

Coaching has given Snow an opportunity to make an impact on up-and-coming players. It also reminds him of when he grew up and learned from people such as Hubbard, Grant, Greer, Stokes, Taylor and his brother Percy.

"It's the love and passion I have for basketball I can see myself doing as long as they allow me," Snow said. "I enjoy doing it. I enjoy teaching and helping people. It's just another way to be involved with the game and at the same time try to help some young men be better men, better people and better players. It's something I'm really enjoying."

JIM THORPE NO. 16

BY STEVE DOERSCHUK

WHERE JIM THORPE RANKS ON THE LIST OF STARK COUNTY'S 20 GREATEST SPORTS ICONS MIGHT MAKE THE PEOPLE OF 1920 WONDER WHAT THE PEOPLE OF 2015 WERE THINKING.

Thorpe is No. 16. In a 1999 ABC poll, he was named Greatest Athlete of the 20th Century. He beat a slugger (Babe Ruth), a boxer (Muhammad Ali), two Buckeyes (Jack Nicklaus, Jesse Owens) and a basketball player (Michael Jordan).

In the 1912 Olympics, Thorpe won the pentathlon, the decathlon and this famous praise from King Gustav V of the host country, Sweden: "You, sir, are the greatest athlete in the world."

Five-time Olympic gold medalist Martin Sheridan said, "Thorpe is the greatest athlete that ever lived."

Thorpe was of mixed ancestry and was raised in a native-American culture, Sac and Fox. At the Carlisle Indian Industrial School in Pennsylvania, he gained renown in track, baseball, lacrosse, other sports and ballroom dancing. In a famous 27-6 win over then-powerful Army, he ran 90-some yards for a touchdown that was called back, then scored for real on the next play.

Army player Dwight Eisenhower said years later, after two terms as U.S. president, "He was better than any football player I ever saw."

Even his punts left crowds gasping.

Thorpe was stripped of his Olympic medals in 1913 because he had been paid to play baseball in Rocky Mount, N.C.

He moved on to a dual career in big-league baseball (New York Giants, Cincinnati Reds, Boston Braves) and pro football. The gold medals were restored in 1983, 30 years after his death.

Thorpe's Stark County story began in 1915. It was no incidental chapter, when you consider he is central to why the Pro Football Hall of Fame is here.

By 1920, his reputation was so enormous that he was named president of a new league organized in downtown Canton. It soon changed its name to National Football League and will celebrate its 96th birthday on Aug. 20.

The league set out to streamline pro football, which Thorpe played for the Canton Bulldogs starting in 1915.

His first game, against the Massillon Tigers, drew a packed house to what already was a bloody rivalry. The game was at Lakeside Park on the east shore of Meyers Lake, about a mile from where decades later the Jim Thorpe statue became the best-known piece in the Hall of Fame.

Thorpe became the best player on Canton teams that won Ohio League pro championships in 1917, '18 and '19. LeBron James might enjoy this: Thorpe also was the coach.

His final game against the Massillon Tigers was a 3-0 win on Nov. 30, 1919.

Massillon did not follow Canton into the NFL—first called the American Professional Football Association—in 1920. But Thorpe never forgot the rivalry.

His thoughts and the flavor of the rivalry are preserved in this recording of his voice:

"It was a professional game played at Massillon. (Knute) Rockne was on the Massillon Tigers and I was on the Canton Bulldogs.

"He played left end, and I was playing left halfback. Consequently I had to go around his end, and he slipped through and tackled me for a couple yards loss. I said, 'Thatta boy, Rock. You're doing fine.' I also said, 'Look at the people came up here to see old Jim run. How about letting old Jim run?'

"And he said, 'Well, if you think you can get away with that, I'd like to see it.' So the next time I carried the ball around, I hit him in the side of the head with my knee, spindled off for a 60-yard touchdown, and on the point after touchdown, why, here came Rock with a player under each arm, all wetted down with a sponge. And I walked up and patted him on the shoulder and said, 'Thatta boy, Rock, you let old Jim run, didn't you?' "

Jim was 32 when the APFA/NFL began in 1920, with him as president of the league while playing for the Canton Bulldogs.

He played elsewhere from 1921-25. He returned to Canton in 1926, the year the Bulldogs faded out of existence.

It would be trite to say Canton never forgot him, but the memory lasted for quite a while. The remembered him at Canton's Onesto Hotel in 1952.

Thorpe had barely more than a year left on Earth when a dinner was conducted in his honor. "Old Jim's" brief remarks blended into a night of speeches.

"I am pleased to think that I am not the forgotten man," he said, "and I appreciate this chance to meet with my old friends. I appreciate Canton, and I love Canton."

During Branch Rickey's speech, he said, "He has received poor recognition of his merits as the world's greatest athlete and a great American."

One can only guess what Rickey might say of Thorpe's No. 16 ranking on the county's top-20 list.

BILL POWELL NO. 17

BY JIM THOMAS

WILLIAM "BILL" POWELL WOULD BE 100 YEARS OLD IN 2016 IF HE WERE ALIVE TODAY.

Powell passed away Dec. 31, 2009 at the age of 93, but his legacy as a minority businessman and benefactor lives on at Clearview Golf Course.

It was the first golf course in the United States to be designed, built, owned and operated by an African-American, according to the Professional Golfers' Association of America. And it still is unique, 70 years after Powell founded the iconic course in 1946 and it opened for play in 1948.

That's but one reason that Clearview is on the National Register of Historic Places.

Powell reached out and touched generation after generation of groups—African-Americans, women, children, military personnel—who could not find a niche in the sport of golf and created programs for them.

East Canton native Alan Page, a former Minnesota Supreme Court Associate Justice and a member of the Pro Football Hall of Fame, worked for Powell in Clearview's infancy.

"When I was a youngster, I was a caddy there," Page said. "All I remember is the heat and long walks carrying heavy bags. (Powell) was a very nice man. Obviously, he was very dedicated to the game of golf."

Powell's vision for the sport was, "That golf should be inclusive of everyone," his daughter Renee Powell said upon her father's induction into the PGA Golf Professional Hall of Fame.

As simple as that might sound, neither golf, nor high finance were readily available to people of color decades ago.

Powell was unable to secure local financing through traditional banks for his dream of building a course after returning to East Canton following his service in the U.S. Army Air Corps in World War II. Through the generosity of two African-American physicians in the area and from his brother Berry, Powell was able to purchase farmland in East Canton. He juggled his jobs at the Timken Co. with moving earth to shape Clearview.

With the help of his wife, Marcella, and later his sons, Larry and Billy, and daughter Renee, Powell was able to open Clearview to the public in 1948. Both Larry and Renee have continued their father's legacy by running and maintaining the course over the past four decades.

"Being an African-American growing up in the last 50 years, two-thirds of the last century, it was a struggle to have the opportunity to do things," Page said. "You have to provide opportunity to others, and he certainly realized that."

Renee Powell, who became the second African-American to play on the LPGA Tour, said her father's course was open to everyone.

"He had over the many years made so many different contributions," she said. "In the 1950s, he started women's golf leagues. Even though women are in the majority (now), they were not participating in golf. My dad was one of those people who paved the way for diversity."

MARTY MULL NO. 18

BY CHRIS BEAVEN

IT'S A TITLE SO FEW EARN, IT SOUNDS FOOLISH TO EVEN PURSUE: "FASTEST SWIMMER IN THE WORLD." FOR A TIME IN THE 1960S, THE WORLD'S FASTEST SWIMMER CALLED CANTON HOME.

Harley M. "Marty" Mull dominated swimming pools—first at McKinley High School and later at Ohio State—in a way few, if any, Stark County athletes dominated their particular sport.

"At one time or another in his career, he held seven national-record times, including four in one year," said R.J. Van Almen, who is on the board of the Greater Canton Aquatics Association and is a member of its Hall of Fame. "From what I've been told, through age-group, high school or the college level, he never lost an individual race in a dual meet or a summer league meet, nothing.

"To have someone from Stark County, from McKinley, to have done what he had done is remarkable."

Mull set national high school records at McKinley. He broke NCAA records at Ohio State. And in the process, "he held the fastest time in the world in the IM," Van Almen said. A seven-time state champion at McKinley and a two-time national champion at Ohio State, Mull's specialty became the individual medley, but he swam it all during his career, leaving an iconic legacy.

Records, though, don't always add up to hype, especially if the record-setter is humble. Mull exhibited none of the look-at-me theatrics found in many an elite athlete in an individual sport today. Asking him about swimming excellence likely would have elicited responses about his younger brothers, both elite swimmers in their own right, or about some of the standouts he coached at McKinley.

"He always deflected, he always talked about everybody else," Van Almen said. "I don't even know if his colleagues knew how great he was."

Most simply knew him as a swimming coach at McKinley for more than 30 years, many of those as the girls head coach. Mull encouraged, listened, protected and cajoled his athletes, all while selling the sport of swimming to them. He earned a spot in the Ohio High School Swim Coaches Association Hall of Fame.

"Stats have always impressed me," Van Almen said. "I'm the keeper of records here in Stark County, so I know their importance to people. But Marty probably made more of an impact as a coach than as a competitor. He won district titles. He had state qualifiers. ... But I think his real talent was caring for his kids, the way he molded them. I don't care if you were the worst swimmer or the best swimmer, you always saw him treat them the same. ... He was something special, not only in the water, but just a special human being."

Mull, who died of a heart attack on Jan. 3, 2011, was a member of the Greater Stark County Aquatics Association's inaugural Hall of Fame class in 1985. He also was inducted into the Varsity "O" Hall of Fame at Ohio State in 2002.

Van Almen got to know Mull first as one of the stars of the boys team at McKinley in the early 1990s, while Mull was coaching the girls. Van Almen's younger sister, Heather, starred for Mull on the girls team. And their dad, Bob, assisted Mull for a few years.

"Marty always had more girls swimming for him than any other team in Stark County," Van Almen said. "He wanted as many kids as possible to have an opportunity. And every home meet at Branin Natatorium, Marty insisted all eight lanes be used. That's before there were JV heats."

Mull's own love of swimming started in 1950 at the Toledo YMCA.

"Marty had way too much energy," his mom, Margaret, recalled. "We thought the YMCA could help him burn off a little bit of it."

Once Mull found the pool, success soon followed. He became a star on the Glass City Aquatics Club, competing throughout the East and Midwest. When the family moved to Canton in 1956, he set records at McKinley from 1957-60 during its run of six straight state titles under Ted Branin.

The NCAA prohibited freshmen from competing, so Mull had to wait until his sophomore year at Ohio State to resume breaking records. Mull won back-to-back 200 individual medley NCAA titles in 1962 and 1963, setting records each year. He also led OSU to a team championship in 1962. As his college career wound down, Mull transitioned to his next phase in life, taking care of his family and becoming a teacher and coach.

As years passed, Van Almen got to know Mull better.

"He shared stories about other people, Ted Branin, the other greats out of McKinley, and his brothers, Gary and Mike," Van Almen said. "He was more proud of his brothers. Mike's a doctor, and Gary's a well-known philanthropist and business owner. ... He was very reluctant to talk about himself. I had to come back with stories I heard from other people and ask him to elaborate."

Mull was eager in retirement to stay involved. "He helped move the (aquatics) association forward and helped come up with ideas to get kids honored."

Van Almen remembers how the McKinley girls used to honor Mull.

"They had the coolest T-shirts," he said. "On the front, they had a Harley Davidson-like logo. On the back, they had 'We Swim for Harley.' "

TODD BLACKLEDGE NO. 19

BY TODD PORTER

MAYBE IF TODD BLACKLEDGE DECIDED HE WANTED TO PLAY BASEBALL, HE WOULD'VE BEEN A CATCHER IN THE BIG LEAGUES. There was a time when Blackledge thought basketball might be his ticket to college. Really, it just depended on the time of year as to which sport Blackledge thought he was going to excel later in life.

"I loved playing all three sports," Blackledge said. "I thoroughly enjoyed football, basketball and baseball. It's one of the reasons why I'm a huge proponent of guys playing multiple sports now. It's healthy. It keeps you fresh and keeps you from getting burned out. I always looked forward to the next season.

"So when I decided to stick with football, I still played a ton of basketball. When I went to Kansas City and played for the Chiefs, I played on their travel basketball team. If it weren't for the fact I was a catcher, I'd have probably played Canton Class A ball in the summers when I was at Penn State, but I didn't want to take a chance on hurting my hand or breaking a finger."

These days, though, more and more people are coming to know Blackledge as ESPN's lead prime time college football analyst. After all, it's been more than 32 years since Blackledge won a national title at Penn State and was the seventh overall player selected in the 1983 NFL Draft, known as the famed QB draft. He was one of six quarterbacks taken in the first round, and the second QB chosen. That draft produced four Pro Bowl quarterbacks, and three Hall of Famers in John Elway, Dan Marino and Jim Kelly. Only Elway was picked before Blackledge.

Growing up the son of a coach, Blackledge lived in various spots across the country before playing high school football at Hoover High in North Canton. His father, Ron, coached in Kentucky, Cincinnati and New Jersey before he was hired at Kent State. It was home. Ron Blackledge is a native of Stark County.

"When I went to Penn State ... I knew I would be a worker," Blackledge said. "I went there with my eyes wide open. I didn't have any false expectations or a sense of entitlement. My goal was to make the travel team at Penn State my first year there and work toward whatever else would happen."

A week before his freshman season was to start, Blackledge got hurt. He likely would have made Joe Paterno's travel team, but he redshirted that season because of an injury. As a redshirt freshman, Blackledge competed against Jeff Hostetler. Paterno went with Hostetler to start the opener against overmatched Colgate, and Penn State beat Texas A&M 25-9 on the road in the second game. Then the Nittany Lions lost against Nebraska in the third game. Paterno made a switch at quarterback, and Blackledge would become the school's starter all the way through winning the 1983 Sugar Bowl and national title. Hostetler transferred to West Virginia after the 1980 season.

When Blackledge's NFL career started, it was 180 degrees different than college. Kansas City drafted Blackledge, and it was an organization, for a period of time, that seemed to be in flux.

"I loved Kansas City. I liked living there. I liked the Chiefs organization," Blackledge said. "But it was tough. There was a lot of turnover in coaches and players. There was instability, but there were also situations where I had opportunities and I didn't take advantage of those, either.

"I started at quarterback for three years at Penn State, and we lost five games during that time. In my first year at Kansas City, I didn't play hardly and we lost 10 games. That was a shock to my system."

Blackledge ended his seven-year NFL career in Pittsburgh in 1989. His father, Ron, was Pittsburgh's line coach. It was the first time Ron Blackledge coached his son's football team.

"It was fun for me to be on the same team as my dad," Blackledge said. "He coached me in Little League, but he was never my football coach. That was the first time we were together in a sport that was a livelihood for both of us."

In 2014, Blackledge signed a new five-year contract with ESPN. The network has exclusive rights to the College Football Playoff and the National Championship Game. He also finished his first season as Hoover's boys basketball coach that winter. On game weeks, when Blackledge is spending his weekends with the ESPN crew, his colleagues ask him about his basketball team.

"As good as Todd is in the booth—and I think he's the best—I honestly believe that coaching is his calling," ESPN play-by-play partner Brad Nessler said in 2015. "I think when these next (four years) are over, I could see Todd walking away and just coaching. And I think he'll be great at it. He will be more impactful in shaping the lives of young men."

BOB COMMINGS NO. 20

BY TODD PORTER

NO ONE PLAYED THE UNDERDOG ROLE AS WELL AS BOB COMMINGS. Not in life, nor in death. Take a look at this iconic list, and there is Commings making an appearance as Stark County's 20th—and final—sports icon. Commings was born an underdog; on Christmas Eve at the height of the Great Depression in 1932. There is something perfectly fitting about Commings filling out the final spot on a who's who of Stark County sports icons.

They told Commings he could never play major college football, maybe even any college football. So he not only made the Iowa football team, he was the Hawkeyes' captain and MVP in 1957, and started in the Rose Bowl that year.

"He was always an underdog," Commings' son, Bob Jr. said. "He shouldn't have done what he did. He was too small and too slow to play major college football, and he did. He liked being the underdog. He liked rooting for the underdog. When he got into coaching, he looked out for those kids who were not given many opportunities in life. He felt for those kids—not just football players, but students—and he tried to help them whenever he could."

After coaching at Iowa for two years as an assistant coach, Commings was hired as a high school coach in Ohio. He landed his first head coaching job at Struthers High School, near his native Youngstown. Commings went 50-16-4 at Struthers. That put him at the front of the line to be hired as Massillon's head coach in 1969. He led the Tigers to a 43-6-2 record the next five seasons, including the school's last state poll titles in 1970 and '72. The 1970 Massillon team outscored opponents 412-29. A year later, the Tigers lost two games each by a point and outscored their other eight opponents 287-18.

His high school coaching track record was so impressive that Iowa hired him to be the Hawkeyes' head coach after Massillon. Commings struggled at his alma mater and was fired with a year left on his contract there.

In 1980, Commings returned to Stark County coaching when GlenOak High School hired him, and Commings put the Golden Eagles on the Stark County football map. In 12 seasons there, Commings went 76-44-1, including a 9-2 season in 1985, which earned GlenOak the Federal League title. His GlenOak teams would win or share four league championships. He also was the first coach to take GlenOak to the playoffs. A sleeping giant in Stark County was starting to awaken.

Commings had a direct way of communicating with players and parents. He often warned parents they could ask him about playing time, but be prepared for an answer they may not like. In the middle of his run at GlenOak, one player's mom asked a question during the booster club's film review.

"She said, 'Coach Commings, my son is a good player and you have him playing third team. I want to know why my son is on the third team!' " Bob Jr. said. "This is in the middle of a big group of people, and he looked at her and said, 'Ma'am, because I don't have a fourth team.' A lot of parents in the room were shocked. There were five or six coaches in the room, and I was one of them. We almost peed our pants it was so damn funny."

Perhaps his signature win as a high school coach came in 1986 when Commings' GlenOak team went to Paul Brown Tiger Stadium and left with a 9-7 win over the Tigers. That win is one of the most legendary in Stark County history. GlenOak players from those years still talk about Commings' pregame speech.

Current GlenOak head coach Scott Garcia played on the 1986 team.

"The gist of it—and I'm cleaning this up—it would be a 48-minute fight," Garcia said, chuckling at the memory of what was really said. "It was a big night, but it was going to be a fun night."

The run at GlenOak came to a tragic end. Commings thought he broke a rib in a game early in the 1991 season. When it didn't heal, Commings had X-rays taken.

"Our team doctor was supposed to give him the results of the X-rays before we played Timken," Bob Jr. said. "Dr. Smith wasn't anywhere to be found before the game. Finally, in the second half, Doc Smith comes walking up, and I was next to my dad on the sideline, and dad looks at him and said, 'Doc, what's the verdict?' The doctor told him they would talk about it after the game. My dad knew right then it wasn't good."

Commings was diagnosed with lung cancer that already had spread to other parts of his body.

More than 700 people attended a service for Commings at Washington High School in Massillon. People from all walks of life came to pay their respects. It would have surprised, maybe even embarrassed, Commings because he was understated. They laughed and cried. To this day, grown men find themselves reflecting back to something Commings told them.

"I was coaching eighth-grade football in 1991," Garcia said. "It was my first year coaching. I went to see him around Christmas with my dad and brother, and Bob was the one lifting our spirits. It was tough to see him like that, but he picked us up. He was always about mental toughness and dealing with adversity. You have to deal with things because they just won't go away. I'm not going to lie. When he was the underdog, he almost always won. The cancer was bad, but I kind of expected he would beat it, too."

> "He was always an underdog. He shouldn't have done what he did. He was too small and too slow to play major college football, and he did. He liked being the underdog. He liked rooting for the underdog. When he got into coaching, he looked out for those kids who were not given many opportunities in life. He felt for those kids—not just football players, but students—and he tried to help them whenever he could." – Bob Commings Jr.

IN THEIR WORDS

BY JIM PORTER

EVERYONE WHO KNEW BOB COMMINGS HAS A COACH COMMINGS STORY. THE STORIES, OFTEN TIMES HUMOROUS, COULD BE PLACED INTO A BOOK ON LIFE LESSONS. I WAS A YOUNG ASSISTANT COACH AT GLENOAK HIGH SCHOOL WHEN BOB ALLOWED ME TO BE ON HIS COACHING STAFF. I LEARNED FAR MORE FROM HIM THAN MY PLAYERS EVER LEARNED FROM ME, I'M SURE.

One day after practice, a man was walking toward Bob. A group of coaches stopped to watch what was about to happen. It looked like it could be a parent encounter, and these could end with an epic line or two.

Instead, this man was a college professor who drove down from the University of Akron to shake Bob's hand. For years, he asked his students to write about the most influential person in their lives.

"I've been reading these papers for years about this Coach Commings who changed lives down here at GlenOak," the man said. "I figured I needed to drive down and shake the hand of the man who has changed so many lives."

That was Bob.

The remarkable thing about Bob is he cared for people. He cared for his players, but as much, he cared for students. Bob was a champion of underdogs.

There once was a story written about Bob after his death. It recounted a conversation Coach had with a vocational student. The student noticed Bob was looking outside on a Friday afternoon in the fall watching the rain fall.

"You going to the game tonight?" the student asked, clearly not understanding Bob was the football coach.

"I'm thinking about it," Commings said.

"Well if you do, take an umbrella," the young man said.

This could have been a chance for Bob to deliver a one-liner. That's not who he was. He didn't have a big ego. He didn't need to tell anyone how strong of a man he was.

He simply lived it everyday.

Jim Porter is publisher of The Canton Repository and CEO of GateHouse Ohio Media. He delivered one of the eulogies at Commings' funeral.

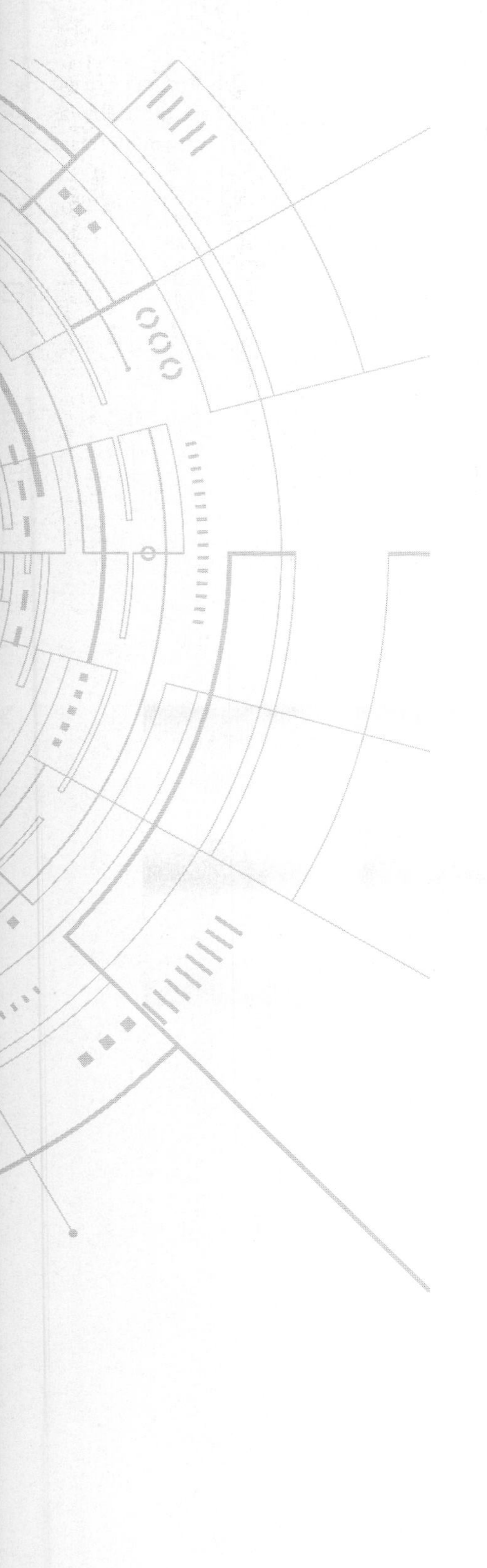

Hoover star Dick Snyder (10) of the Cleveland Cavaliers reaches and scores a basket in the first quarter against the Boston Celtics in the NBA playoff at Boston Garden Thursday, May 6, 1976.

ALLIANCE

CANTON SOUTH

CANTON CENTRAL CATHOLIC

EAST CANTON

FAIRLESS

GLENOAK

HOOVER

JACKSON

LAKE

LEHMAN

LINCOLN

LOUISVILLE

HIGH SCHOOL GREATS

MARLINGTON

MASSILLON

MCKINLEY

MINERVA

NORTHWEST

PERRY

SANDY VALLEY

ST. THOMAS AQUINAS

TIMKEN

TUSLAW

CHRISTIAN SCHOOLS

ORIGINS OF A LEGEND

BEFORE THE PRO FOOTBALL HALL OF FAME. BEFORE THE SUPER BOWL. BEFORE EVEN ALLIANCE HIGH SCHOOL. THERE WAS GOAT HILL.

The old field at Morgan Avenue and Garwood Street in Alliance was, in many ways, where the athletic career of legendary quarterback and Alliance icon Len Dawson began.

"I was 10 or 11 years old, and I'd always go up to Goat Hill," said Dawson, reflecting back more than six decades during a telephone call from his home in the Kansas City area. "There were a lot of kids in the area, and that's where they all hung out. It was never hard to find a game of some kind going on there. There were always nine guys around to play baseball."

It was a place that always had a special allure to Dawson. The thrill of competition and the sound of bats hitting baseballs may as well have been the sound of a siren singing, drawing Dawson closer to the game.

"I have many fond memories from that time," Dawson said. "I had a paper route, and I remember on Sundays that I would be three to four blocks into it and see kids playing baseball up at Goat Hill. I would drop the papers and go join in. One of the neighbors would see me up there playing and they would call my home and my sister would have to come and pick up the papers and finish the route for me."

It was those Goat Hill games that gave the Alliance area glimpses at what would be the finest athlete the community has ever produced. Dawson was a natural athlete and displayed skills beyond his age. That was not by happenstance. There were challenges that came with being the ninth of 11 children, but there were also benefits.

"I had six older brothers," Dawson said. "One was very good at basketball. He was in charge of the basketball leagues over at the Methodist church. I would go down,

and he would teach me the fundamentals. I ended up being very advanced at basketball for a 10-year-old. It was the same with baseball. I had another brother that took me out and showed me how to run the bases and everything. I was way ahead of a lot of other kids, and I was fortunate to have had those experiences."

Those fundamentals transferred over to high school at Alliance. By the time Dawson was a senior, he was first-team All-Ohio in both football and basketball.

It is his time on the gridiron that Dawson is remembered for the most. And with good reason. His senior year was highlighted by leading the Aviators to a win over McKinley.

"I remember that game well," Dawson said. "It was at Mount Union Stadium. They had the old wooden goal posts back then. I remember when the game ended, everybody stormed the field, and we watched the crowd take those old goal posts down. It was a really powerful moment."

The meaning of the moment was not lost on Dawson as he watched the crowd at Mount Union carry off the goal posts.

"It was certainly better than getting our butt kicked by them the previous 18 times," Dawson said with a laugh. "That was the first time in 19 years we defeated McKinley. We were never able to defeat Massillon when I was there. Those schools were powerhouses, and the atmosphere in the county for football was always hot and heavy with them in it."

Dawson's play at quarterback caught the attention of college teams nationwide. He remembers being recruited by Ohio State and legendary head coach Woody Hayes.

"I remember Coach Hayes sitting me down to show me the offense," Dawson said. "He told me I was going to line up under center and run towards the line of scrimmage. If there was room up the middle I was supposed to give it to the halfback. If there wasn't, he wanted me to continue down the line of scrimmage and play the option. I remember asking what that is.

"He told me that if the defensive end chased me to pitch it to the running back. If he chased the running back I was supposed to keep it. I just remember thinking I was going to be putting my life in the hands of some very big defensive ends. I just kept thinking I was going to get crushed by one of those guys."

Dawson ended up at Purdue. The precision passing offense of the Boilermakers was a better fit for him. It's also where he met a little-known assistant coach at the time: the great Hank Stram.

Stram played a huge role in getting Dawson to the Dallas Texans once he turned pro. The franchise later moved to Kansas City and became the Chiefs.

"I had lunch with Coach Stram and he told me, 'You know Leonard, if you are able to get free, we would really love to have you in Dallas.' " Dawson said. "I was a backup with the Cleveland Browns at the time. I ended up asking Paul Brown for my release after that."

Before Dawson was free to sign with the Texans, he had to pass through waivers.

"I was granted my release in June," Dawson said.

"Luckily a lot of teams and scouts had gone home for the summer. I passed through the waiver wire before anyone had known I was really on it. When teams got back from the break in the fall, more than one told me, 'If we had known you were available, we'd have definitely brought you in and taken a look.' It ended up working out best for me that they didn't."

Reuniting Dawson and Stram was instant magic. Dawson delivered the AFL Championship to Dallas in his first year with the franchise in 1962 and also was the AFL MVP that season.

After a move to Kansas City, the best was yet to come for Dawson and Stram. The two delivered a Super Bowl victory for the Chiefs in Super Bowl IV. Dawson was named the game MVP.

"The rest as they say is history," Dawson said. Dawson's achievements saw him inducted into the Pro Football Hall of Fame in 1987. His portrait hangs in the Alliance High School gymnasium. A reminder that even the biggest of dreams can begin on Goat Hill.

—CLIFF HICKMAN

SCORING MACHINE

MANY GREAT BASKETBALL PLAYERS HAVE COME THROUGH THE ALLIANCE HIGH SCHOOL PROGRAM. NONE PUT UP MORE POINTS AND FEW WORKED AS HARD AS J.J. KUKURA.

The 2014 graduate poured in 1,681 total points in his career. That is good for third place all-time in county history, according to Repository records. Only Jami Bosley (Jackson, '95) with 2,077 points and LeRoy Thompson (Waynesburg, '53) with 1,746 points scored more.

"My main thing has always been scoring," said Kukura, who averaged 28.1 points and 9.0 rebounds per game as a senior. "It's a huge honor to be that high on a list with all the great players in this county. Ultimately, it was all about winning for me, though. That's what drove me. If we needed 20 or 30 points in a game to win, I wanted to get it."

There were plenty of wins along the way. Alliance was a perennial power with Kukura, Parrish Martin and Kordelle Phillips on the roster. The trio's biggest accomplishment came as sophomores when the Aviators put together a 20-0 regular season. Overall, the Aviators were 63-12 during Kukura's final three years, including 38-4 in the Northeastern Buckeye Conference. He was a three-time All-NBC pick and helped his teams win two league titles.

"It was a great four years," Kukura said. "That 20-0 season was a real highlight, though. Our whole team just loved to play. I was in the gym all the time. So were Kordelle and Parrish. We all put a lot of work in."

Kukura wasn't just in the gym hoisting jump shots. He was always making additions to his game. By the time he was a senior, Kukura was far more than the perimeter threat he was known for being early in his career. He added a tough post game and had mastered scoring with either hand.

"That was big," Kukura said. "A lot of kids can go right or go left. Not many can do both. I would say if a young kid is looking to be an elite player, that's a key thing to work on."

That addition did nothing but fuel Kukura's post game.

"It became easier to get my points in the post," Kukura said. "A lot of teams would try to guard me on the perimeter with guards. I was 6-foot-3, so I would take them down low and post them up and that was a matchup problem for them."

Kukura played his high school ball for his father, Alliance head coach Larry Kukura. Larry Kukura never had to talk his son into putting in extra work while J.J. was on the roster.

"He was in the gym constantly," Larry Kukura said. "He was always around the game. I never forced him to be around it. I didn't have to push it. From his freshman year on, he was always asking me to take him back to the gym so he could shoot and rebound."

That love of the game was contagious and was one of the driving factors of the success that permeates the Alliance program to this day.

"He was the best leader I've ever coached," Larry Kukura said. "They knew he wasn't in it for numbers. He was in it to win. He would get on teammates when they weren't working as hard as he was, and they respected that because they saw how hard he worked."

That role as a leader didn't afford J.J. Kukura any days off.

"You have to do it every day if you want your words to carry any kind of weight," Larry Kukura said. "When you're a leader like that, people watch you close. ...There was never a lack of effort and he never seemed to have a bad day that affected his effort at practice."

Though working with family can be difficult in some circumstances, it wasn't for the Kukuras. It's a pairing that both miss, though, each remains successful.

Larry Kukura guided Alliance to a league title and a 22-3 season this past winter, earning honors as the state's Division II coach of the year. J.J., meanwhile, has taken his brand of instant offense to Mount Union, where he stars for the Purple Raiders. As a freshman, he helped them reach the NCAA Division III tournament.

"My dad was great," J.J. Kukura said. "I think he's one of the best coaches in the entire state. He put in a ton of work and he was a big reason for our success. He always put us in a position to win."

Larry Kukura shares a similar sentiment.

"I miss coaching him," Larry Kukura said. "He's one of a kind. He's a player that really had no weaknesses. He was a good passer, he could post up and he could score with both hands. You won't find many players out there like him." —CLIFF HICKMAN

1

LEN DAWSON A lot of people are familiar with Dawson's exploits on the gridiron as a Pro Football Hall of Famer but don't discount his contributions in other sports at Alliance. He also starred in basketball and baseball for the Aviators. As a senior, Dawson was a first team All Ohio selection in football and basketball.

<<< 2

MEL KNOWLTON Knowlton spent 24 years as the head football coach and athletic director at Alliance High School. He did more than just coach Len Dawson with the Aviators. Knowlton played under Paul Brown at Massillon in the 1930s and that knowledge showed. Knowlton won a state title with Alliance in 1958 and had a top 10 program in the state six times. Knowlton was named Ohio Coach of the Year in 1954 and is an Ohio High School Football Hall of Famer.

3

ANTHONY BLAIR Track and field records tend to fall frequently in Stark County with the amount of talent that makes its way through the area. The lightning-fast Blair set records that have stood the test of time. He still holds the county record in the 200 (20.8) and the 400 (46.5), which were set in 1976. Blair won three state titles in the 440 during his career at Alliance, helping the Aviators win a share of the 1976 team state championship.

<<< 4

HARRY FAILS JR. Fails was a legendary basketball coach for 16 years in the '70s and '80s. During that time, the Aviators never had a losing record. Alliance made two trips to the regional tournament during his tenure. How much did the contributions of Fails mean to Alliance High School? The school renamed the gymnasium after him in 2007.

>>> 5

JOHN BORTON How good of a quarterback was John Borton? Good enough to hold off a young Len Dawson for the starting job with the Aviators. Borton started as a junior and senior for Alliance and was a first team All Ohio pick in his final year with the Aviators. Borton went on to play for Woody Hayes at Ohio State, where he set the single-game record for touchdown passes in a game with five. Borton also excelled in basketball and baseball for Alliance.

<<< 6

DAVE CLEGG A legendary figure in cross country and track in field in the county. Clegg coached track for 23 years and started the cross country program at Alliance, coaching it for 17 years. He led Alliance to three top-10 finishes at the state meet in cross country. Clegg also coached numerous standouts such as cross country state champion Lowell Terrell and state champion sprinter Anthony Blair.

7

KENDALL DAVIS-CLARK Best known for his success in football as a running back, Davis-Clark was a Division III All-Ohio pick as a senior. He averaged 11 yards per carry that year and had 1,108 yards and 11 touchdowns in just seven games. Davis-Clark had 3,300 yards and 30 touchdowns total. Davis-Clark also was a decorated sprinter. He won state titles in the 100 and 200 in 2004, helping the Aviators to a team state title. He went on to have a successful career as a defensive back at Michigan State.

8

JEN WOLLAM One of the greatest cross country runners in county history before going on to star in college at Malone. Wollam capped her Alliance career with back-to-back Division I state championships in 1996 and 1997—a feat no one duplicated in Division I until Centerville's Jen Studebaker won her second straight title last fall.

9

J.J. KUKURA During the course of his varsity career, Kukura became the third-all time leading scorer in county history with 1,681 career points and tied the school's single-game mark (46 points). He also helped the Aviators reach three straight Division II district finals, two league titles and compile a 20-0 regular season his sophomore year.

>>> 10

CHARLES BABB No county quarterback has thrown for more yards than this four-year starter (2003-06). Babb left Alliance after throwing for 6,801 yards and tossing 73 touchdowns. He also broke Dawson's single-season record for touchdown passes in a season with 19 along the way. Babb lettered in basketball and track and field, too.

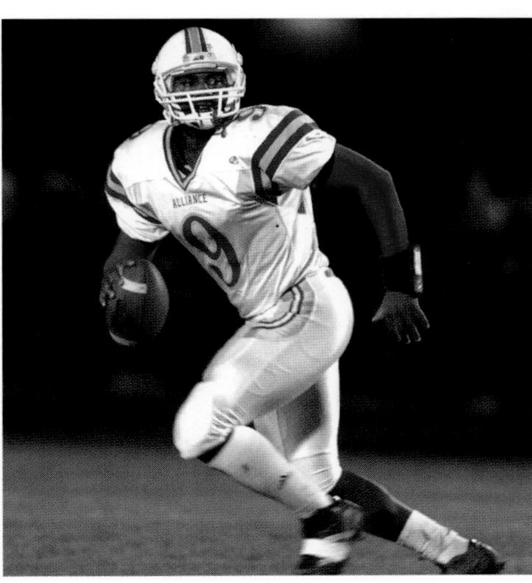

HONORABLE MENTIONS

MARC ANDERSON
JAMES "SONNY" BRABSON
TOM GOOSBY
JAIVON HARRIS
CHARLIE KING
RANDY AND RON KUCEYESKI
CHUCK LARSUEL
E.J. LILLY
SHAWN WATSON
CHRIS ZURBRUGG

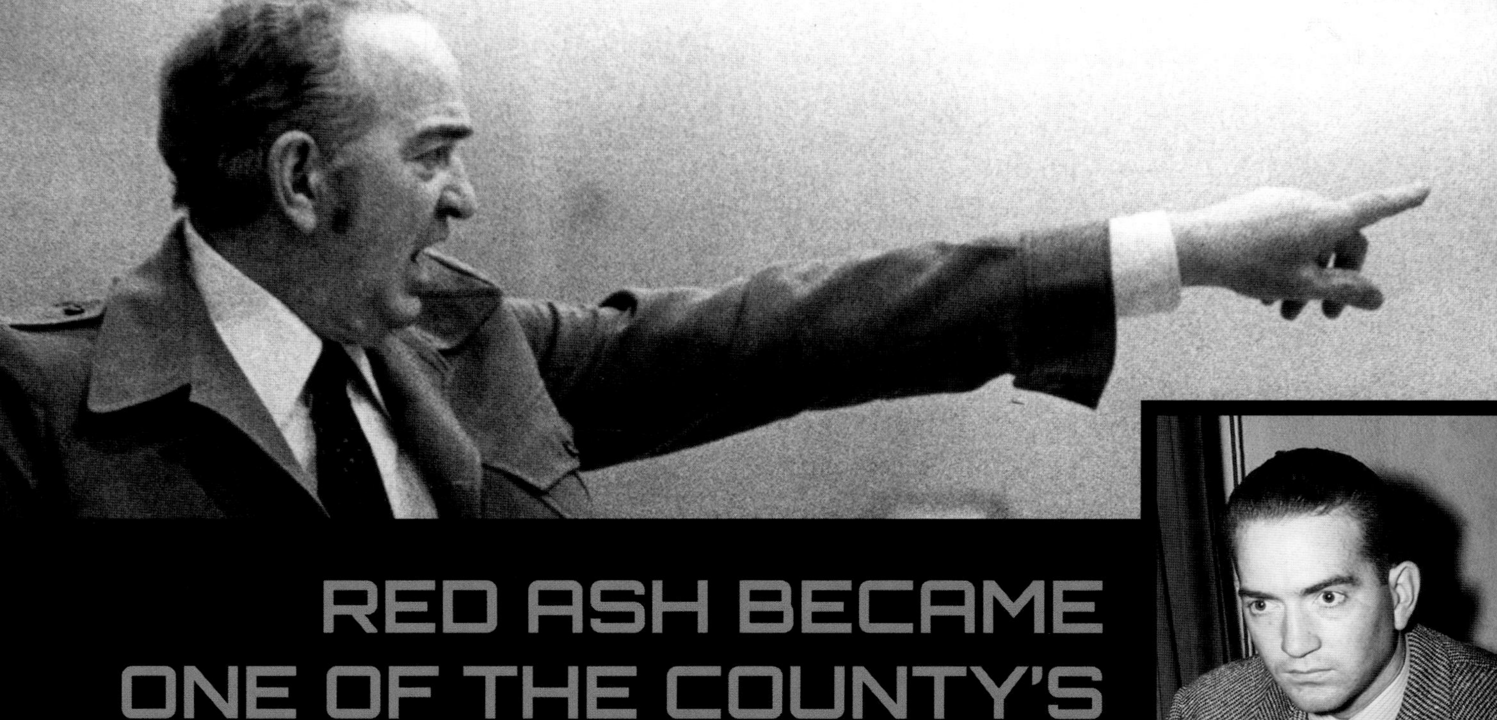

RED ASH BECAME ONE OF THE COUNTY'S MOST COLORFUL AND SUCCESSFUL COACHES

THE GYM ALWAYS WAS FULL. The team always was good. The coach always was Red.

So it went during the best era—touching five decades—of Canton South High School athletics. It was the age of Charles "Red" Ash, who took turns as head coach of the football and baseball teams, but forever will be remembered for turning basketball into the community's long-running, much-celebrated winter festival.

Bo Hysong, a South student during the 1960s, was smiling when he used one of Ash's other nicknames to sum up a phe-

Ash's 1955-56 basketball team went 23-1 behind future NBA player Howard Jolliff, who was a junior on the 1954-55 team that won 16 of its last 18 games. Larry Gerzina, who later had a strong run as head coach at Timken, was a senior on the latter team.

"Everybody was afraid of Red," Gerzina says. "If you got in trouble, you'd rather face the Gestapo than face Red.

"He controlled everything. Nobody fooled around much. You went to school and shut your mouth.

"But Red also was a lot of fun. You had never been in an environment like that. The place was full, and it was intense.

"On one play one of our guys got driven into the wall behind a basket. (Lincoln coach) Ken (Newlon) and Red squared off with one another."

Haverstock was a senior in 1965, the year Ash's Wildcats beat state No. 1-ranked McKinley in the sectional tournament prior to knocking off Lincoln in the district finals.

Mark Miller, who later became a record-setting quarterback at Bowling Green en route to getting drafted by the

1977-78 season, his record as an Ohio high school head basketball coach was 634-200. It was the most wins in state history at the time. Many of Ash's players became community icons in their own rights.

The unbeaten 1944-45 team, for example, included Hayden (future Canton Local school superintendent), Ed Palmer (future principal at Faircrest Middle School) and county scoring leader Floyd Meers (father of Kevin Meers, who coached South to a regional girls basketball appearance years after playing for one of Ash's better teams).

Jolliff from the 1950s and Dick Cunningham from the 1960s made it to the NBA. Cunningham won a championship ring with the Milwaukee Bucks and later was head coach at Central Catholic. Jolliff became a head coach at Jackson and eventually was principal at Canton South.

Ash's list of Repository first-team all-county players who played for him included Palmer, Cunningham, Bob Garrett, Al Bungard, Dale Snider, Fred Filliez, Tom Eibel, Jerry McKinney, Larry Hackenberg, Tom Lagodich, Denny Leach, Jim Eckinger, Vic Watkins, Paul Ash (one of Red's four sons who played for him) and Bud Fontes.

Some of his second-team all-county players (as selected by the newspaper) could have made the first team. That list included Benny Battista, Mervin Hill, Roger Baker, Bud Harbold, Walt Hall, Gary Crowe, Jim Bardine, Ed Lenzy, Sheldon Cunningham, Terry Miller, Rick Nunley, Dan Ross, Len Watkins, Keith Allerton and Greg Williams.

In Ash's time, Canton Township was more populous, and the Wildcats competed in the Federal League. From 1965-74, the league's first 10 years, his Wildcats were 20-2 against Jackson, 17-5 against Perry, 19-2 against Glenwood, 16-4 against Louisville, 12-2 against Oakwood, and 11-1 against Hoover.

"Everybody knew who Red Ash was," said Miller, who was a senior on a team that featured Vic Watkins and went 13-0 against the schools mentioned above. "Everywhere we went, the signs we saw weren't about beating South. They said things like 'Kick Red's Ash.' "

Many of his games were blowout wins—the 1948 team that reached the state final four beat Stow and McKinley in regional play by a combined 99-45. Plenty of games had thrilling and sometimes bizarre finishes.

In 1974, Ash's 600th victory was by a 54-52 score, preserved only when it was ruled a last-second heave that went through the basket had deflected off the roof at Oakwood. Old Wildcat Lou Mikunda was among boosters waiting at the locker room with a cake after officials ruled "no basket."

In 1969, Massillon came in with perhaps its best big man ever, Brian Westover, and led 49-48 in the final seconds. A foul was called with seconds left. Watkins went to the line by himself, with 0:00 showing on the clock, and made two foul shots for a 50-49 win. A fight broke out at the scorer's table. In 1964, with a loaded lineup, South faced a McKinley team that came into the district finals with a 21-1 record. McKinley won 58-56 on a last-second tip-in by Bo Peep Jackson. Everyone from South thought Jackson committed an obvious foul while going through Cunningham for the tip. Cunningham always has said, "I'm still waiting for my (free) throws."

The endless wins and the thrilling finishes, win or lose, have smoothed into the sands of time. Left is the glow of one of the most colorful figures in county sports history. Mostly, Canton South people who remember him smile at the utterance of that syllable worth a thousand words, "Red."

Hayden recalls a generous man who worked hard to get kids into college, whether or not they went to South.

After coaching, Ash stayed in Canton Township and got elected to the Ohio House of Representatives.

He wasn't hard to find. He remained in the house where he lived when he was the coach. He had the most famous face around. He was a large man who drove a red Mustang.

One time, he spotted Gerzina, by then the head coach at Timken, walking along Cleveland Avenue near Gerzina's house. Ash whipped the Mustang across traffic, hitting the brakes at a spot near his former player.

"Hey," he told a slightly startled Gerzina, by way of congratulations. "If you don't quit winning, you're going to pass me."

Ash was in his mid-70s when he fell ill. He died March 3, 1991.

Near the end, there were days when the door on his hospital room said "no visitors."

One of the last orders the old coach gave came when he overheard a nurse talking in the hall to someone whose voice sounded familiar.

"Open that door now," came the voice from inside the room.

Ronnie Young, a star of the famous 1965 tournament win over McKinley, found his way in. The old player and the old coach shared one last meeting on Earth.

"It wasn't until after I was an adult," Young says, "that I came to believe he could have coached at any level.

"As a man? I cared very much about Charles 'Red' Ash."

—STEVE DOERSCHUK

A STAR FOR EVERY SEASON

RONNIE YOUNG DOESN'T FEEL LIKE A LEGEND NOW, AND HE CERTAINLY DIDN'T THEN.

He was a third-grader who had never thrown a football or caught a baseball when his family moved to Canton Township, on Sherman Church Road, near Paradise Hill.

During recess at his new school, Prairie College, he watched the older kids shooting baskets—he had never done that, either.

He asked if he could join in. After a while, a member of "the junior police"—sixth-graders of high character—sent Ronnie inside. His crime: Playing better than the older boys.

In time, Ronnie was better than all of the boys, from all over.

Before high school, he pitched all six tournament games for a team that won a Hot Stove state championship.

He was a Canton South freshman when he scored 16 points in a tournament win that ended with him blocking a shot by North Canton star Dick Snyder.

As a South sophomore, he intercepted 12 passes for a football team that went 9-1.

As a Wildcat junior, he threw three straight no-hitters.

The exclamation point came in the 1965 basketball tournament, when he was a senior. An incredible cast that had forged a 36-5 record across the previous two seasons was gone, save for Young. He was the 6-foot-5 leader of a team that steadily improved with four new starters, Tom Lagodich, Frank Gonzales, Jerry Eibel and Tom Becker. The ride seemed doomed when the Wildcats made it to a game against McKinley, which was 20-0.

"There's no way we're supposed to beat McKinley," Young recalls. "They're the No. 1 team in the state of Ohio, and here come the old country boys up the road, and ... that was a good day."

South won 61-57 in double overtime.

Young was tall, confident, athletic and instinctive. He relished the requisite practice work, and he loved to play.

The thought of accepting a full basketball scholarship at Tennessee thrilled him. Baseball scouts were all over him. He was a big lefty with a body and a fastball like Cleveland's "Sudden" Sam McDowell.

He was drafted out of high school by the Pittsburgh Pirates, but there was trouble behind. He had thrown too many baseballs, in an era before it was understood how that could tear up a young arm.

"That senior season of baseball was the worst season of my life," Young said. "My arm hurt so bad. I started a game at Sandy Valley, and it was like 29 degrees. I just felt something snap. It felt like my left arm just fell off my body."

Young signed with the Pirates, telling no one how much he hurt when he threw. Nothing seemed the matter when, in his first minor league season, he struck out 18 two different times and 19 in another game.

He was invited to the Pirates big-league camp in his third year, but by then, he says, his arm was "meat."

"If I had it to do over," said Young, 69, "I would never have signed a professional baseball contract. I would have gone on to Tennessee and played basketball.

"When you're 18 years old and someone offers you thousands of dollars and you live on Sherman Church Road out in the country, you think you're a millionaire."

In his early 20s, Young thought about returning to basketball. He received letters of inquiry from two NBA teams, but he didn't follow up.

"I was kind of fighting the depression thing," he said. "I lost hope for a while.

"And then God entered my life in a big way, when I was 26. I got baptized in the name of Jesus, and God filled me with his spirit. I'm 69 now. My life has never been the same. Nor have I ever been any happier in my life."

The story winds back to Sherman Church Road.

Young's family lived near Canton Lincoln High School for the first six years of his life and then moved to Louisville. In second grade, he met a girl named JoAnn Manse.

They might never have seen each other again, except, after the Youngs moved from Louisville to Canton Township, so did the Manses.

"It was like fate," Young said. "We celebrated 50 years in December (2015)."

Ronnie and JoAnn have a large family now.

He became an electrician, working for years out of a home in Canton Township. He says he would still be stringing wire but for an ailment that makes it hard for him to stand for more than a few minutes at a time.

"I've had a great life," he said. "I have four amazing kids that have never given me five minutes trouble, 11 wonderful grandchildren, four wonderful great grandkids. And my wife is the best human being I've ever met ... numero uno."

He says any regrets about anything in athletics are gone, while the good memories (the McKinley game is No. 1) still bring a smile.

"I just feel like sometimes God has different plans for people," he said. "I want to make him happy. If I make him happy, I know I'm OK." —*STEVE DOERSCHUK*

CANTON SOUTH TOP TEN ICONS

1

RED ASH (RIGHT)

RED ASH His 37-year career as a Canton South coach stalled in 1943, when the Wildcats did not play football because of World War II. It took off when his 1944 football team and his 1945-46 basketball team went undefeated. Gave up football in mid-1950s, but his run in basketball was just heating up. Retired as winningest coach in Ohio high school basketball history.

2

RONNIE YOUNG Six-foot-5 basketball player who sank shots from corner like they were layups. Dominated every other aspect of court in 1960s. From sophomore through senior years, Wildcats went 41-9 in regular season and 12-3 in tournament games. Feared left-handed pitcher. Started on offense and defense for football team.

3

DICK HIMES Stark County's football MVP in 1963 while playing on offensive and defensive lines. Also made coaches' 11-man all-county team as junior in 1962. Starting forward on basketball teams that compiled 36-5 record in his last two seasons. Two-time, All-Big Ten tackle at Ohio State. Played 10 years for Green Bay Packers.

4

HOWARD JOLLIFF Was still growing as junior on a 17-5 basketball team and blossomed on 1955-56 team that was 23-0 before losing in regional finals. Averaged 16 points and 18.7 rebounds for first Ohio University team to win a MAC hoops title. Had 29 points, 16 rebounds in NCAA Tournament win over Notre Dame. Played for Los Angeles Lakers. In Ohio Basketball Hall of Fame. Head basketball coach at Jackson before 25-year run as principal at Canton South.

5

FRANK DUGAN Stark County's MVP for 1962 football season. Man-among-boys runner who scored county-record 192 points for Wildcats team that went 9-1. Starred as a junior on 1961 team that shared Class AA League championship. Began college career at Michigan State before transferring to Alabama.

6

DICK CUNNINGHAM Six-foot-10 center on 1962-63 and 1963-64 teams that went 36-5 and lost two district-final thrillers to McKinley. Gregarious giant with huge hands he used to palm teammates' heads, for sport. Led NCAA in rebounding as senior at Murray State. Had seven-year NBA career highlighted by key role in rotation of Milwaukee's 1971 NBA title team.

7

RONNIE BOURQUIN Broke Ronnie Young's career scoring record in basketball. Led Wildcats to state basketball final four. Four-year football letterman who stood out at quarterback and defensive back. Baseball star who, at Ohio State, was 2006 Big Ten Player of Year. Second-round MLB draft pick. Represents one of school's best-known athletic families.

8

BENNY BATTISTA Viewed by Canton Township old guard as equal of any of the great all-around athletes school produced. Never left field for 1944 football team that went undefeated and outscored its last seven opponents 301-25. Standout on 1944-45 basketball team that went 19-4. Baseball star remembered for belting home runs into Nimishillen Creek. In Stark County High School Football Hall of Fame.

9

TIM MILLER Head coach of South baseball team for 29 years (1965-93), posting 404-244 record. Jersey No. 25 hangs on outfield fence. Versatile South athlete who returned to alma mater shortly after college. Younger brother Mark became record-setting Bowling Green QB drafted by Cleveland Browns.

10

ART FACH Quality representative of South's girls athletic programs. Longtime Canton Local teacher who quietly and with class steered tennis teams to excellence. Won more than 400 matches across quarter century before retiring after the 2015 season. Omnipresent, decades-old green van (tennis wagon) was most iconic vehicle in Wildcat sports.

HONORABLE MENTIONS

JACK FULLER
HERB HACKENBERG
FLOYD MEERS
LOU MIKUNDA
ED PALMER
SHAVON ROBINSON
DEVON TORRENCE

FOOTBALL WAS JUST STARTING POINT FOR PAGE TO MAKE DIFFERENCE

ALAN PAGE ALWAYS HAS TRIED TO MAKE THE WORLD A BETTER PLACE.

He did it during a football career that stretched from Central Catholic High School to the steps of the Pro Football Hall of Fame in his hometown. He did it during his career as a lawyer and state supreme court justice.

Even in retirement, Page never stops touching lives, especially today's youth.

"There are a lot of kids who have simply given up hope," Page said during a visit to Kent State University's Stark campus in 2016. "I think to the extent we can create hope for a better future, the future will be a bright one."

An All-Ohio offensive tackle in high school, Page is one of the most influential people who graduated from Central. He played defensive end on Notre Dame's 1966 national championship team and never missed a game during his 237-game Hall of Fame career with the Minnesota Vikings and Chicago Bears.

Page, however, spent the majority of his professional life working in the judicial system. He earned his law degree while he played in the NFL and worked

"I THINK TO THE EXTENT WE CAN CREATE HOPE FOR A BETTER FUTURE, THE FUTURE WILL BE A BRIGHT ONE."
—ALAN PAGE

(LEFT TO RIGHT) JIM MARSHALL, ALAN PAGE, GARY LARSEN AND CARL ELLER, THE "PURPLE PEOPLE EATERS."

for a Minneapolis law firm during the offseason. In 1992, he became the first African-American to be elected an associate justice on the Minnesota Supreme Court, a position he held until the mandatory retirement age of 70.

The base for his life's work was formed at home.

"I was influenced by my parents and family," Page said. "They're the ones who laid the foundation for the person I am."

Page also was a great football player.

At 6-foot-4, 230 pounds when he played at Central, Page possessed speed and strength. He was a dominant defensive end who helped the Crusaders record 16 shutouts during his sophomore, junior and senior years. Central posted seven shutouts and allowed just 33 points during a 10-1 season in 1961.

"He was an intense football player," John McVay, his first head coach at Central, said in 2002 before Page was inducted into the Stark County High School Football Hall of Fame. "He had all of God's gifts: size, speed, strength and quickness.

"As a high school player, he was big. Way big. He was an imposing sight."

Page played three seasons at Notre Dame. He was named an All-American in 1966, when the Fighting Irish won a national title. He also scored a rare touchdown against Purdue in 1964 when he blocked a punt, recovered the ball and ran 67 yards to the end zone.

The Vikings made Page their second pick in the first round of the 1967 NFL Draft. He won the starting job at right defensive tackle in the fourth game of his rookie season, beginning a streak of 234 straight starts that ended when he retired.

Page became just the second defensive player voted NFL Most Valuable Player in 1971. He was a three-time NFL Defensive Player of the Year, a six-time All-Pro selection and was voted to nine straight Pro Bowls.

As the right tackle on the famed "Purple People Eaters" defensive line of the Vikings, Page played in four Super Bowls. Minnesota lost all four games, but Page has no regrets.

"My professional football experience ... what I think about, what I remember the most is the people I played with," he said. "Jim Marshall, Carl Eller, Bobby Bryant, Charlie West, Chuck Foreman, a whole host of people who were great teammates, worked hard and were exceptionally talented football players. We were fortunate enough to all end up at the same place at the same time."

The Vikings waived Page after the 1978 season, but he quickly moved on to division rival Chicago. He started every game for the Bears during the final three seasons of his career.

Page recorded 173 sacks and recovered 28 fumbles during his 15-year NFL career. In 1988, he became the first Canton native elected to the Pro Football Hall of Fame. —*MIKE POPOVICH*

KLINEFELTER IS SYNONYMOUS WITH CENTRAL CATHOLIC

THE STADIUM HE COACHED IN FOR WELL OVER HALF HIS LIFE BEARS HIS NAME. THE STREET THAT SURROUNDS IT IS APPROPRIATELY NAMED "KLINEFELTER BOULEVARD."

Lowell Klinefelter is synonymous with more than just Central Catholic football. He spent 41 years as Central's head football coach and athletic director. He was a teacher at the school for almost half a century.

He was a success in everything he did.

Klinefelter won 257 games and led the Crusaders to two state championships. His win total ranks him No. 1 all-time among Stark County head football coaches. He is also the only football coach to win multiple state titles at a county school.

Never expecting to stay at one school for as long as he did, Klinefelter is grateful for the opportunity Central gave him.

"I kind of knew I was where I should be," he said in 2015 before he was inducted into the Stark County High School Football Hall of Fame. "I was happy there, and that's where I wanted my family to be brought up. That's where we stayed.

"At Central I got to teach kids who wanted to learn. If they weren't great athletes, they sure tried hard and gave everything they had. It was a great place to be."

"AT CENTRAL I GOT TO TEACH KIDS WHO WANTED TO LEARN. IF THEY WEREN'T GREAT ATHLETES, THEY SURE TRIED HARD AND GAVE EVERYTHING THEY HAD. IT WAS A GREAT PLACE TO BE."
—LOWELL KLINEFELTER

Klinefelter grew up in Marion and studied chemistry and mathematics at Ohio State. One of his other college courses was the fundamentals of coaching ... taught by Woody Hayes.

Seeing the Buckeyes head football coach in the classroom inspired Klinefelter.

"I thought if it was good enough for Woody Hayes, it was good enough for me," he once said.

Central was the only school that offered Klinefelter a chance to teach and coach at the high school level. He arrived in 1966 and became the Crusaders' head boys basketball coach in 1970. He also coached freshman football and was on varsity head coach Joel Spiker's staff in 1971 and 1972.

A new era began in 1973 when Klinefelter took over as head football coach. It stretched until his retirement after the 2013 season.

Klinefelter led the Crusaders to a winning record (7-3) in his third season and their first playoff appearance in 1977. Central lost to Cincinnati Wyoming in the Class AA state semifinals.

The best years were ahead of him.

Central went to the playoffs under Klinefelter 10 more times. The Crusaders won the Division IV state championship in 1988 with a power running game. Twelve years later, they won the Division III state title on the strength of a spread offense with speedy playmakers.

"We had some great teams that didn't make it to the state championship we were really proud of," Klinefelter said. "But boy, the state championships we had. I sure hope everybody felt they were a part of them."

Klinefelter's teams never shied away from tough opponents. Some years were challenging, but others were very satisfying. One of his final senior classes went from two wins as sophomores in 2009 to eight wins and the playoffs as seniors in 2011. It was the last team he led to the postseason.

Two years later, Klinefelter announced his retirement.

"I've enjoyed the journey," he said then.

In the Stark County high school football coaching circles, it was a journey like no other. —*MIKE POPOVICH*

1

ALAN PAGE Defensive force on a 10-1 Central football team that shut out seven opponents in 1961. Anchored the Minnesota Vikings' famed "Purple People Eaters" defensive line and was elected to the Pro Football Hall of Fame in 1988. Served as an associate justice on the Minnesota Supreme Court for more than 20 years.

2

LOWELL KLINEFELTER Stark County High School Football Hall of Famer who coached the Crusaders for 41 seasons. Won a Stark County-record 257 games and led the Central to 11 playoff appearances, including state titles in 1988 and 2000.

3

BOB BELDEN Ahead-of-his-time pro-style quarterback who earned All-Stark County honors in 1964. Earned a scholarship to play at Notre Dame and was selected by the Dallas Cowboys in the 12th round of the 1969 NFL Draft.

4

DOUG MILLER Has led Central's baseball team to three state championships in 35 seasons as head coach heading into the 2016 postseason. One of the state's all-time winningest coaches, he surpassed the 700-win mark during the 2016 season. Announced during the season that he had accepted a buyout to leave Central, following a disagreement with the school's administration over his continued role as athletic director.

5

RENEE POWELL Became the second African-American woman to play on the LPGA Tour in 1967. Head golf pro at Clearview Golf Club in East Canton. The course was built by her father, Bill, the only African-American to design, build, own and operate a golf course in the United States.

6

ROGER DUFFY All-Ohio center who starred with his twin brother, Pat, on the Crusaders football team. Helped lead Penn State to a national championship in 1986 and played 12 seasons in the NFL with the New York Jets and Pittsburgh Steelers.

7

JIM THOMAS Won Division II state tennis singles titles in 1991 and 1992. Played four years at Stanford, where he earned All-American honors and helped lead the Cardinal to an NCAA title as a senior. Turned pro in 1996 and reached the U.S. Open semifinals in doubles in 2005. Has won six career ATP doubles titles. Also has played at the Australian Open, French Open and at Wimbledon.

8

DAN MINOCCHI Won the Division II state shot put championship as a senior in 2000. His winning throw of 61 feet, 9 3/4 inches remains a Stark County record—erasing the decades-old mark that had been held by Dan Dierdorf. Played football all four years and was a two-time All-Ohio offensive lineman.

9

MARGARET PETERS Multi-sport athlete who earned 11 varsity letters during her high school career. Leapt 17 feet, 9.75 inches to win the Class AAA state championship in the long jump in 1979. Second team All-Ohio selection in basketball as a senior. Helped the Crusaders finish as Class AA state runners-up.

10

KELLE SAXEN Won a state track and field title in 1994 when she finished first in the Division II high jump. Holds the school's high jump record by clearing 5 feet, 7 3/4 inches. Still holds the girls basketball team's career scoring record with 1,387 points. Was a second team All-Ohio selection as a senior.

HONORABLE MENTIONS

PAT DUFFY
KEVIN FINEFROCK
TOMMY HENRICH
JOHN MASSARELLI
KATIE MOKROS
DAVE MONNOT
DICK PROEBSTLE
MICHAEL RUBIN

DAVIS MADE WIZARDS BIG, HAPPY FAMILY

IT WAS ALMOST MARDI GRAS TIME DOWN IN N'AWLINS. TOM DAVIS AND HIS WIFE, JEAN, HAD FLOWN THROUGH A VICIOUS THUNDERSTORM FROM THEIR HOME IN SOUTH CAROLINA TO SPEND SOME TIME IN THE CRESCENT CITY.

"You can do that when you're retired," Davis said, the smile on his end of the phone evident. "It was a horrible flight. I was green."

For anyone who ever spent any time in East Canton, it was hard to picture Tom Davis in anything other than a shirt and tie, often surrounded by girls basketball players clad in blue, yellow and white.

For 60-plus years, Davis was the heart and soul of the Osnaburg community. He was an All-Ohio football and basketball player at East Canton High School. After graduating from Denison University, the son of a teacher/coach came home to East Canton and plied his trade for four decades, eventually rising to superintendent in the district while becoming one of Ohio's winningest basketball coaches with 624 victories in the girls program he founded in 1975. When he finally retired from coaching after the 2010 campaign, his name was emblazoned across the new basketball court of the recently completed high school.

Nobody ever cared more about East Canton, its students and its athletes than Tom Davis. How to know that? Davis once coached a season while battling colon cancer, wearing a colostomy bag, fighting chemo and radiation treatments and never missing a game. Outside of the district and family, nobody knew of Davis' battle.

"The colon cancer, it probably shortened my coaching

career," Davis said, recalling that 2002 season and saying he is now cancer-free. "But I coached right through it. I had chemo and radiation in the summer. I remember I missed something. We were in a summer league. My son Jarrod, he took the team when I (couldn't). My wife, she ran the weightlifting program three times a week. And I'm sure my daughter Tara helped, too.

"It was a real family affair."

Tara Davis was one of a multitude of star players to score 1,000 points under Tom Davis. Even now, there are five East Canton players among Stark County's top 10 career scorers. Davis treated them all like family, then and now, easily rattling off the names of 20 players who had left their mark. In the summer of 2015 alone, he made it back to the area to attend the weddings of four of his former players.

"I try not to miss any of them," Davis said of the weddings. "We have Facebook; we stay in touch. Now, I get to follow the girls."

For 36 seasons, East Canton girls followed the lead of Davis. His first season, as both head coach and junior varsity coach, the team won one game. The second season, it won six times and a sectional championship. East Canton would win 34 straight sectional titles under Davis. Three times his peers chose Davis as the state's Division IV Coach of the Year—1995, 2001 and 2007. His teams never did win a state championship, but the Wizards played for the title in runner-up finishes in 1995 and 2006.

It is the players that Davis remembers moreso than the games, the wins and losses.

"I had so many great players," he said. "There were very few seasons I didn't have a great player, or two. But I don't have a No. 1 (favorite). They all did so many things. Linda Krider, she was the first All-Ohioan. She got the ball rolling. Jodi Dobransky, she was tremendous. Tara Johnson was a tremendous scorer, and she did it on a bum leg. She blew her knee out her junior year and averaged 29.9 points a game her senior year. The next-high scorer averaged four points—and we still won games.

"There was Beth Sternberg, Deb Ketchum. Katy Arick, Caitlin Sharp. Shelly Wright, she was incredible. She won a state high jump title and went to Youngstown State. She walked on to the basketball team and played (both sports)."

Davis said he was not a fan of the offense most teams run now, the motion or flex. His teams ran and pressed, and they scored.

"I always thought that kids had roles to play," he said. "If you are a scorer, it took the burden off the other kids. Every kid can not shoot the basketball. Why run the flex offense to have someone get the ball who doesn't shoot? We ran plays to get specific kids shots. That allowed the others to concentrate on what they could do."

That is how Davis had some 10 girls score more than 1,000 points.

None of that would have been possible without the support of the Osnaburg administration and the boys basketball teams, Davis said.

"I wanted to be the boys basketball coach (in 1975)," he said. "I applied for the job, didn't get it. They asked if I wanted to be a the girls coach. I said, 'I don't think I want to do that.' The girls phys-ed teacher tried to start teaching the girls (basketball), and I kind of enjoyed watching that, so I went back and said I would do it.

"They always treated us equal. We had the same facility as the boys, the same schedule, the same number of assistant coaches. We were never treated as second-class. We never fought over money or uniforms. Those guys always treated us with respect. I give a lot of credit to the board at that time, and the boys teams. We had different nicknames, but the boys supported the girls, and the girls had always supported the boys.

"It was just a real good situation."

East Canton always was for Davis. It all began when he was in high school. He was All-Ohio in football and basketball.

"Football was my favorite sport," he said. "I started the last game of my freshman year and played every game. Then I went to college and started my first game—seven-plus seasons and never missed a game. I always thought I was going to be a football coach. My dad coached football and basketball at Lincoln. I always loved football best."

Stark County was and always will be a football hotbed. Davis helped make it a girls basketball area. He said it was the players who made East Canton, not him.

"They bought into what we were doing," he said. "They were willing to work in the offseason. And they were talented. They were athletic kids who bought into the program. I had a lot of fun coaching them."

These days not too many people in East Canton recall Davis' football days. They will, however, always remember Davis and his Wizards. *—JIM THOMAS*

EAST CANTON CROSS COUNTRY OWES EXISTENCE, SUCCESS TO STERNBERG

FIRST-YEAR TEACHERS FRESH OUT OF COLLEGE ARE EAGER TO HIT THE GROUND RUNNING. LEE STERNBERG WAS NO EXCEPTION WHEN HE GRADUATED FROM OHIO STATE AND WAS OFFERED AN ELEMENTARY PHYSICAL-EDUCATION POSITION IN THE OSNABURG LOCAL SCHOOLS.

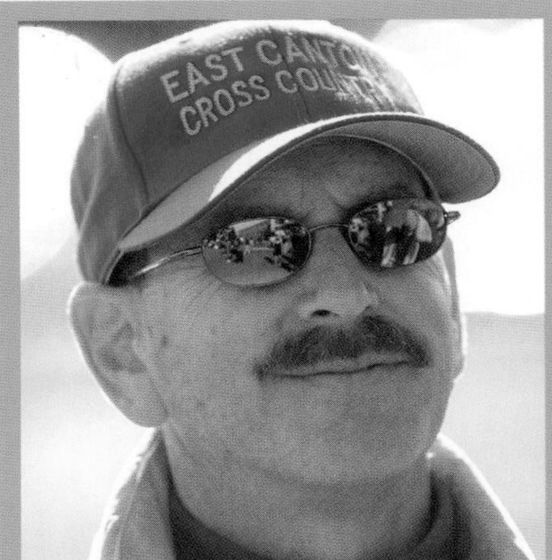

"IT IS ABOUT SEEING A KID IMPROVE AND REACH GOALS. I ALWAYS TELL THEM IF YOU PUT THE WORK IN YOU SEE THE REWARDS."

—LEE STERNBERG

"My first question to the principal was, 'Do you have a cross country team?' " Sternberg said of that day in 1973. "He said, 'No, we have a track team.' He said the board wanted to do either cross country or wrestling.

"I did a cost analysis for cross country and figured it cost $100—and told the board I'd do it for free. Then they talked about wrestling ... five people signed up, not enough for a team.

"They said we would have a cross country team, and I'd get $100 to do that. I was so excited."

Sternberg is still excited some 42 years later. His Hornets have qualified 18 boys teams to the state meet, produced one state championship team, three state runner-up teams and a myriad of individual qualifiers and placers. He was inducted into the Ohio Association of Track and Cross Country Coaches Hall of Fame in 2001.

He also will tell you that he's just excited about the time of his eighth man as the one who crossed the finish line first.

"It is about seeing a kid improve and reach goals," said Sternberg, who outside of one year as head coach has been a track assistant since 1973, too. "I always tell them if you put the work in you see the rewards."

Sternberg came from Akron, where his father had a shop called Akron Felt and Chenille that made letter jackets, T-shirts, and even shirts for the Cleveland Cavaliers. And Sternberg was a runner at Firestone High School, earning his letter jacket, part of the team's state runner-up squad in 1966.

He qualified for state in cross country twice and took fifth in the 800 in track as a senior after an injury cost him his cross country season. He set the Firestone 800 mark at the regional meet with a 1:55.2, clocked a 1:56.5 for his fifth at state and then went to OSU to run.

"But I got hurt," he said, a partial tear of his Achilles tendon, the demon. "But I ran today, and I'm still running 50-some years later."

He credits three Firestone coaches for getting him involved in coaching: Bill Heideman, who nearly made the US Olympic team in the 800, Alex Adams, the head cross country coach, and Don Hammit, the track coach.

"(They) were three gentlemen who really spurred me on to be a coach," he said. "When I got to college (and couldn't run) that's where I wanted to be, coaching."

Sternberg can tell you about the three state runner-up finishes of 1987, 1988 and 2006 in excruciating detail, moreso than the 1998 championship team.

"In 1987, we got blown out by Caldwell," he said. "They had Brian Hesson. They also had Jason Benzel. I'll never forget him."

Benzel was in Sternberg's sixth-grade PE class.

"On sixth-grade track and field day he told me, 'I've got to leave the school, my dad's got a job.' It was in Caldwell. He was the one that got away."

Benzel was coached by Dugan Hill, a good friend of Sternberg. When the 1988 state race boiled down to their two teams, Sternberg said he pulled out his pocketful of tickets his finishers had handed him and asked, "what's the ticket total?'

"It was 67-67," Sternberg said of the tie. "Back then you decided it on the sixth man's time. His beat mine by a second."

"That was tough, but it gave us the opportunity to realize we could be pretty good."

Or great, as in 1998, the championship year.

"We had a good team, some good senior leadership," Sternberg said. "My son was part of that team and that made it special. Mike Aukerman—he's the head coach at Carrollton now—was a really good leader."

The last runner-up finish was agonizing, both because it was by a single point and because it came at the hands, and feet, of St. Thomas Aquinas in 2006.

"Nick Dysle ran well for us (finishing as the individual runner-up), St. Thomas just ran better," Sternberg said. "One point again."

Neither the losses nor the wins got Sternberg too high or low. He has simply enjoyed coaching, teaching, seeing kids develop discipline and going after their goals."

"We've been fortunate," he said. "We had talent. We had kids who were motivated.

"Believe me, not every day was easy," he added. "But (coaching) gets in your blood." *—JIM THOMAS*

TOM DAVIS He started the girls basketball program at East Canton in 1975. In his 36 seasons as coach, his teams won 624 games (sixth-most all-time in Ohio), went to 15 regionals and were state runner-up twice. The 1970 graduate of East Canton also was All-Ohio in both football and basketball for the Hornets.

DAVE THELEN The 1953 graduate starred for nine seasons in the Canadian Football League, making five all-star teams. Drafted by both the Cleveland Browns and Indians, the two-time Mid-American Conference all-star back from Miami led the CFL in rushing with 1,407 yards in 1960, ran for 8,463 career yards and was inducted into the CFL Hall of Fame in 1989.

LINDA KRIDER Krider was East Canton's first three-time All-Ohioan, its first two-time first-team honoree and was the 1981 Class AA Player of the Year as a senior. When Krider graduated, she had scored 1,931 points—a Stark County record that stood for 30 years.

BILL NARDUZZI
Lettered in football, basketball, baseball and track at East Canton—was a Class B all-county tackle in 1953—but made his mark as a head football coach at Youngstown State from 1975-85. Narduzzi led the Penguins to two Division II playoff appearances and the championship game in 1979. Narduzzi also coached at Benedictine, Sandy Valley and Ursuline high schools, and was a college assistant at Pitt, Brown, Yale, Miami and Kentucky. His son, Pat, is the head football coach at Pitt.

JOE BRADLEY The first Stark County athlete to sweep the sprints at a state track meet. Bradley achieved that feat in 1981 as a senior, winning the 100 (10.89), 200 (21.79) and 400 (47.94), all in Class A record times. His 30 points gave the Hornets third place as a team.

LEE STERNBERG
The founder of the boys cross country team in 1973, Sternberg steered the Hornets to the 1998 state Division III state championship. His 1987, 1988 and 2006 boys teams were state runner-up and 18 teams qualified for state in his 42 seasons. Sternberg was inducted into the OATCCC Hall of Fame in 2001.

MACK YOHO
Earned Class B All-Stark County honors at end in 1952 and then starred at Miami of Ohio. Yoho played in all 14 Buffalo Bills AFL games each season from 1960-1963. The 6-2, 230-pound defensive end was agile enough to intercept two passes, running one back for a touchdown his rookie season.

CODY MARSHALL After a fourth-place state finish in the pole vault as a junior, Marshall went to No. 1 in 2010, winning state and setting the county mark at 15-7 in Columbus. Marshall then stayed in town, starring at Ohio State and winning the Big Ten outdoor title in 2011 with a vault of 16-7.75 on his way to a personal-best 17-0 clearance. He also made All-Ohio in football for the Hornets.

CAITLIN (SHARP) DeROSA A dual threat as a runner and guard on the basketball team. A two-time All-Ohio selection on the court, Sharp's 1,666 points rank seventh in county history. The 2008 graduate earned All-Ohio in both track and cross country. Sharp played basketball and ran track and cross country for Malone.

KATY ARICK She helped the Wizards reach the 2006 Division IV state championship game her senior year, scoring 33 in a semifinal win. Arick was The Repository Player of the Year, a two-time All-Ohioan and finished her career with 1,789 points, fifth in county history. She then lettered four years for NCAA Division II University of Charleston.

HONORABLE MENTIONS

CHASE CLINE
JARROD DAVIS
JODI DOBRANSKY
NICHOLAS DYSLE
TOM LOY
JOE PANGRAZIO
BETH STERNBERG
BOB WERLEY

PROVOST WENT FROM FAIRLESS TO NATIONAL TITLE AT OSU, PROS

A HALF-CENTURY LATER, TED PROVOST'S LEGACY AT FAIRLESS HIGH SCHOOL REMAINS STRONG.

Provost arrived there in the early 1960s, shortly after the consolidation of Beach City, Brewster and Navarre schools formed the Fairless district. It didn't take long for him to become the school's first true star.

"He was a great athlete in any sport," said Ron Rankin, Provost's head football coach. "Football, basketball, track. He didn't play baseball when he got to high school, but he was also good in baseball.

"He could do it all."

Provost was an all-around athlete when the Falcons played in the Federal League. His best sport was football, where he played quarterback and safety.

"He was about 6-3 and had good speed," Rankin said. "... We didn't keep him in the pocket. We were a roll-out type of team with him as our quarterback. If things were clogged up, he could always run out.

"He really stood out as a defensive back. He never came off the field."

Former Fairless athletic director and golf coach Ken Youngman was Provost's teammate. He remembers Provost as a team player with no ego.

"Everything came natural to him," Youngman said.

Provost was a quiet, reserved person

"HE WAS A GREAT ATHLETE IN ANY SPORT. FOOTBALL, BASKETBALL, TRACK. ... HE COULD DO IT ALL."

—RON RANKIN

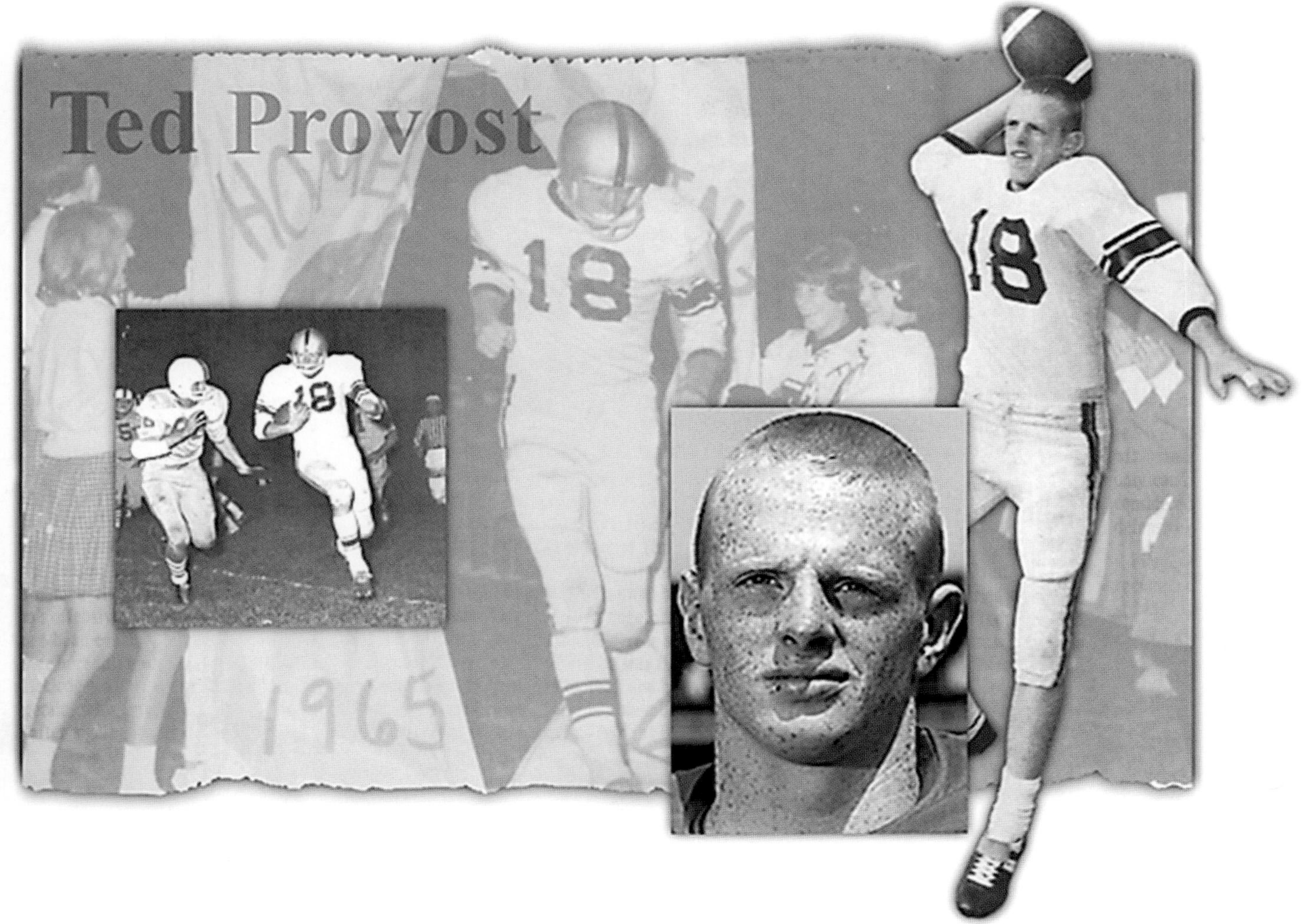

off the field. On the field, it was different. Teammates, even in practice, saw a fierce competitor.

"We avoided him in tackling," Youngman said. "He would really hit you."

Provost was one of the area's top hurdlers and reached the state track and field finals. As a basketball player, he led the Falcons to a near-upset of McKinley in a 1966 sectional final. A Fairless turnover and a McKinley basket in the final seconds led to a 62-61 Bulldogs win.

Football, though, was Provost's future. Ohio State head coach Woody Hayes didn't need to see him in person to be convinced.

"The story goes Woody Hayes saw him on film and said, 'I want him,' " Youngman said.

The athlete that Buckeyes assistant coach Lou McCullough saw when he watched Provost play basketball reaffirmed Ohio State's decision to sign him.

"That set it off," Rankin said. "They knew they wanted him for sure then, but they were going to commit to him whether they had seen him play basketball or not."

Provost was an All-Big Ten defensive back in 1968 and 1969, his final two seasons with Ohio State. He also earned All-American honors in 1969.

As a junior, Provost helped lead the Buckeyes to a national championship. The breakthrough win came in the third game, when Ohio State shut out top-ranked Purdue 13-0.

Provost broke the ice after a scoreless first half.

"Mike Phipps, who later played with the Browns, threw a pass intended for Leroy Keyes," Youngman said. "Ted read everything. He intercepted it and went for a touchdown."

The Los Angeles Rams selected Provost in the seventh round of the 1970 National Football League Draft. They later traded him to Minnesota, where he played seven games with the Vikings. He also played two games with the St. Louis Cardinals in 1971.

Most of Provost's pro football career was spent in Canada. He played five seasons with the Canadian Football League's Saskatchewan Roughriders and was a two-time CFL West All-Star.

A Stark County High School Football Hall of Fame inductee in 2004, Provost came a long way from the early days of Fairless High School.

"Ted was one of those guys who convinced us to set our bars a little higher," Youngman said. "We never thought anybody from Fairless would play pro football. That was Massillon.

"All of a sudden, here's a guy who made it."

—MIKE POPOVICH

MARCHAND GAVE UP FOOTBALL TO BECOME DISTANCE RUNNING STAR

FAIRLESS' GREATEST DISTANCE RUNNER STARTED HIS HIGH SCHOOL CAREER PLAYING FRESHMAN FOOTBALL FOR KEN YOUNGMAN.

Even Youngman, who later became the school's athletic director, is thankful Joel Marchand had a change of heart.

"I was dumb," Youngman said. "I convinced Joel to give up cross country and play freshman football. How smart was I?"

Marchand remains the most decorated athlete in Fairless history. He became the school's first state champion in 1978 when he won the Class AA title in cross country and added four more state titles before he graduated.

A player since his pee wee years, cutting ties with football wasn't easy. Head cross country Tim Stith told Marchand he would have to tell head football coach Dave Dourm himself he was giving up football.

"I go stumbling up to him and I'm like 'Hey, coach. I don't think I'm going to play football. I'm going to run cross country,' " Marchand said. "He was cool about it. He said 'Hey, you have to do what you have to do.'

"It was pretty intimidating, but I do respect (Stith) that he made me do the right thing instead of just quitting or writing a note telling him."

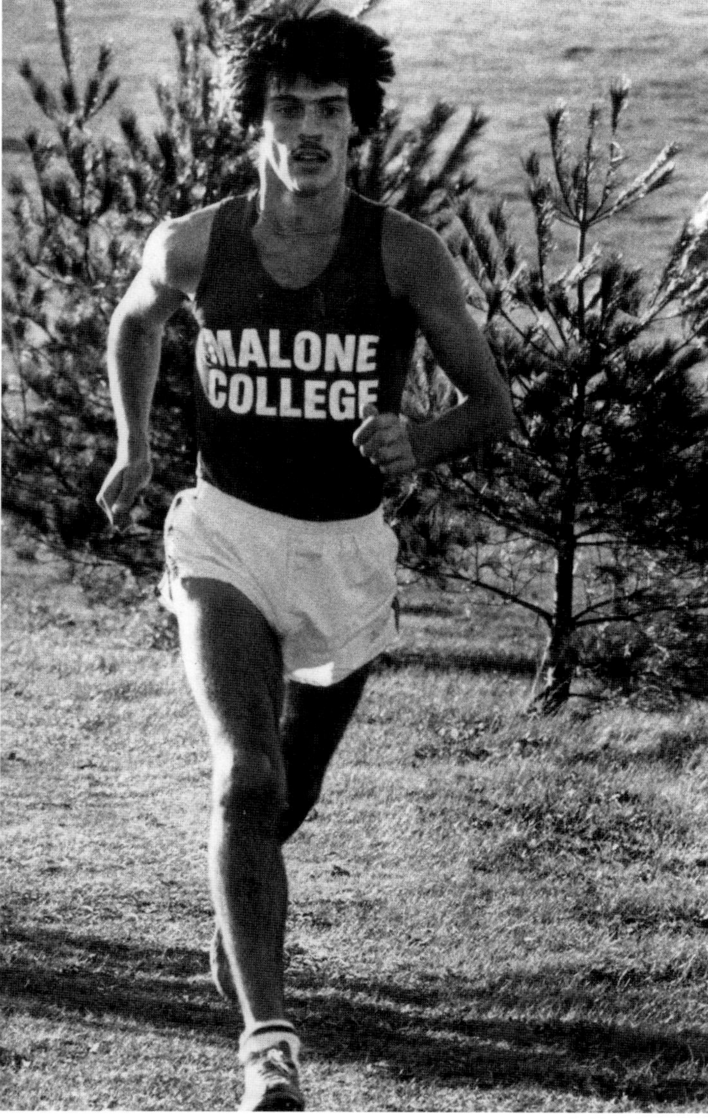

Marchand led one of the state's top distance programs in the late 1970s. His win at the 1978 state cross country meet led Fairless to a runner-up finish in the team standings.

The Falcons did not qualify for the state meet the following year, but Marchand won the individual qualifiers race by just over 32 seconds. His winning time of 12:11.9 was the second fastest in all divisions.

The thought of being Fairless' first state champion didn't hit Marchand right away.

"As any other kid at the time, I didn't really know what I did until later on and people started to talk about it," Marchand said. "I was just a kid doing what I loved to do. It just happened for me."

Marchand also won three state championships in track and field. He won the Class AA title in the 3,200-meter run in 1979 and swept the 1,600 and 3,200 in 1980. He is the only Stark County boy or girl to win both distance races at a state meet.

"It was pretty grueling," Marchand said. "I remember it was 100-some degrees on the track that day. Of course they help you out by posting that right by the track so you know how hot it is."

Marchand won his state track championships at Ohio Stadium. He grew up wanting to play football for Ohio State. Little did he know he would win state titles at the Buckeyes' stadium.

"At least I got to run around Ohio State's football field," Marchand said. "I never got to play on it like every Ohio kid who wants to play for the Buckeyes."

Marchand was a four-year letterman in cross country and track at Malone. He became the school's second NAIA individual national champion when he won a pair of indoor two-mile indoor titles and an indoor three-mile title.

A six-time NAIA All-American, Marchand still holds the Malone cross country school record on an 8,000-meter course (23:57). *—MIKE POPOVICH*

FAIRLESS TOP TEN ICONS

1

TED PROVOST Three-year letterman as a quarterback and defensive back. Was voted to the Stark County High School Football Hall of Fame in 2004. Reached the state finals in track his senior year. Played safety on Ohio State's 1968 national championship team and was named an All-American in 1969. Played two seasons in the NFL with the Minnesota Vikings and St. Louis Cardinals and seven years with the Canadian Football League's Saskatchewan Roughriders.

<<< 2

JOEL MARCHAND Became the school's first state champion in 1978 when he led the Falcons cross country team to a runner-up finish in Class AA. Won two state titles in cross country and three in track. Went on to star in college at Malone.

3

FRED BRIDEWESER Coached football, basketball and baseball at Navarre High School beginning in 1931. Led the baseball team to five state tournament appearances, including a pair of runner-up finishes. Named the first athletic director and baseball coach at Fairless when the school opened in 1960.

<<< 4

ALLYSON SIMMONS Won Division II state track and field titles in the pole vault in 2013 and 2014. Her winning vault of 13 feet, 4 1/2 inches in 2014 was an OHSAA girls record at the time. First Fairless girl to win a state championship.

>>> 5

HUNTER WELLS Stark County high school football's career passing leader with 8,344 yards. Also holds county record for career completions with 617 and ranks second in touchdown passes with 67. Named Stark County Player of the Year, Northeast Inland District Division V Offensive Player the Year and first team All-Ohio as a senior. Led the Falcons to their first playoff berth in 14 years and their first-ever postseason victory.

^^^ 6

AARON MELHORN Won back-to-back Division II cross country state titles in 2005 and 2006 and a Division II track state championship in 2006 when he finished first in the 3,200 meters. Won individual titles in the 3,000 steeplechase at the NAIA Outdoor Track and Field Championships as a freshman and sophomore at Malone. Helped lead the Pioneers cross country team to three straight national championships from 2007-09.

7

LINDSEY GAUT The Fairless girls basketball team's all-time leading scorer with 1,709 points, sixth-most in Stark County history. Three-time PAC-7 Player of the Year, two-time Stark County Player of the Year and three-time All-Ohioan. Led the Falcons to a Division II district title in 2005. Returned to Fairless in 2012 to become the girls basketball team's head coach.

8

BARB SPURGEON Voted Class AA Player of the Year in 1980 when she led the girls basketball team to the state tournament. Three-time All-Ohio selection who ranks second on the Falcons' career scoring list with 1,429 points. Member of the volleyball team that qualified for the state tournament in 1978.

9

BILL GAUT Became the first Fairless wrestler to compete for a state title in 1979. Finished second at 185 pounds. All-Stark County middle guard who helped the football team earn a share of the 1978 All-Ohio Conference championship, the first league title in program history.

10

TERRY GRIFFITH Coached the Fairless baseball team from 1977 to 2000. School's winningest coach with 259 victories and seven league championships. Team's baseball facility, the Terry Griffith "1" Baseball Complex, was dedicated in 2015 in his honor.

HONORABLE MENTIONS

KELLY HYSONG
CHAD MERCER
TYLER NEFF
LINDSAY SALSBURG
KEN WOHLHETER
KEN YOUNGMAN
ATHLETIC COMPLEX TEAM
(VOLUNTEERS WHO CONSTRUCTED THE ATHLETIC COMPLEX NEXT TO THE HIGH SCHOOL)

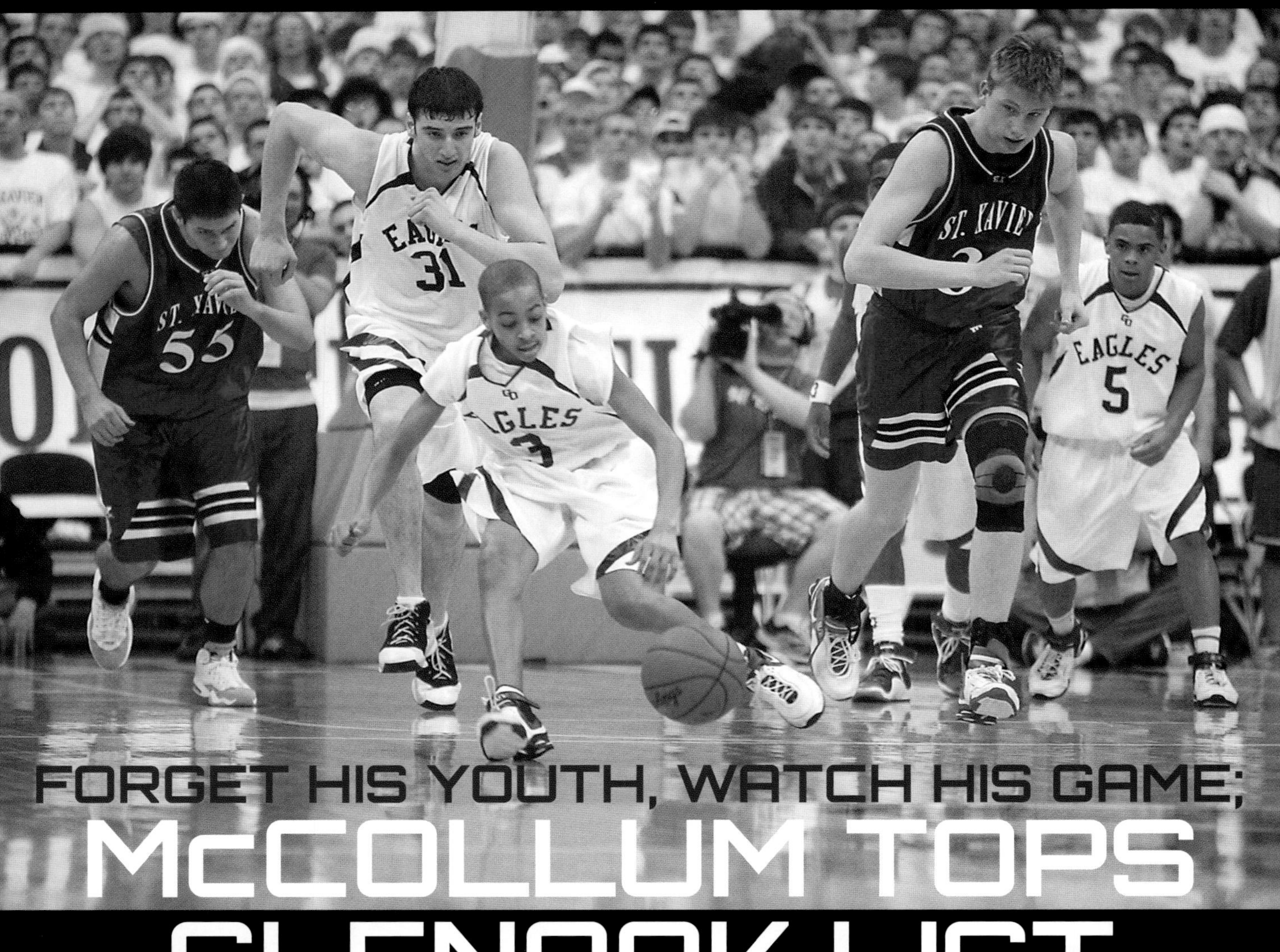

FORGET HIS YOUTH, WATCH HIS GAME; McCOLLUM TOPS GLENOAK LIST

TWENTY-FOUR-YEARS OLD SEEMS YOUNG FOR ICON STATUS.

But don't be fooled by C.J. McCollum's baby face.

McCollum is all grown up. His game. His demeanor. His identity.

The 2009 GlenOak High School alum is emerging as an NBA star with the Portland Trail Blazers, and he is doing it with the same style and character that he exuded while lighting up gyms in Stark County and later at Lehigh University.

McCollum's first two NBA seasons were stunted by circumstance.

His rookie year was marred by an injury to his left foot—the same foot and the same broken bone that cost him the stretch run of his senior year of college.

His second year saw him struggle for consistent minutes on a talented playoff team, although he offered a glimpse of his capabilities late in the season when Portland was ravaged by injuries.

Year No. 3 has brought a breakthrough.

McCollum averaged 20.8 points per game during the 2015-16 season, the highest scoring average ever by a Stark County native in the NBA, He surpassed North Canton native Dick Snyder's 19.4 with the Seattle SuperSonics in the 1970-71 season.

He also easily earned NBA Most Improved Player, helped form one of the league's highest-scoring duos and helped the Blazers win a first-round playoff series over the Clippers.

"Being raised in Canton, Ohio, making it to this stage, it's means a lot to me," McCollum said the day he earned Most Improved Player.

His scoring average increased by 14 points from 2014-15, the largest points-per-game improvement in the league in 26 seasons. He also averaged 4.3 assists and 3.2 rebounds to go with 41.7 percent shooting from 3-point range, good for eighth in the NBA.

McCollum believes his emergence is more about opportunity than improvement.

The only starter Portland returned from 2014-15 was two-time All-Star Damian Lillard, providing McCollum—the 10th overall pick of the 2013

GlenOak's 2007 run to the state tournament as a sophomore, McCollum grew at least four inches heading into his junior season.

If anyone had questions about his potential, he answered those with a school-record 54 points in GlenOak's 2008 season opener. He followed that with 44 points in game No. 2.

McCollum led Stark County in scoring for two years, totaling 1,226 points in those two seasons alone en route to a school-record 1,405 points for his career.

His senior season was like performance art for offensive basketball: He averaged 29.3 points with shooting percentages of 50.7 from the field, 40.0 from the arc and 85.7 from the foul line. He was runner-up to future NBA colleague Jared Sullinger in Ohio's Mr. Basketball voting and won Ohio Gatorade Player of the Year.

Still, his slight frame and late-bloomer status had Division I programs in Ohio late to the recruiting party, if they came at all.

So McCollum went to Lehigh, a Patriot League school in Bethlehem, Pa. And he carried a large chip on his shoulder since all the Ohio schools ignored him.

"That's a lot of motivation," McCollum told The Repository back in a 2009 interview for his Stark County Player of the Year story. "They passed on my brother (Errick). They passed on me. I want to make them wish they would have got me."

Payback is hell. McCollum scored 42 points at Kent State as a Lehigh sophomore. The Golden Flashes and every other Ohio school chose not to schedule the Mountain Hawks again.

The vengeance thing aside, McCollum is about as kind and gracious as a star athlete can be. He's also smart and forward thinking, as evidenced by the fact he already has a post-playing career in journalism in the works.

McCollum hosts a weekly radio show in Portland and writes for Derek Jeter's web site, The Players' Tribune. He has started a mentoring program for students at Portland's Madison High School called "C.J.'s Press Pass." It gives kids interested in journalism a chance at "real-time experience," as McCollum puts it.

He's a darling in Rip City.

Is it any wonder he's already an icon back home? *—JOSH WEIR*

draft—a chance to prove himself as foundation piece.

"I knew an opportunity would come at some point," McCollum said before a December 2015 game against the Cavaliers in Cleveland. "I just prepared for that, mentally and physically, just making sure I would be ready. I knew I wasn't going to blow an opportunity. ... I felt like when the time came, I'd be ready.

"Having to go through that process over the course of my first two years, I understand exactly what it takes to be successful. I've got to watch Dame's rise to stardom. I've seen the type of work he puts in every day. That prepared me for this."

McCollum and Lillard form a tandem Cavs superstar LeBron James described as "the two-headed monster they have, there's only a couple of backcourts in our league like that."

They averaged a combined 45.9 points a game, a figure trailing only Stephen Curry/Klay Thompson of Golden State and Kevin Durant/Russell Westbrook of Oklahoma City in terms of highest scoring duos in 2015-16.

"Those guys are producing every single night," James said, "and C.J. ... I think he used that playoff experience and the way he played 2015 and just turned it up another notch."

The production is there. So is the style.

There is a rhythm and a pace to McCollum's game, almost like rehearsed dance steps. He glides through sets before unleashing a dizzying array of offensive moves: Crossovers into step-back jumpers. Spin moves into scoop shots. Hesitation dribbles into running bankers. Fading jumpers. Three-pointers off the bounce or off the catch.

The 6-foot-4, 200-pound McCollum works very well off ball screens. Portland head coach Terry Stotts believes increased strength has been key to McCollum blossoming.

"The other technical aspect is he has really improved his ball-handling," Stotts said. "He's really got a great handle. He can get where he wants to go with the ball. He's always been able to shoot, but I think his strength and ball-handling have really helped."

The skill set has evolved, but the basic beauty and fluidity to his game has been there since McCollum's body finally started catching up with his talent.

After being one of the shooters stationed around Kosta Koufos during

SPOTLESON EXCELLED WHATEVER THE SEASON

W*HATEVER THE SPORT AT GLENOAK HIGH SCHOOL, SUZI SPOTLESON EXCELLED AT IT.*

She was a setter for the Golden Eagles' state-ranked volleyball team.

She scored 1,260 points on the basketball court—a school record that still stands 32 years after she graduated.

Her all-league, all-county talents on the softball field led to a college career that included competing in the College World Series for Northwestern.

And after all that, in her mid 20s, she finally picked up a golf club.

Spotleson might have saved her best sport for last. Her 11 Women's Akron District Golf Association championships and numerous Stark County amateur titles attest to that possibility.

Today, the 49-year-old Spotleson, who works for Synchrony Financial, is regarded as one of the best female golfers in the area.

SUZI SPOTLESON
SUBMITTED PHOTO

She knew nothing about golf when a friend encouraged her to give it a try in the early 1990s.

"That was it," Spotleson said. "I was hooked."

So began a love affair with a game that's not always easy to love.

Spotleson spent a few years as a double-digit handicap. Her progress sped up rapidly once she hit single digits.

She played in her first state tournament in 1998. By 2001, she was competing in a U.S. Amateur.

Spotleson guesses her hand-eye coordination from softball played a role in how she took to golf. She also believes Mike Emery, an instructor at Brookside Country Club, was vital.

Spotleson met Emery around 2000. She soon could call herself a scratch golfer.

"I really do owe him a lot of credit for some of the success I've had in golf," said Spotleson, who hovers from scratch to a 2 handicap these days. "I still pick his brain. You learn in this sport every time you go out."

Spotleson has been a member at Brookside since 1998 and set the course record of 63 a few years back.

As for her high school accomplishments, Spotleson is shocked that her scoring record still stands.

"I want an asterisk besides that because we had no 3-point line and we had no girls (sized) basketball," joked Spotleson, who, as a 5-foot-4 guard, "would fire from anywhere."

Being a Division I college athlete was her goal, and softball presented the best opportunity to do that. A talented outfielder known for her defense, Spotleson went the preferred walk-on route at Northwestern and eventually earned her way to a scholarship. She put together a career that included four letters, two Big Ten championships and a second-team All-Big Ten nod as a junior. She also was All-Academic Big Ten three times.

Spotleson traded in her bat for a 9-iron as she entered adulthood. As much success as she has enjoyed on tee boxes and putting greens, golf has meant much more than accolades to her.

"I've met my best friends on the golf course," Spotleson said. "It's challenged me constantly, so I'm never bored with it. As soon as you feel like you have something mastered, you go back out and it's a disaster. It's just a challenge for me every single time. That to me is very motivating." *—JOSH WEIR*

GLENWOOD & OAKWOOD PRODUCED THEIR STARS, TOO, HERE'S A FEW

1 DAN DIERDORF Big kid gradually grew into a big star. Two-time all-county football player who helped Glenwood to 9-1 record as a senior two-way lineman. His shot put of 60 feet, 8 inches stood as a county record until 1999. An All-American offensive lineman at Michigan, Dierdorf went on to five All-Pro nods and six Pro Bowls for the St. Louis Cardinals and was enshrined in the Pro Football Hall of Fame in 1996. Longtime NFL broadcast analyst.

2 TIM FOX Three-year letterman in all three sports at Glenwood. First Team All-American safety at Ohio State, where he served as co-captain his senior year. Buckeyes went 40-5-1 and played in four consecutive Rose Bowls during his tenure. First-round draft pick who played 12 years in NFL with Patriots, Chargers and Rams. Selected to one Pro Bowl.

3 TOM ECREMENT WHBC Stark County MVP and first team All-Ohio as a senior, leading Glenwood to a 9-1 record. Eagles won two Federal League titles and finished as runner-up in his three varsity seasons, which included the linebacker/end starting every game offensively and defensively. Career at Ohio State cut short by a back injury.

4 MARK MURPHY Late-blooming athlete, whose senior year was the first year of GlenOak, earned All-American football honors at West Liberty and played 11 years in the NFL with the Green Bay Packers. Member of West Liberty Hall of Fame and Packers Hall of Fame.

5 JIM REICHENBACH A standout lineman for Massillon and Ohio State, Reichenbach coached Glenwood to a 53-35-2 record over nine seasons, including a 9-1 record and a Federal League title in 1966.

GLENOAK TOP TEN ICONS

1 **C.J. McCOLLUM** One of the smoothest, most skilled players ever to grace Stark County's basketball courts. GlenOak's all-time leading scorer with 1,405 points. While at Lehigh, authored memorable first-round NCAA Tournament upset of Duke and became Patriot League's all-time leading scorer with 2,323 points. The 10th overall pick of the 2013 NBA Draft, he just finished a breakout third season with the Portland Trail Blazers.

>>> **2** **BOB COMMINGS** Hard-nosed coached who earned fierce loyalty from his players. Guided GlenOak to a 76-44-1 record and four Federal League titles over 12 seasons before succumbing to cancer in February 1992. School's football field named after him in 2007.

3 <<<

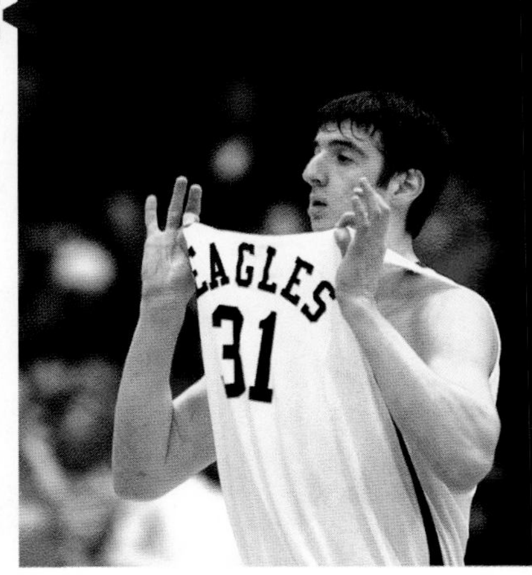

KOSTA KOUFOS
Seven-feet worth of skills and smarts who played inside and out at GlenOak. McDonald's All-American his senior year when he led the Golden Eagles to their only state tournament appearance. Spent one year at Ohio State, during which he was named MVP of the NIT. A former first-round draft pick now in his eighth NBA season. Has grown into a rotation player, now with the Sacramento Kings.

<<< **4**

DUSTIN FOX The ultimate quick-twitch athlete with explosive speed and hops. First team All-Ohio twice in football. Part of team that still holds the county record in the 400-meter relay. Starting cornerback on Ohio State's 2002 national championship team. Played parts of four seasons in the NFL.

5 **JOE GILHOUSEN** Stoic, commanding figure of baseball in Plain Township for 33 seasons. Gained 575 of his 601 career wins at Oakwood and GlenOak, winning 17 Federal League titles, 10 district titles and two state championships. The 1966 Lehman grad led GlenOak to become the only public school to win consecutive big-school division state titles (1995-96). School's baseball field dedicated to him in 2007.

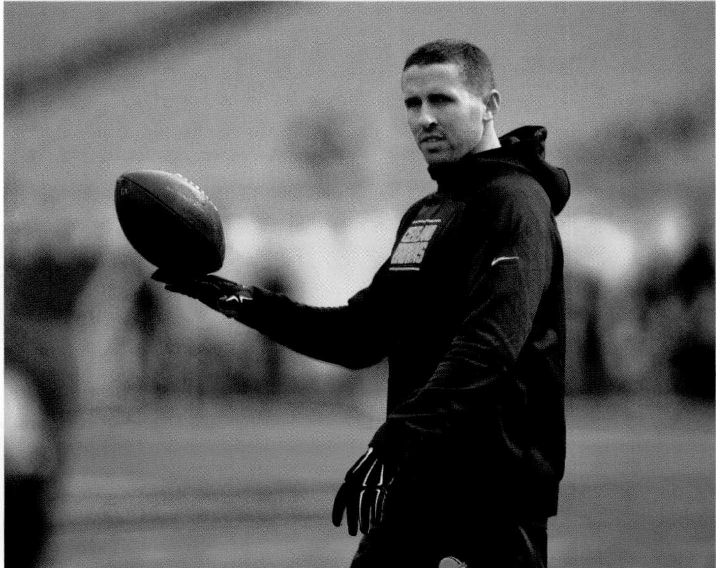

6 **BRIAN HARTLINE** Recovered from gruesome leg injury in football his senior year to win state track titles in the 110 and 300 hurdles that spring. Successful tenure at Ohio State has led to arguably the best NFL career by a county native since Chris Spielman. Owns two 1,000-yard receiving seasons in his seven years in the NFL.

7 **SUZI SPOTLESON** All-league/all-county softball player who contributed to state-ranked volleyball team and still holds GlenOak's girls basketball scoring record (1,260). Four-year letter winner for the Northwestern softball team. Competed in a College World Series and was part of two Big Ten championships. Picked up golf after college and has become one of the area's best amateur golfers.

8 **HEATHER LYKE** Three-sport star who was part of GlenOak's 1988 state runner-up basketball team. Four-year letter winner, two-time All-Academic Big Ten honoree and captain her senior year for the Michigan softball team. First female to be the full-time athletic director at Eastern Michigan University highlights successful career in athletic administration.

9 **JOANN ZERGER** Versatile, unselfish athlete led the Golden Eagles to Columbus three straight years, winning a state championship in 1989 and finishing as runner-up in 1988. First-team All-Ohio as a senior. Played four years at UNC Greensboro, starting two. Fourth most assists in UNCG program history.

10 **MIKE MUZI** All-Stark County defensive back who made his biggest impact on the pitcher's mound, going 25-0 in his career and helping GlenOak to consecutive Division I state baseball championships. State coaches association player of the year as a senior. Two-time All-Ohioan. Pitched collegiately for Bowling Green and gained third-most saves in BG history.

HONORABLE MENTIONS

JIM BOLLAS
BRIONTE DUNN
DEREK FOX
GARY ISLER
ERRICK MCCOLLUM
ERICH MUZI
LOUIDAJEAN (HOLLOWAY) PAYTON
SAM SEIPLE
T.J. SUTTON
KANDACE THOMAS
RICK THOMPSON
DERRICK WILLIAMS

SNYDER STILL THE STANDARD

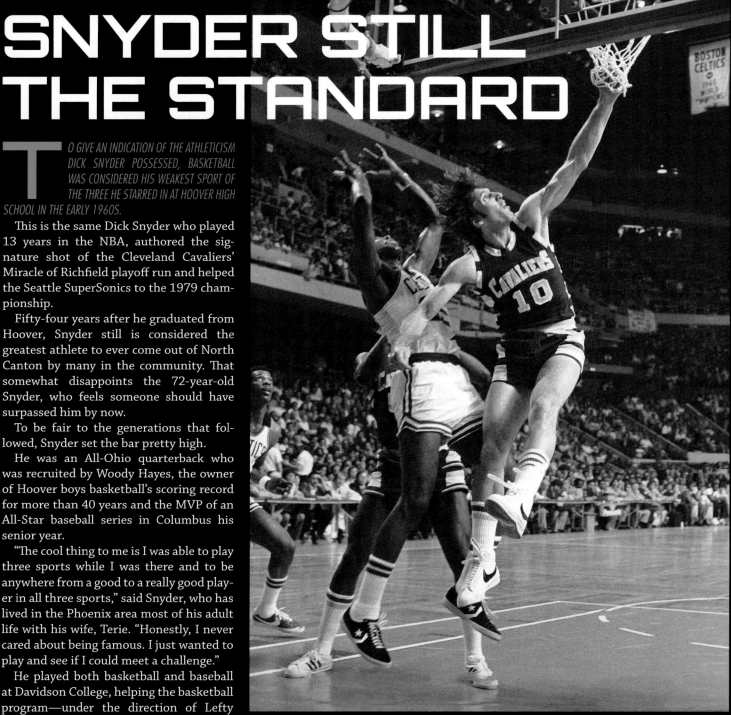

TO GIVE AN INDICATION OF THE ATHLETICISM DICK SNYDER POSSESSED, BASKETBALL WAS CONSIDERED HIS WEAKEST SPORT OF THE THREE HE STARRED IN AT HOOVER HIGH SCHOOL IN THE EARLY 1960S.

This is the same Dick Snyder who played 13 years in the NBA, authored the signature shot of the Cleveland Cavaliers' Miracle of Richfield playoff run and helped the Seattle SuperSonics to the 1979 championship.

Fifty-four years after he graduated from Hoover, Snyder still is considered the greatest athlete to ever come out of North Canton by many in the community. That somewhat disappoints the 72-year-old Snyder, who feels someone should have surpassed him by now.

To be fair to the generations that followed, Snyder set the bar pretty high.

He was an All-Ohio quarterback who was recruited by Woody Hayes, the owner of Hoover boys basketball's scoring record for more than 40 years and the MVP of an All-Star baseball series in Columbus his senior year.

"The cool thing to me is I was able to play three sports while I was there and to be anywhere from a good to a really good player in all three sports," said Snyder, who has lived in the Phoenix area most of his adult life with his wife, Terie. "Honestly, I never cared about being famous. I just wanted to play and see if I could meet a challenge."

He played both basketball and baseball at Davidson College, helping the basketball program—under the direction of Lefty Driesell—gain success not seen again until a guy named Stephen Curry wore the Wildcats' uniform four decades later.

He went on to put together arguably the best career of any Stark County native in the NBA. At the time of his retirement, Snyder possessed the 17th most points in NBA history.

However, his first true taste of stardom probably came on the football field.

Snyder was first team All-Ohio his senior year as a quarterback who preferred running to passing. He also played safety, punted and returned kicks as the Vikings went a combined 17-2 in his junior and senior seasons, which happened to be the first two seasons of 21 for Don Hertler Sr. as head coach.

The late Hertler Sr. called Snyder the best athlete he ever coached.

Colleges took notice. Snyder was recruited by Ohio State, Michigan and Notre Dame, among others.

As he explained, "I was a 6-(foot)-5 quarterback that had enough speed that he could eventually play in the backcourt of the NBA."

His high school teammate, Bob Esmont, told the Repository in a 2003 story for Snyder's induction into the Stark County High School Football Hall of Fame, "One time, halfway through our senior year, I had an early block on a sweep that took me out of the play. I was just standing there watching the way he moved down the field—his quickness, the way he set up his blocks. Sometimes you don't realize what a superior athlete you're playing with until you just watch him like that."

For all his ability on the football field, Snyder's passion wasn't there. So he had to say no to all the football coaches, including Hayes, which stunned local fans at the time.

"I didn't have the love of the game," Snyder said. "... It just came down to the point where I realized I don't care how good you are, assuming you're as good as everyone says. If I go down there and I'm competing against the other guys that love the game, they're going to beat me out."

Snyder's heart was on the hardwood. He found himself excited at the mere thought of practice, let alone a game.

However he thought his future was baseball.

His father, Dick Snyder Sr., excelled at baseball and, the story goes, had a chance to play minor league ball before settling into a career at the Hoover Company.

The younger Snyder, who was drafted by the Washington Senators in the 30th round of the 1966 Major League Baseball draft despite not playing baseball his senior year at Davidson, was an outfielder and pitcher in the Canton Class A League during the summers.

"If you'd seen him play baseball, you'd say that was his best sport," said Ron Blackledge, a longtime college football and NFL coach who actually managed Snyder on the Class A Black Label team.

Snyder led the league—highly competitive in those years with talent such as Thurman Munson in it—with a 1.05 ERA in 1965. He also hit three home runs and finished second in the league with 18 RBIs.

Snyder said he chose Davidson—another stunner for locals and one of the few schools to recruit him for basketball—because he figured he could just have fun playing basketball while getting his degree. Then he could pursue a baseball career after that.

Instead, he became arguably the best basketball player in Davidson history before Curry came along.

Snyder helped the Wildcats to their first NCAA Tournament berth as a senior in 1965-66, the same season he was the Southern Conference Player of the Year and an All-American averaging 26.9 points. He finished his career with 1,693 points (in three years since freshmen weren't allowed to play varsity at that time).

"I didn't expect to play at the level we did there or to have the success I had," said Snyder, who also was an academic All-American in college. "That wasn't remotely in my mind. I didn't even know until halfway through my senior year that there were some NBA teams considering me and had scouts at games."

Snyder credits the aggressive man-to-man defense that Driesell demanded for making him capable of playing guard in the NBA. He is considered the best defensive player Driesell ever coached at Davidson.

"When it came to athletics, Dick could do just about anything he wanted to," Driesell said in a Davidson media guide. "That even included riding a bicycle better than anybody else."

Snyder was the fourth pick of the second round in the 1966 NBA Draft by the St. Louis Hawks.

He averaged 12.1 points for the Phoenix Suns in his third NBA season, starting a string of eight consecutive years in which he averaged double figures. He peaked for Seattle in the 1970-71 season, when he averaged career highs of 19.1 points on 53.1 percent shooting and 4.3 assists. His points-per-game average was the highest in an NBA season by a Stark County native until GlenOak grad C.J. McCollum averaged 20.8 points per game this season for Portland, in the 2015-16 season.

Snyder described his job this way: Guard the likes of Oscar Robertson, Jerry West and Walt Frazier on the defensive end, run the floor hard and knock down jump shots on the other end.

Snyder killed opponents softly with his jumper, which was described as "softer than a Carolina sunrise" by one sportswriter during an era without the 3-point line. He specialized in the pull-up jumper off the dribble but eventually developed a good catch-and-shoot game, a facet he credits to playing off the penetration of Lenny Wilkens in Seattle.

Snyder got good elevation on his jump shot, which had a slight fade to it, making it a nightmare for opponents to defend.

"They could put a hand up, but it was virtually impossible for them to get to my shot," Snyder said. "After a while you realize that and you don't even think about them."

The most famous of the 11,755 career points he scored in the NBA certainly displayed his deft touch. Snyder's driving bank shot with four seconds left highlighted the Cavs' Game 7 win against the Washington Bullets in the 1976 Eastern Conference semifinals.

Snyder drove around Wes Unseld, leapt from outside the left block and kissed the bank shot over Phil Chenier for one of Northeast Ohio's most iconic pro sports moments.

Not bad for a reluctant football star and a potential baseball star.

After his playing days were over, Snyder spent 35 years as a State Farm insurance agent. He has fond memories of his native North Canton and returns fairly regularly to visit friends and family.

"I feel guilty for not settling back there and doing more for the community," Snyder said, "but not guilty enough to leave Arizona." —*JOSH WEIR*

WOOLBERT THE BIG FISH IN LOCAL SWIMMING

UPON ARRIVING AT HIS DORM AS AN LSU FRESHMAN IN 1989, THE BIG FISH IN STARK COUNTY SWIMMING MET THE MAN WHO WOULD LATER BECOME THE BIG ARISTOTLE, AKA WILT CHAMBERNEEZY, AKA SHAQ FU.

Yes, the first person Hoover High School swimming legend Gordy Woolbert saw was Shaquille O'Neal, who just happened to be flanked by another future NBA player and 7-footer, Stanley Roberts.

"I thought I was in the wrong place," Woolbert said.

Woolbert later tutored O'Neal in accounting and quickly recognized the star power in the fun-loving giant.

As for giants in local swimming, they don't get much bigger than Woolbert.

"From the perspective of having kids who are now reaching the high school age, it's fun that my name is still bandied about in sports circles," said Woolbert, a lawyer for Day Ketterer in downtown Canton. "I can at least point them to the fact their father used to be a decent athlete."

It is with slight disappointment that Woolbert reports that none of his six children have followed him into the pool.

That might be for the best, though. Woolbert likes that they've chosen their own paths. Swimming in dad's wake would have been a challenge.

Woolbert was good enough to have Olympic aspirations. He registered the fastest 100-meter backstroke time in the nation as a high school junior and earned All-American honors in each of his four years at Hoover.

"IN THE NEW ERA, IN THE LAST 55 YEARS, GORDY WOOLBERT IS YOUR GOLD STANDARD."
—R.J. VAN ALMEN

Woolbert won three individual state championships and one relay state championship. He led the Vikings to a state runner-up finish as a team in 1988. And he did all this without swimming "shaved and tapered" his senior year.

A shoulder problem—which went misdiagnosed for years and plagued his college career—kept him from competing in the tournament his final high school season.

Still, Woolbert's career is the stuff of legend in the county swimming community.

"Certainly in the post-McKinley dynasty era, he's the best," said R.J. Van Almen, the president of the Greater Canton Aquatics Association. "I always say the best ever is going to be a Marty Mull, a Ben Ledger and a Tom Whiteleather. But you're talking about three guys who swam before 1960. ... In the new era, in the last 55 years, Gordy Woolbert is your gold standard."

Just imagine what that standard would be like with a tournament run his senior year. He still owns county records in the 100-yard backstroke and 100 butterfly. He finished his college career at Stanford, where he was part of the Cardinal's 1993 national championship team.

"I've done some what-if scenarios in my head had I been able to swim my senior year of high school," Woolbert said.

"I had some state records I was gunning for. And the race I was going to swim in addition to the backstroke was the 50 free. I really wanted to do a 50 freestyle shaved and tapered. And it never quite happened."

—JOSH WEIR

HOOVER TOP TEN ICONS

1 DICK SNYDER

DICK SNYDER One of the best athletes in Stark County history by any measure. A 13-year NBA veteran who scored 11,755 career points. Owned Hoover's scoring record for more than 40 years. All-Ohio quarterback who was coveted by Ohio State, Michigan and Notre Dame among others. Star outfielder/pitcher who played baseball and basketball at Davidson College. Drafted by the Washington Senators in 1966.

2 DON HERTLER SR.

DON HERTLER SR. Known for calm demeanor and innovative pro-set offense. Put Hoover football on the map, guiding Vikings to seven Federal League titles, two undefeated seasons and a 163-43-3 record in 21 years. Never experienced a losing season. Memorial Stadium's playing surface named in his honor in 2011. Also coached baseball program to 220 wins from 1954-70. Son, Don Jr., later guided football program to 136 wins in 19 years.

3 TODD BLACKLEDGE

TODD BLACKLEDGE Three-sport star who shined brightest on the basketball court at Hoover, where he averaged 20.0 points in 1979 and led Vikings to their first Federal League title. Went football route in college, quarterbacking Penn State to 1982 national championship and winning Davey O'Brien Award. Seventh pick in legendary 1983 NFL Draft. Played seven seasons in NFL. Respected college football analyst and current head coach of Hoover boys basketball.

4 JENNA LILLEY

JENNA LILLEY Her team and individual accomplishments on the softball field are staggering. While leading Hoover to four consecutive state championships and a 123-9 record, the lefty-swinging Lilley batted a career .576, including .697 as a junior. Now at Oregon, was Pac-12 Freshman of the Year and one of three finalists for NFCA Freshmen of the Year last season as she batted .427. Member of Team USA.

5 JEFF LOGAN

JEFF LOGAN Fast, powerful running back whose county record for career scoring stood 30 years and whose county record for single-season scoring stood for more than 40 years. Led Hoover to its first 10-0 season in 1972. Four-year letterman at Ohio State who waited his turn behind Archie Griffin before busting out for 1,248 yards as a junior.

6 WALT TOLARCHYK

WALT TOLARCHYK Made Hoover into public-school wrestling power. Spent 27 years atop program, guiding nine individual state champions and team runner-up finishes in 1982 and '83. Member of the Ohio High School Wrestling Hall of Fame and the National Wrestling Hall of Fame's Ohio chapter.

7 BRITTANY (ORBAN) WEBB

BRITTANY (ORBAN) WEBB Relentless, overpowering forward who led Hoover to three Federal League titles and two district titles. Went 81-15 in four-year career, including 38-0 against Stark County teams. Program's career scoring and rebounding leader. Ranks fourth in county history with 1,887 points. Three-time first team All-Ohio, two-time county player of the year. Also a state qualifier in track and field. Three-time Academic All-Big Ten at Northwestern, where she started all but three games in her career.

8 GORDY WOOLBERT

GORDY WOOLBERT Maybe the finest Stark County swimmer of the past 50 years. Won three individual state championships and a relay title despite not competing as senior because of injury. Registered fastest 100 backstroke time in the nation in 1988. Still holds county records in 100 back and 100 butterfly. Part of 1993 national championship team at Stanford. Four-time Greater Canton Aquatic Association Swimmer of the Year.

9 ASHLEY (MUFFET) DUNCAN

ASHLEY (MUFFET) DUNCAN One of only two female athletes in county history with three individual track and field state championships. Still owns county records in the shot put and discus. Former state record holder in the shot (50-10). Four-time All-American at the University of Kentucky. Competed in two U.S. Olympic Trials. Assistant coach at Ohio State. Also tended goal for Vikings soccer team.

10 CHARLIE GRANDJEAN

CHARLIE GRANDJEAN Three-time letterman in both football and basketball for Vikings. Starred on the football field, where he led Hoover to 27-3 record, including 10-0 as a senior in 1975. Named first team all-county at RB. Helped 1978 Navy Midshipmen to Holiday Bowl win against BYU. Transferred to Kent State, where he was two-time first team All-MAC DB. Member of Golden Flashes' Varsity "K" Hall of Fame. Played one season in USFL for Birmingham Stallions.

HONORABLE MENTIONS

NYLES EVANS
JEFF HITE
DOM IERO
JERRY GOODPASTURE
JUD LOGAN
KATIE (CHAIN) MILLER
JANET (BAUGHMAN) PEARE
TIM POWELL
ALEX RAMSEY
STEVE SCHICK
DAN SHETLER
BRET WACKERLY
DAN WILLAMAN

TWO DECADES LATER, LEGEND LIVES ON FOR BOSLEY

WIDE-SPREAD PLAYER INVOLVEMENT IN THE JUNIOR HIGH AND YOUTH LEVELS HAS ALWAYS BEEN A POINT OF EMPHASIS FOR LARRY TAYLOR WITHIN HIS PROGRAMS.

The more kids who played, the better. In the spirit of getting kids interested and excited about basketball, Taylor did not want one player dominating the action.

So when he heard that a seventh grader by the name of Jami Bosley scored 41 points in a game, the long-time Jackson High School head coach paid a visit to the junior high staff.

"They said, 'Umm, Coach, he only played the first half,' " Taylor recalls. "That was the first time I realized he was something special."

It's been 21 years since the Era of Bosley in Jackson, since a teenage basketball savant became a focal point of the growing township.

And Bosley, now a 38-year-old husband with two kids and a mended knee after tearing his ACL earlier this winter, still feels a warmth when he thinks about a community and a school that nurtured him, protected him and celebrated him.

"I love Jackson," Bosley said. "I love what we did there. I love what they do now. Would I do some things differently? Sure. Maybe. I don't know.

"I'm glad I'm from there."

Bosley, who lives in the Wadsworth area and works in safety and medical equipment sales, actually was born in Shelby and spent his elementary years in Massillon. His family moved to Jackson in the sixth grade. His four varsity years for the Polar Bears (three as a starter) included four Federal League championships, three district titles, the school's first appearance at state and his scoring a Stark County-record 2,077 career points—a mark that no one else has really sniffed.

His college career paled in comparison to high school and was marred by him being kicked out of Ohio State. But, in fairness, it was almost impossible for college to measure up to his high school days.

"It was like we were rock stars," Bosley said. "It was unbelievable. Larry Taylor was our leader. You knew everything was going to be OK because we trusted him and he led us.

"I never felt pressure. I never did. I felt like I was amongst people that cared about me and that would take care of me. I never really had to put on airs. I was still goofy, a little bit immature with a good heart."

Bosley averaged more than 20 points a game his final three years at Jackson, including 25.8 points, 9.4 rebounds and 3.2 assists as senior in 1994-95. He also set Jackson career marks for rebounds and assists.

He was not athletic in the traditional basketball sense of long, lean players who operate above the rim. He had a quick first step, quick instincts and quick hands. He was a master of angles in a 6-foot, 200-pound body.

And he was strong. So, so God-gifted strong.

How much lifting did Bosley do in high school?

"Zero. Nothing," he said. "I never went into a weight room until Ohio State."

Bosley made the occasional 3-pointer (13 as a senior) and scored from all over. But the vast majority of his damage was done in the paint, whether on downhill drives or off offensive rebounds.

Bosley's playing style was part instinct, part heart and part wrecking ball. He originally patterned himself after his brother, John, who was three years Jami's senior. But he soon developed his own style.

"I always felt like I had a particular way I got things done," he said. "... I always felt like I was stronger than most players I played against. I felt like I just had more energy and basketball was a way that I could release that energy."

"I ALWAYS FELT LIKE I WAS STRONGER THAN MOST PLAYERS I PLAYED AGAINST. I FELT LIKE I JUST HAD MORE ENERGY AND BASKETBALL WAS A WAY THAT I COULD RELEASE THAT ENERGY."

—JAMI BOSLEY

Bosley sees the same voltage running through his 11-year-old son Maxx.

"We have this nervous energy," Bosley said. "... It's like when they say someone has a motor. My motor got me into all kinds of trouble in my life. But basketball was a way my motor got me all kinds of positive feedback."

Basketball was very much a contact sport with Bosley on it. That led to a lot of trips to the foul line.

His 685 career free throws trail only Luke Kennard and Geno Ford in Ohio history, according to unofficial OHSAA records.

"I have so many referees that I meet now and they say, 'You were the hardest guy to ref,' " Bosley said. "I think I just put a lot of pressure on them. I forced them to make a call. My mindset was, I have the ball and if our bodies are touching and I'm not barreling you over with my shoulder, you have to give the advantage to the guy with the ball."

Refs were puzzled. So were college basketball coaches.

"It was fun watching Jami be recruited," Taylor said. "They were just baffled. They were, like, staring at me. I remember Rick Barnes was at Clemson. He was like, 'Do I really want to sign this kid?' "

Bosley's college choice did not require much thought despite him getting letters from across the nation. He watched Jay Burson and Jimmy Jackson growing up. He knew he wanted to be a Buckeye.

"Literally my second college choice was Malone because I liked Hal Smith," Bosley said.

He vividly remembers when his Ohio State dream became true. It was June 17, 1994, the day of the infamous OJ Simpson police chase. Jackson was at an Ohio State team camp. Buckeyes head coach Randy Ayers told Bosley that he wanted to meet with him and Taylor later to offer him a scholarship.

Bosley laughed as he remembered Taylor encouraging him to wait and talk to Cincinnati's Bob Huggins later that day.

"I was like, 'Larry, I'm not dating. I'm telling him yes,' " Bosley said.

It seemed like a fairy tale for Bosley. But this is real life, and real life is complicated.

Bosley held his own on the court for the Buckeyes, averaging 5.6 points and 2.3 rebounds as a true freshman. But no longer in the cocoon Jackson provided, he struggled to handle adversity.

He recalls sitting in his jeep with Taylor and weeping after a loss to Minnesota.

"I just cried because it was hard," Bosley said. "I look back at that and I think, 'Damn, what was I crying about? I was at Ohio State.' "

Bosley, whom Taylor described as "his own person," still needed a support system, a framework from which to operate.

He had that at Jackson. He did not at Ohio State.

He found himself partying and drinking too much.

It was the weekend of Mother's Day in 1996 when he got in trouble in connection with three cars being broken into in a campus parking lot. He was booted from the team.

"It was bound to happen," Bosley said. "It was a series of bad choices at a bad time in my life. Honestly, I love Ohio State. I love to go to Ohio State football and basketball games now."

Bosley transferred to Akron and enjoyed good success, averaging 18.6 points as a junior and earning first team All-Mid-American Conference. He scored 1,435 points in his college career.

But he was burnt out by the end and ready to move on from basketball.

He enjoys being a fan these days and rooting on current Jackson stars Kyle Young and Logan Hill, two Division I college prospects. Young has offers from Big Ten and ACC schools, among others.

"You're going to be watching him on ESPN. He's not going to Akron," Bosley said, sounding almost like a proud parent. "... There's a good chance that kid is going to be playing in the NBA someday. I believe that. That kid's a stud. I love that kid."

Young fits the mold of a basketball prospect: 6-7. Jumps out of the gym. Range beyond the 3-point line.

Bosley never fit a mold.

But he fit at Jackson, and Jackson got the opportunity to experience a supremely unique athlete.

"There may be a pure point guard. There may be a 7-footer that comes around that is agile and can do a lot of things," Taylor said. "But I don't know if we're going to see another Jami Bosley." *—JOSH WEIR*

LONG BEFORE LEBRON, CABLE TOOK HIS TALENTS SOUTH

LONG BEFORE LEBRON TOOK HIS TALENTS TO SOUTH BEACH, ONE OF JACKSON TOWNSHIP'S GREATEST ATHLETES ALSO VENTURED TO THE SUNSHINE STATE.

The son of a coach/educator, Randy Cable experienced few vacations growing up.

So he lived vicariously through his cousins' photos of their Florida trips.

"I'd think, 'God, if I ever could go to Florida,' " said Cable, who grew into a three-sport star for a Jackson High School that was much more rural than suburban in the mid 1960s.

His athletic talents, specifically those on the basketball court, offered him the chance to head south.

Cable fell in love with Florida State on his recruiting visit—his first time on an airplane—and basically never left Tallahassee. After joining a redheaded All-American by the name of Dave Cowens on Seminoles teams that went 60-19 in his three years as a letterman, Cable did some coaching before settling into a career with pharmaceutical giant Bristol-Myers Squibb.

"I'm glad I came here," said the now-retired Cable, 67, who, along with his wife Kay, spends much of his time these days tracking nine grandchildren. "I loved it and I stayed."

Before that, he left quite a mark behind in Stark County.

Cable's 1,202 career points stood as Jackson's scoring record for almost 30 years until Jami Bosley's reign in the 1990s. The 6-foot Cable led the county in scoring as a junior and finished as runner-up his

senior year to Minerva's Jim Elliott while also leading Jackson in assists both seasons.

Massillon native Don James, who later went on to a legendary coaching career at the University of Washington, was an assistant football coach at Florida State at the time. James saw Cable tear up Massillon in a basketball game and mentioned to Seminoles basketball coach Hugh Durham that he might want to take a look at this high-scoring guard from Ohio.

Cable averaged 23.7 points a game his senior season, which included putting 42 points on Sandy Valley in his final game of the regular season.

"Randy is the best high school guard I've ever seen," said Rich Thomas, then-Jackson's coach, in a press release touting Cable's All-Ohio credentials.

Interestingly enough, Cable was called a 1960s version of Bosley by Larry Hackenberg, a long-time area coach who shared All-Stark County first-team status with Cable as a prep player for Canton South.

Cable was accurate from the outside in an era without a 3-point line, but Hackenberg remembers Cable more as a strong, versatile athlete who scored from anywhere on the court.

"We'd play a 2-3 zone against them, but it was the kind of 2-3 where we always knew where he was," Hackenberg said. "He was thicker than most basketball players. He had that football body."

Which he put to good use in the fall.

Cable, a running back/defensive back, led the Federal League in scoring and was second in the county only to Louisville star Tom Chlebeck as he led Jackson's football team to a 10-0 record as a senior. Jackson still is waiting for its next 10-0 season. The '65 Polar Bears pitched four shutouts and allowed 34 points through eight weeks before beating Canton South 26-13 in Week 9 and Hoover 22-17 in Week 10.

"Our defense was phenomenal," Cable said, "and we didn't have anybody over 185 pounds."

In baseball later that spring, Cable starred at shortstop as the Polar Bears made a surprising run to regionals. They lost 1-0 in a semifinal to West Holmes at a field in Philo that Cable described as a "cow pasture."

"We never expected to be as good as we were, but, good gracious, several of us hit the ball like crazy," Cable said. "We didn't make many errors and we had two guys who could pitch—Bruce Peters and John Weisz. They probably couldn't break a plate of glass, but they were precision pitchers. ... I think I hit about .460. Peters and Dickie Booth hit over .400. We had a good team."

Cable played freshman baseball at Florida State but did not continue the following year after being exhausted from basketball season.

"It was the biggest mistake of my life that I didn't keep playing baseball," said Cable, whose father, Don, believed it to be his son's best sport.

Cable averaged 5.3 points in 76 career varsity games at Florida State. He wishes he could have accomplished more individually on the basketball court there. But he was part of some great Seminole teams that had a distinct Midwest flavor.

Jeff Hogan, an Ellet product, was a year ahead of Cable. Columbus Linden-McKinley's Skip Young, maybe Ohio's most sought player in 1967, was a year behind Cable.

Cable recalled trips to Cowens' Newport, Ky., home each summer when they were still in college. Said Cable, who roomed with the future NBA MVP in college and remains friends with him to this day, "Those are stories, a few of which I don't want going in the newspaper."

The NCAA banned Florida State from playing in the postseason Cable's senior year, preventing a 23-3 squad from a potential tournament run. (Two years later, Florida State lost in the national championship game to an undefeated UCLA team led by sophomore Bill Walton.)

The official reason for the punishment was Durham having a hand in getting recruits summer jobs. Cable believes it also had something to do with Florida State being one of the first colleges in the South to recruit black athletes.

"The NCAA decided to make an example of us," Cable said.

"You can speculate on the reason why." *—JOSH WEIR*

JACKSON TOP TEN ICONS

1

JAMI BOSLEY Bosley is one of the most unique and dominating basketball players in Stark County history. A mix of power, quickness and tenacity in a 6-foot, 200-pound frame. County's all-time leading scorer with 2,077 points. Led Jackson to three straight district titles and one state appearance. Two-time first team All-Ohio and a 1995 McDonald's All-American. Spent a year at Ohio State and three at Akron in a college career that produced 1,435 points.

2

JAY ROHR The toughest guy in purple, or any color for that matter, when he was on the field. Linebacker/running back holds special place in heart of Jackson football fans. Four-year starter and two-time All-Ohio first teamer who graduated as Jackson's all-time leader in tackles and rushing yards. Stark County Player of the Year in 2001 when he led Polar Bears to Federal League title. In college, an All-MAC linebacker who led Akron to first Division I-A bowl game. Now an assistant coach at Jackson.

3

ROBERT FIFE Patriarch of football in Jackson Township. Posted a 111-41-1 record as head coach from 1945-61. School's football stadium named after him in 1975. Never experienced a losing season after his debut campaign. His 9-0 team in 1955 never punted. Named to Stark County High School Football Hall of Fame in 2009. Also coached baseball. Passed away of a heart attack in 1968.

<<< 4

CHASE KINNEY Most decorated girls swimmer in Stark County history. Three-time state champion, winning the 50 freestyle twice and the 100 freestyle once. Holds Stark County records in 50 free and 100 free. Previously held state record in 100 free. Earned All-Ohio and All-America honors each of her four years in high school. Also a state qualifier in cross country and track, and a letter winner in softball at Jackson. Through her junior season at Wisconsin, Kinney is a four-time All-American who has been first team All-Big Ten twice and second team once.

5

LARRY TAYLOR Fiery, tough-love coach who cut an imposing figure on Jackson's sideline for 21 years. Built Jackson into one of the strongest basketball programs in Stark County. Led the Polar Bears to 307 wins, eight Federal League titles, five district titles and two state tournament appearances.

>>> 6

RANDY CABLE Remarkable all-around athlete who starred in football, basketball and baseball for Jackson in the mid 1960s. Running back/defensive back led Jackson to 10-0 season in football as a senior while leading Federal League in scoring. In basketball, was a guard whose school scoring record of 1,202 points stood until the Jami Bosley era. Played shortstop for a Jackson baseball team that advanced to regionals. In college, played hoops at Florida State with Dave Cowens.

<<< 7

KERI SARVER Best player in the storied history of Jackson girls soccer. Scored 50 goals her senior year when Jackson made it to state semifinals. Three-time All-Ohioan and a Parade All-American. Two-time All-ACC player at Maryland and member of ACC 50th anniversary team. Played professionally for the Cleveland Eclipse, Washington Freedom, New York Power and Carolina Courage. Member of the Ohio Soccer Hall of Fame.

>>> 8

MIKE FUNK Perfect on the mat and in the classroom. A 4.0 student, Funk won consecutive Class AAA state championships in 1985 (175 pounds) and '86 (185), during which he never lost a match, going 74-0. Followed his older brother, Dan, also a state champion, to wrestle collegiately at Northwestern, where he was the first four-time All-American in program history. Big Ten champion at 190 pounds in 1991.

9

MARK HENNIGER Steady, efficient big man led Jackson to 2010 Division I state title and ranks as the county's seventh all-time leading scorer with 1,552 career points. The 6-foot-8 Henniger was first team All-Ohio and player of the year for All-Northeast Inland District, Repository All-Stark County and All-Federal League teams as a senior, when he averaged 20.9 points and 8.9 rebounds. Lettered four years at Kent State, playing in 123 games, 56 of them starts.

10

JENNY (WOODWARD) MALANDRO Almost 30 years after her graduation from Jackson, still holds several school records in basketball, including the career scoring mark of 1,403. Federal League Player of the Year and third team All-Ohio as a senior in 1987. Later that spring, won the Class AAA high jump state championship. Followed in the footsteps of former Jackson great Holly Seimetz and played basketball at Youngstown State, where she totaled 897 points and 226 assists as a four-year letter winner.

HONORABLE MENTIONS

EVAN BAILEY
JASON BAKE
ROB DEWOLF
DAN FUNK
CARLIN ISLES
EMILY (HALM) JENKINS
TED ROHRER
HOLLY SEIMETZ
NATE STRONG
SCOTT WILES

"ONE OF THE BIGGEST MOTIVATORS WAS YOU DIDN'T WANT TO LET THE GUYS NEXT TO YOU DOWN AND YOU DIDN'T WANT TO LET COACH DURBIN DOWN. IT WASN'T JUST A FEAR OF GETTING YOUR BUTT CHEWED ON SATURDAY MORNING WATCHING FILM, BUT IT WAS BECAUSE YOU KNEW HE PUT A LOT INTO IT, TOO."

—CRAIG DUES

AFTER SCARY START, DURBIN BUILT LAKE INTO STATEWIDE POWER

BEFORE HE BECAME THE WINNINGEST COACH IN SCHOOL HISTORY, BEFORE HE LED LAKE TO THREE STATE CHAMPIONSHIP GAMES AND TWO OTHER STATE SEMIFINAL BERTHS, BEFORE HE BECAME JUST THE SECOND STARK COUNTY COACH TO WIN AT LEAST 150 GAMES WITH THE SAME SCHOOL, JEFF DURBIN WAS JUST A FIRST-YEAR HEAD COACH RELYING ON A SKILL HE DEVELOPED AS AN ASSISTANT COACH AT THE UNIVERSITY OF AKRON: RECRUITING.

It was the summer of 1990 and, like a lot of school districts in Stark County, Lake was mired in levy hell. Township voters had rejected six straight levies, the school district had just canceled a season of spring sports and there was talk of canceling fall sports, too. Durbin knew he had a special junior class, but Division I prospects like Matt Christopher (who went on to play linebacker at Ohio State) and Craig Dues (a future all-conference linebacker at Toledo) were looking to transfer to schools such as St. Vincent-St. Mary, Massillon, Hoban and St. Thomas Aquinas.

Ultimately, Lake settled on a $242 pay-to-play fee.

"I thought that might kill us," Durbin said.

The opposite happened. The players did fundraisers—Christopher remembers volunteering to bag groceries at the Hartville IGA—and when they started practice that summer, Durbin had 53 players who had bought in, literally and figuratively.

"Those kids were at practice every day," he said. "I never had a practice with less than 50 guys. I think a lot of that had to do with paying that money. I think it strengthened us with a bond and I really think it was a catalyst for us. And I do think our success from there was kind of a unifying factor in the community."

Lake went 7-4 that season, losing to Steubenville in the second round of the playoffs for the second time in three years. Lake finally passed a levy in May of 1991,

the school dropped the fee and the Blue Streaks started the 1991 season 13-0 (with a win over Steubenville in the state semifinals) before falling to Fostoria in the Division II state championship game. By the time he retired in 2012, Durbin had won 163 games (against 99 losses) with 14 playoff appearances, state runner-up finishes in 1991, 1993 and 1997, state semifinal appearances in 1999 and 2010 and four Federal League titles.

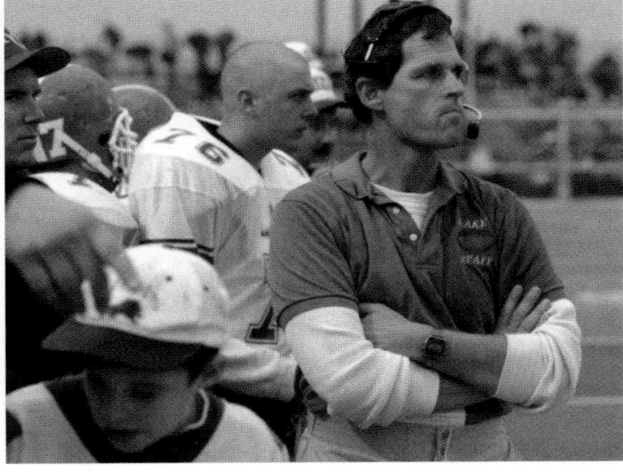

"He had the respect of all his players," said Dues, who now lives in St. Henry on the western side of Ohio. "He was very intelligent and he knew football inside and out. He never played games and you knew where you stood with him. If you weren't playing, it was probably because you shouldn't have been playing.

"I just think there was a sense of unity at Lake. It's a small town cliché, but you're playing with your best friends, the guys you grew up with. One of the biggest motivators was you didn't want to let the guys next to you down and you didn't want to let Coach Durbin down. It wasn't just a fear of getting your butt chewed on Saturday morning watching film, but it was because you knew he put a lot into it, too."

Schematically, Durbin was more Vince Lombardi than Bobby Petrino. He didn't try to outsmart his opponents, running essentially the same offense (I-formation) and defense (50 shade) during his tenure, with subtle tweaks based on his personnel.

"You always knew what your job was," said Dues, who played safety and wide receiver at Lake. "It wasn't guys at some schools that freelanced a bit because they wanted stats and tackles. That doesn't always work. You might make a lot of plays, but if you aren't in your gap, you'll make a great play on one down and the next play goes for a touchdown. That wasn't the case under Durbin."

Added Christopher, the team's leading rusher with 1,470 yards in 1991, "We basically lined up and it was 3 yards and a cloud of dust. That was it. The biggest thing with him (Durbin) was, he got the most out of guys. Maybe the guys that would have been average at other schools were good football players because they played for him. We were never the biggest, never the fastest, but we lined up and hit you and that's still the philosophy over there."

After Durbin retired in the spring of 2013, Lake promoted his longtime offensive coordinator, Dan DeGeorge. A year later, Durbin was lured out of retirement by his son, Luke, who was hired as the head coach at North Ridgeville. Durbin has spent the past two years as the Rangers' offensive coordinator, making the 70-minute drive each way.

"It's been great to work with Luke, but it's frustrating in some ways because I haven't felt we've changed the culture yet," he said. "At Lake, we felt like we did establish the culture where the expectations were to get in the playoffs and make a run every year."

That's true of the district, too. While North Ridgeville did make the playoffs in 2015, going 7-4 and losing in the first round, "the attendance is not where it is in Stark County, Durbin said. "The passion for football there, that's part of what I cherished over the years. It's been a special place for myself and my family."

"No matter where I am, I'll always be a Blue Streak." —*JOE SCALZO*

DESPITE CONCUSSIONS, CHRISTOPHER RELISHES FOOTBALL CAREER

IN EARLY NOVEMBER 2015, MORE THAN TWO DECADES AFTER HIS FATHER'S ONCE-PROMISING OHIO STATE CAREER WAS CUT SHORT BY CONCUSSIONS, CHARLIE CHRISTOPHER AND HIS MOTHER VISITED OHIO STADIUM FOR THE BUCKEYES' 28-14 WIN OVER MINNESOTA.

"He absolutely loved it," said Matt Christopher, a former standout linebacker and running back at Lake High. "I mean, who wouldn't love it?"

Well, Christopher's oldest son, for one. Even though his dad is generally considered the best football player in Lake history, and even though his mom, Lori, was Lake's head cheerleader as a senior, 12-year-old Marcus Christopher veered into action sports. He's one of the top-ranked freestyle BMX riders under the age of 15.

"He knows about my career, but it's not his thing," Christopher said. "And that's cool."

Charlie is a different story. He's only 9, but, like Matt, he loves football and basketball. He's already asking his dad about playing at Ohio State and reveling in the celebrity that comes with being "Matt's son."

"He's the one following in my footsteps," he said. "But he's his own person. Just like anyone else, I tell him if he wants to be good at something, he has to dedicate himself."

> "WHAT HAPPENED TO ME MAY HAPPEN TO ONE OUT OF 10 KIDS. I HAVE FRIENDS WHO PLAYED IN THE PROS FOR 15 YEARS AND I HAVE FRIENDS WHO PLAYED ONE YEAR BECAUSE THEY WERE SO BEAT UP. IT'S THE SAME THING IN COLLEGE AND HIGH SCHOOL."
>
> —MATT CHRISTOPHER

Few in Stark County history were better than Christopher, a 6-foot-1, 230-pound linebacker/running back who rushed for 1,470 yards on Lake's 1991 Division II state runner-up team while earning Ohio Division II Lineman of the Year honors from the Associated Press. But Christopher also suffered seven concussions over his high school and college career, which ended after butting helmets with Buckeye tight end Rickey Dudley in practice in 1995.

With that background, you might think Christopher would steer his son away from football, especially with all the research that's been done in the past 20 years on the concussions. But he still loves the game and won't deprive his son of the same opportunities he had.

"What happened to me may happen to one out of 10 kids," he said. "I have friends who played in the pros for 15 years and I have friends who played one year because they were so beat up. It's the same thing in college and high school. You don't know.

"The game has made a lot of good changes, things that were shunned off before or swept under the rug. If you teach proper tackling, you go from there."

Besides, Christopher said, "Kids can get hurt doing anything. You can get hurt walking your dog."

Christopher, who turned to bodybuilding after his playing career ended, still lives in Hartville. (One of his neighbors is former teammate Steve Lippe, who played at West Virginia and is now the associate principal at Lake High School.) For the past 12 years, Christopher has owned a lawn treatment company called Weed Man. He's also the west coast sales representative for Blackout Distribution, which sells BMX bikes and parts. He was inducted into Lake's Athletic Hall of Fame in 2002 and the Stark County High School Football Hall of Fame in 2004.

"He's probably the best guy I've ever coached anywhere," said his high school coach, Jeff Durbin.

People in Stark County won't be surprised to hear that. They saw his talent firsthand. Christopher just wishes the people in Columbus could have seen it, too.

"Football is the greatest game in my mind that's ever been created," he said. "I'd do anything to play again." —*JOE SCALZO*

LAKE TOP TEN ICONS

1 **JEFF DURBIN** Durbin went 163-99 with 14 playoff appearances as Lake's football coach from 1990-2012, three state runner-up finishes (1991, 1993 and 1997), two state semifinal appearances (1999, 2010) and four Federal League titles. Selected the Ohio Associated Press co-coach of the year in Division II in 1993. Inducted into the Stark County High School Football Hall of Fame in 2015.

2 **MATT CHRISTOPHER** Christopher rushed for 1,710 career yards, including 1,470 in 1991 to help the Blue Streaks go 13-1 and advance to the Division II state championship game. Associated Press Division II Lineman of the Year as a senior in 1991 for his work at linebacker. Played linebacker at Ohio State from 1992-94 before concussions ended his career. Inducted into the Stark County High School Football Hall of Fame in 2004.

BRIAN BOWERS
Bowers rushed for 3,012 career yards, leading the Blue Streaks to two straight 10-0 seasons in 1969 and 1970. Associated Press Class AA player of the year as a senior in 1970. Lettered two years at linebacker at Ohio State, starting as a senior in 1974. Inducted into the Stark County High School Football Hall of Fame in 2011.

4 **MICHAEL MILLER** Miller is a three-time wrestling state champion from 2003-05. Went 164-11 overall. Earned All-American honors at Central Michigan in 2007 and 2009.

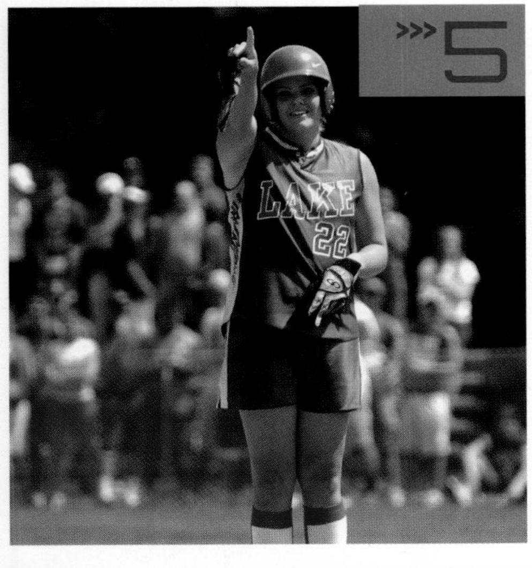

JULIE BOYES
Ohio Pitcher of the Year and Federal League Player of the Year as a senior in 2005 after leading the Blue Streaks to the Division I softball state title. Helped Lake finish as the state runner-up in 2004. Second team All-Mid-American Conference selection at Akron in 2006. Ranks in the top 10 all-time for the Zips in RBIs and pitching strikeouts and first in grand slams.

RON VISCOUNTE Viscounte holds Lake's career receiving yardage record with 1,332 from 1982-84. Rushed for 1,039 yards and caught 29 passes in 1984 to earn Stark County MVP honors. Finished with 48 career TDs, third all-time in Lake history.

ROB STRADLEY
Stradley threw for 1,240 yards in 1982 as a senior. Holds Lake's career interceptions record with 13. Was a four-year letterman at linebacker at Michigan State and captain of the 1988 Rose Bowl team.

ERIC COBLENTZ
Coblentz is the school's all-time leading scorer with 1,177 points. Second team All-Ohio in Division I as a senior in 2007. Led Malone in scoring his final three seasons of college basketball.

TOM TSCHANTZ
Tschantz was the school's all-time scoring leader in basketball until Eric Coblentz broke his record. Earned All-Ohio honors as a senior in 1961. Tschantz also played baseball.

10 **CRAIG DUES** The second-best player on Lake's best team, Dues starred at receiver and free safety, earning first team all-conference as a senior. The 1992 Lake graduate was a three-year starter at linebacker at Toledo, earning second team all-conference honors as a junior and senior. Also a three-time academic all-conference pick.

HONORABLE MENTIONS

DAN BAILEY
BONNIE BERTSCH TANKSLEY
STEVE LIPPE
TOM MCBRIDE
ERIN REESE
AARON VANDERKAAY

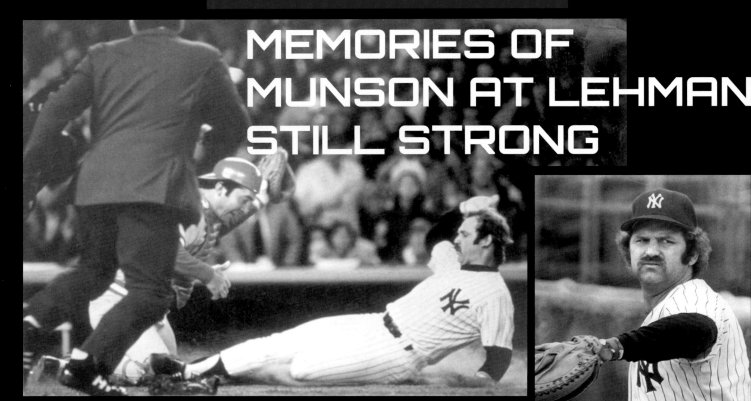

MEMORIES OF MUNSON AT LEHMAN STILL STRONG

"THURMAN WAS A NATURAL WHO DIDN'T LOOK LIKE A NATURAL."

—DAVE CADY

THE SHINING JEWEL ON THE HILL IS DARK, CLOSED AND DOOMED.

"Canton may have the money to demolish former Lehman High School," a 2014 Repository headline said.

Until it actually happens, the gaunt behemoth dominates a city block between 14th and 15th streets, still. The fortress leaves the impression it could stand for 1,000 years, Coliseum style, if left to its own devices.

Its monolithic architecture and sheer size exude a classic strength to older eyes. This goes unnoticed by neighborhood kids laughing on an Oxford Avenue sidewalk on a warm spring day. What is Lehman to them? It hasn't been open as a high school for 40 years. Whatever remains inside is hidden by boarded-up windows.

What do children know of the thousands who sat on the cement steps descending to an ancient football field? The crumbling steps look ghostly with no people on them.

A rusty set of goalposts protrudes from overgrown grass. Along a wall that separates the field from 14th Street, someone spray painted, "MY MOM IS BEAUTIFUL."

These impressions are taken in by someone attempting to reset the scene of Thurman Munson's youth. It was the writer's first drive through the neighborhood in years, tied to an arbitrary choosing of each Stark County high school's top 10 sports icons. Lehman was included for posterity's sake. Munson is Lehman's obvious No. 1.

The back story is Munson's relationship with his father. It was not beautiful. It may help explain why Thurman made it from the cement steps to the top of the baseball world.

The Cleveland Indians could have used Thurman Munson. He loved the Cleveland Browns and the Cleveland Indians. His favorite baseball player was Rocky Colavito.

In Canton youth baseball games, he would clutch his bat with both hands, lift it parallel to the ground above his head, and dip it behind his back to his shoulders. It was the Colavito stretch.

The New York Yankees came to admire Munson's take on it. There is a Thurman Munson monument behind center field in The Bronx. There is a Thurman Munson Memorial Stadium that traces to the 1979 plane crash about 10 miles northwest of where Munson settled his family in the Canton area.

He was 32 years old, not long removed from helping the Yankees reach three straight World Series. He was a fledgling jet pilot motivated to shorten the distance between New York City and his Stark County home.

Munson's wife and children were his adult family. In his first family, he was the youngest of four children. He was young when the Munsons moved from Akron to Frazer Avenue, within a mile of Lehman.

When he died, he was estranged from his father, and his mother lived in a seniors complex next to Canton's Palace Theatre.

There are different views of why Munson came off to many people as blunt, gruff and arrogant. One is that the expressions were ways of railing against his home life.

He became a clutch-hitting catcher for big-time Yankees teams. He seemed to

REGGIE JACKSON (LEFT) AND THURMAN MUNSON (FAR RIGHT)

vaporize every pitch any Cleveland Indian threw him.

On his way up, he attended Worley School and became a paperboy carrying The Repository. One bridge to self-esteem was sports. Another was his relationship with the neighborhood girl, Diana Dominick, who would become his wife.

He was as good in football and basketball as he was in baseball.

He could make teammates laugh. He would do impersonations of the cartoon character, Huckleberry Hound. He would brag, and he would back it up.

His father was a long-distance truck driver. Thurman was a truck.

Dave Cady was a Lehman kid who grew up to be a coach in the city, eventually the head basketball coach at McKinley some years after Lehman was swallowed up in a consolidation.

Cady was a young adult when he watched Munson's Lehman career unfold in the mid-1960s.

"Thurman was a natural who didn't look like a natural," Cady said. "He was a stocky guy, and to see him you wouldn't have guessed the kind of player he was.

"He was an excellent football player. He was an excellent basketball player. For people who saw Jami Bosley play at Jackson ... Thurman was very similar to that in basketball.

"He was as intense as anybody you'll ever see. He was an intelligent player in everything he played. He had a self-confidence I never saw rivaled."

More than 30 years before Joe Gilhousen coached GlenOak to two state baseball championships, he was Munson's pal and teammate at Worley School when they were little boys, and later at Lehman and Kent State.

One time Lehman was facing an excellent Lincoln basketball team in an all-city madhouse in Memorial Field House.

"At the end of the game, we needed a couple of foul shots to win the game," Gilhousen recalls. "Thurman was very calm. He told us he was going to make the shots, and he did."

Baseball is the sport in which body shape means the least, and Munson excelled the most. He was an All-Ohio shortstop with a batting average close to .600 as a Lehman senior in 1965. He was a shortstop before he was a catcher. It was a stroke of luck, perhaps, that Jerome Pruett pitched for the Polar Bears.

Pruett soon would be on a fast track in the St. Louis Cardinals system, and no one at Lehman could catch him. Munson became Pruett's catcher and later caught other Lehman pitchers.

Munson always loved to hit, but the craft of catching began to fascinate him and to pave a way for a pro career. He had plenty of college options but opted to stay close to Canton. He played baseball and basketball at Kent State. The Yankees made him the fourth overall pick of the 1968 draft, less than three years after he graduated from Lehman.

He got to the big leagues in a hurry and hit .302 as the Yankees' starting catcher when he was just 23 years old.

He was one of the biggest stars on the planet from 1975-78, named American League MVP in 1976.

His clutch hitting was evident to anyone who watched him play and is recorded for posterity in his .357 batting average in 30 postseason games.

The No. 1 sports icon in Lehman Polar Bears history came home in 1979. He was in his 11th season in New York, but he would never go back.

The jet crash was one of the county's all-time stunners.

While the tale would have changed had he been a Cleveland Indian, Canton and Lehman High School were always going to be at the heart of the Thurman Munson story. Lehman was a high school from 1932 through 1976. Somewhere behind the boarded-up windows, the fascinating aura of Thurman Munson lingers in the shadows. *—STEVE DOERSCHUK*

LEHMAN TOP TEN ICONS

1 THURMAN MUNSON Rugged competitor in football, basketball and baseball. Led Lehman to 68-65 upset of strong Lincoln team in his final all-city basketball game in the Field House in 1965. Averaged 19.4 points that season. Played baseball for Kent State and soon after the New York Yankees. Was on his way to the Hall of Fame as a catcher and clutch hitter before he died in a 1979 plane crash.

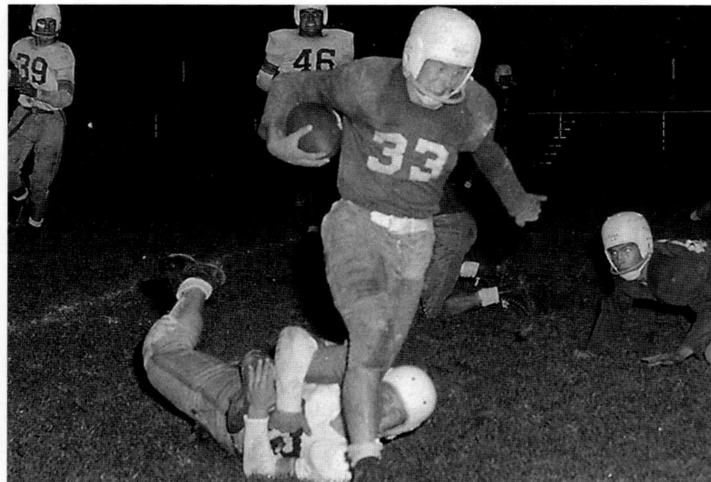

2 BILL WENTZ Scored 13 TDs for 1955 football team that won all eight games it played. Won 10 Lehman letters in football, basketball, baseball and track. Became a starter at Ohio State and had a 103-yard kickoff return in a win over No. 4 Illinois in 1960. Part of the Stark County High School Football Hall of Fame's Class of 2008.

3 DON EDDINS Graduated from Lehman in 1947. Went to Mount Union and returned to Canton for a long coaching career in football, basketball and baseball. Made his mark as head coach of Canton's first state basketball champion in 1971. Old-school drill sergeant who wanted players' hair short and practices long. Lehman team was ranked first in Ohio at end of 1973 season. Moved to North Canton and coached Hoover to its first Federal League boys basketball title in 1979.

4 STEVE WATSON Presented Bup Rearick Award as city's best basketball player on All-City Night of his senior year, 1973. Accepted award prior to a game Lehman needed to complete 18-0 regular season and solidify the Polar Bears' No. 1 ranking in the Class AAA Ohio poll. Played his best game of the season. Made all-county with junior Dan Finn. Followed footsteps of his father, Jim, into baseball. Played four years at Ohio State and later became a Canton Class A League MVP.

5 JIM ROBINSON Coaching reign spanned from the 1930s into the 1950s. Posted 121-59-9 record as head football coach and 142-53 mark as head basketball coach. Head football coach at McKinley for three years. Directed North-South All-Star Football Game during a 20-year run at Fawcett Stadium. Did high school radio shows with WHBC announcer Jim Muzzy.

6 JIM DORLAND Dominant basketball player on war-time teams that beat McKinley in 1942-43 regular season before losing regional final thriller to Bulldogs team that went to state finals. Avenged loss by knocking McKinley out of 1943-44 tournament. Set county scoring record in 1944. Made five-man all-county team both years. Coached basketball at Lehman for 10 years. Became local and national champion of continuing adult education.

7 JACK YUN It was 6-foot-8 center John Mills who made first team all-county, but it was the second-teamer, Yun, who had a game for the ages the day Lehman beat Warren Champion in the 1971 Class AA state championship game. Yun put on a shooting display en route to 36 points in a 68-63 win. Lehman became first Canton city school to win a state basketball crown. Mills was an inside presence throughout the season and the tournament run.

8 DICK BOWMAN All-county end on 11-man 1959 all-county football team picked by coaches. All-city in basketball as both junior and senior. Led Polar Bears to 54-39 win over McKinley and a 48-45 win over Lincoln on All-City Nights in 1960.

9 BOB ARNOLD First of two Lehman players to be Stark County football MVP (Arnold in 1951, Jack Nichols in 1953). First team All-Ohio halfback. Initially went to Michigan State to play football but enlisted in the Marines during the Korean War. Settled in Wadsworth and was 79 when he died in 2014, leaving 13 grandchildren and 13 great-grandchildren.

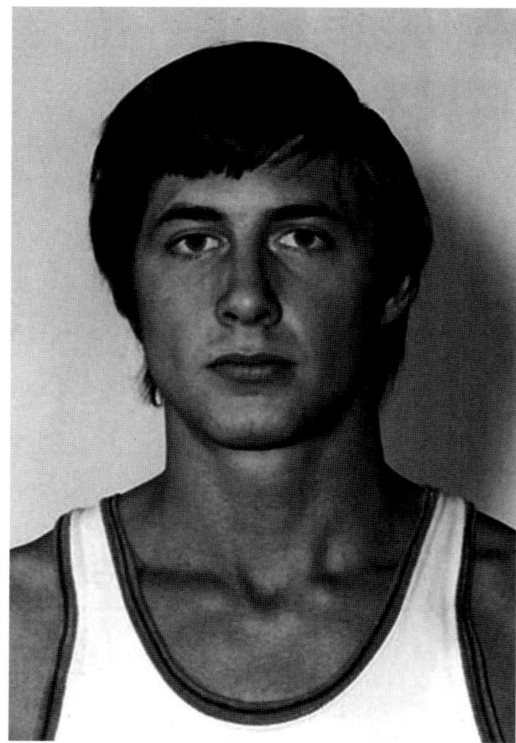

10 MIKE BARR

Six-foot-3 all-around player who emerged as a senior in 1968. Continued to develop at Duquesne, where he made the school's All-Century team in 2016. Worked his way into a pro career in the ABA and the NBA. Played alongside Julius Erving with the Virginia Squires and later played in St. Louis in the ABA and with the Kansas City Kings in the NBA. Also starred in baseball at Duquesne, hitting .477 as a junior.

HONORABLE MENTIONS

DICK BOWMAN
CAMPBELL TWINS *(DEAN AND DOUG)*
BOB DELAP
DAN LOVER
BILL MEOLA
JEROME PRUETT
DAVE SCOTT

DON NEHLEN (FAR LEFT)

NEHLEN'S RIDE TO THE COLLEGE HALL STARTED AT LINCOLN

DON NEHLEN MUST HAVE PUT 100,000 MILES ON HIS BICYCLE BY THE TIME HE WAS OLD ENOUGH TO DRIVE TO LINCOLN HIGH SCHOOL.

He pedaled that baby all over Canton, right up to the time he convinced himself he was going to quit riding it to Lincoln football practices.

During his sophomore year, a football collision left him feeling as if he rode from the top steps of the McKinley Monument to a crash at the bottom. A broken collarbone convinced him to quit football and attend to his other Lincoln loves, basketball and baseball.

A Lincoln football coach named Bill Doolittle called Nehlen's dad with some pointed advice: Get him back on his bike and point it to football.

"EVERYBODY PLAYED FOOTBALL IN A PHONE BOOTH, WOODY-STYLE. IF I WOULD THROW 15 PASSES IN A GAME, DOYT PERRY WOULD SAY, 'WOAH ... AN AERIAL CIRCUS.' CANTON PEOPLE DON'T REALIZE HOW GOOD A BALL CARRIER VIC DEORIO WAS. HE WOULD FLAT OUT HONK IT UP IN THERE."

—DON NEHLEN

The kid got back on his horse and rode it to the College Football Hall of Fame.

Don Nehlen became one of the better all-around athletes Lincoln would see. In football, he quarterbacked the Lions to a victory over big, bad McKinley.

He was really good at everything, and he was in demand among coaches. One spring, he hopped back and forth from playing infield for the baseball team to pole vaulting for the track team.

But he never did get big, physically. He weighed about 160 pounds as a senior. The college offers that came around weren't of the Ohio State variety. He wound up with a three-way athletic scholarship to Bowling Green, one-third for football, one-third for basketball, one-third for baseball.

It was fine by him, the lark of a lifetime. He went away to live the college life with two of his best Lincoln pals, Vic DeOrio and Larry Kelly. They became Bowling Green roommates and football teammates.

When they got there, Bowling Green football was in gutterball mode.

The dad who talked Don back into football was visiting Bowling Green not long after his son enrolled. The Falcons were getting smeared in their homecoming game.

The old man said something sarcastic like, "Nice school you picked, son."

It turned around after Bowling Green hired Doyt Perry, who had been working for Woody Hayes at Ohio State. The Falcons became a national power at their level, recruiting Canton heavily.

Those were the days of the running back.

"Everybody played football in a phone booth, Woody-style," Nehlen said. "If I would throw 15 passes in a game, Doyt Perry would say, 'Woah ... an aerial circus.' Canton people don't realize how good a ball carrier Vic DeOrio was. He would flat out honk it up in there."

After Don's senior year at Bowling Green, an old ally from Canton, Earl Schreiber, wanted him to come home to work in a recreation program operated by the Timken steel company.

Don's athletic prowess wasn't enough to make him a pro prospect in any of his sports. He set his heart on becoming a coach. Schreiber, who had a million connections, understood. He helped Nehlen land the head football coaching job at Canton South.

Nehlen was only 23, but veteran coaches weren't itching to take over a program in a seven-year losing streak.

Nehlen got the job and worked as if he had just replaced Hayes at Ohio State. He visited the homes of every prospective player. He was overjoyed when he got to hire Kelly as an assistant coach.

One of the first things Nehlen and Kelly did was to clean up a dirty football locker room. The lights in the school were blazing on a Saturday night while the old Lincoln pals mopped and swashed. The cops came to see who had broken in. It took a while to convince them they were the new football coaches.

Nehlen visited Massillon to check out training techniques. He set up an isometric workout room. Inheriting an 0-9 team, his first two games as head coach were wins over Jackson and Perry by a combined 34-6 score.

"Our attitude was, don't give me this malarkey about you can't get the job done," Nehlen says. "Where there's a will, there's a way."

The Wildcats were 9-1 in his fourth season. He was pretty fired up about a team that had been added to the schedule for the season opener: Lincoln. His team beat his alma mater 32-12.

Nehlen then made a move to expand his résumé, taking a college job at Cincinnati. It gave his buddy, Kelly, a chance to take over as South's head coach.

The McKinley head coaching job came open in 1964. Old ally Schreiber pulled more strings. The next thing Nehlen knew, he was back in Canton, not yet 30, as head coach of the 1964 McKinley team that went 9-1.

Nehlen's ride as a coach was just starting.

He had other connections. Bo Schembechler, who had been on Doyt Perry's staff at Bowling Green, brought him to Michigan.

The Michigan job led to the head coaching job at West Virginia in 1980. Nehlen was inducted into the College Football Hall of Fame in 2005.

He sometimes wonders what might have happened if he hadn't gotten back on his bicycle at Lincoln.

—STEVE DOERSCHUK

>>> 1

DON NEHLEN

Voted outstanding athlete in 1954 graduating class. All-city quarterback for two years. Leading scorer on 1954 team that set school record for points. Multi-year starter in baseball. Posted 21-2-4 record as Bowling Green's starting QB in 1955, '56 and '57. Head football coach at Canton South and then McKinley en route to long head coaching run at Bowling Green and West Virginia. In College Football Hall of Fame with 202-128-8 record.

<<< 5

MIKE REJINA

Sensational ball carrier in football who doubled as ferocious linebacker. Lincoln's leading basketball scorer as junior and senior. Was as good in baseball as the other sports, known for hitting home runs. Killed in Germany while serving in Army within year of graduating from Lincoln. In Stark County High School Football Hall of Fame.

<<< 2

GEORGE SAIMES

"Saimes may not have the size for the pros," a scout said when he was Michigan State's All-America fullback in 1962, "but my goodness he has guts." Enjoyed long pro career and wound up on the American Football League all-time team at safety. Helped Buffalo Bills to titles the last two years before the AFL winner went to the Super Bowl. All-county fullback for Lincoln in 1958 and standout on basketball team that beat McKinley in 1959 district finals. Track star. Spent decades as a top NFL scout.

<<< 6

STU WILKINS

Member of the Stark County High School Football Hall of Fame. Standout on Lincoln's war-years teams who was only 17 years old when he began his football career at Michigan. All-Big Ten guard for 1947 Michigan team crowned national champ after a 49-0 rout of USC. Settled in Canton as a business leader and board member at the Pro Football Hall of Fame.

3

KEN NEWLON

Became Lincoln's best basketball coach in 1956, replacing Bob Flanders and going 17-4 in his first year. Coached at Stone Creek and Strasburg before Lincoln and at McKinley after Canton City Schools consolidation, but best known for 20 years with the Lions. Teams went to final fours in 1962 and '67. Overall head coaching record was 527-227, with nine district championships. Tail gunner in Europe during World War II.

7

JOHN ANDREADIS

First team all-county in basketball in the 1960-1961 season as a junior and first team all-county on an 11-man football team picked by coaches later in '61, when he was a senior. Second team all-county on 1961-62 basketball team that reached state final four, with teammates Bill Gribble and Dave Kosht making first team. Played college football at Miami (Fla.).

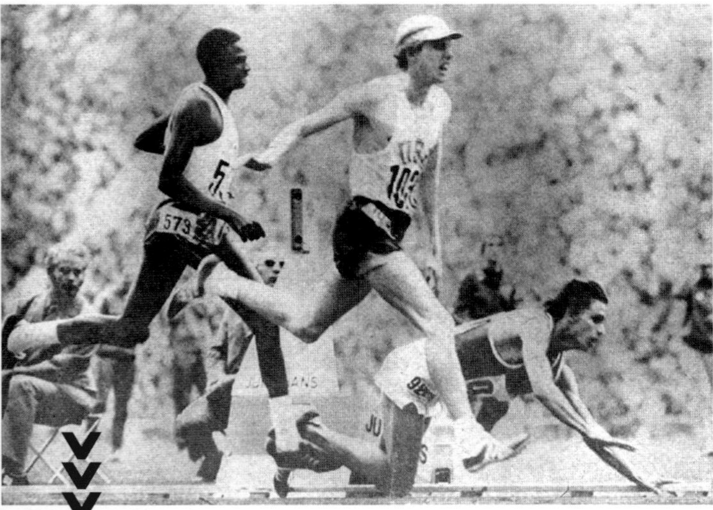

4

DAVE WOTTLE

Olympic gold medalist in 800-meter run at 1972 Summer Olympics in Munich. Began ascent as track star at Lincoln and developed into national name at Bowling Green. Finished second in NCAA nationals in mile in 1970 behind Marty Liquori. Later was national NCAA champ in mile. Famous for race-winning kicks and wearing a golf cap as he motored along.

8

DANNY TODD

Shooting star on 1966-67 basketball team that reached final four. Between All-City Nights and tournament games, Lions beat Lehman 56-33 and 75-51, Timken 94-59, and McKinley 59-44 and 56-50 (district final). Deadly shooter from 25 feet and in before there was 3-point line. Won full ride to Bowling Green. Also stood out in baseball.

9

BRUCE FOWLER

Big, tough football player whose charismatic side was more conspicuous in basketball. Started as sophomore on district championship basketball team and was junior on 1966-67 team that reached state final four. Established enforcer by 1967-68 season, when Lions led Stark County in defense.

10

DON BUTTREY

Was "Boot" to those who knew of him, and almost everyone did. Remembered for stunts and carnival tricks, which led to pizza-eating contests on TV and novelty-act work with the Cleveland Cavaliers, but known to his closer friends for his soft-spoken, serious side. Popular choice to play Santa Claus, with perfect body shape for job. Accomplished baseball hitter who delivered in clutch and never struck out. Deceptively fast. Longtime player and manager in Canton Class A League.

HONORABLE MENTIONS

BRUCE BEATTY
BILL GRIBBLE
RICK HAVERSTOCK
JIM OSBORN
DICK TEEL
MIKE TONEY
RON WORSTELL
LOU VENDITTI

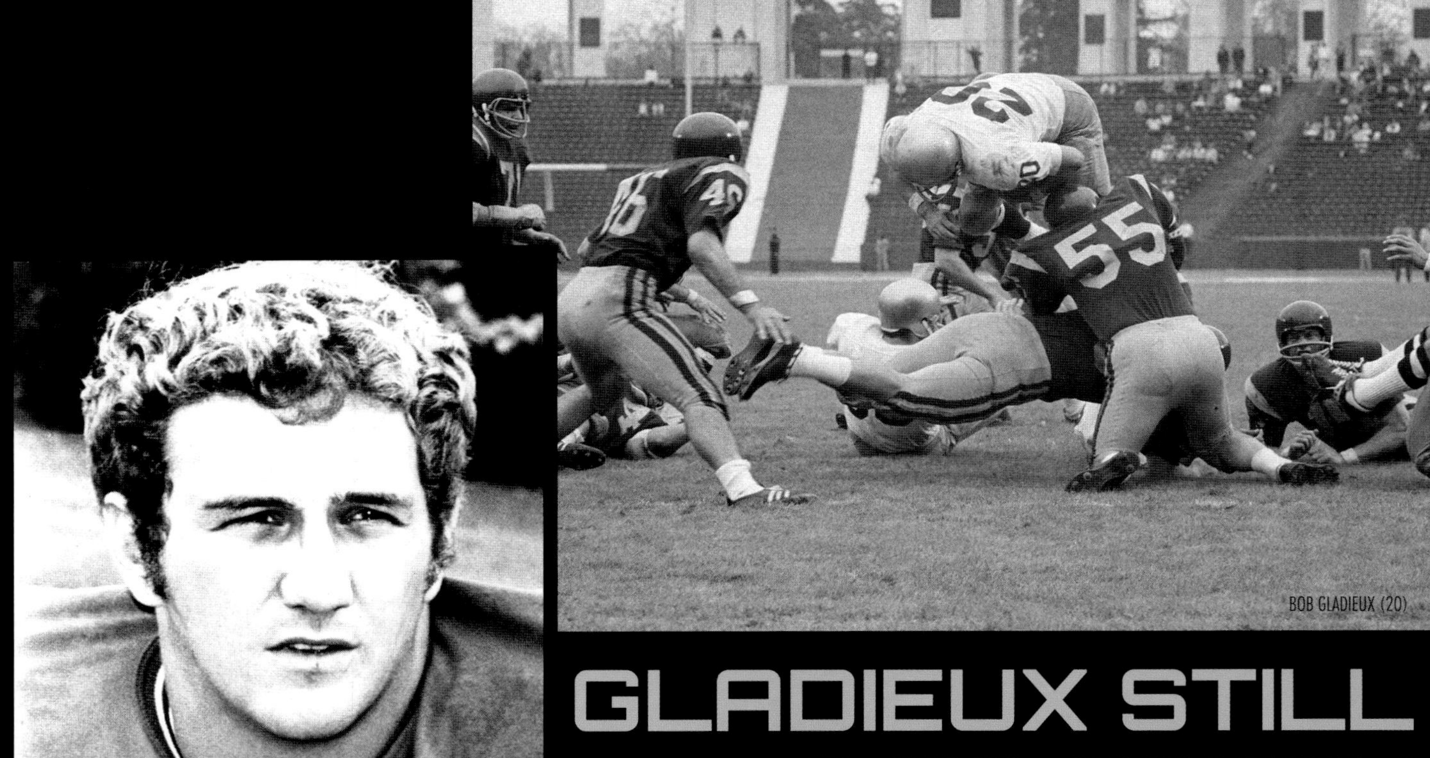

BOB GLADIEUX (20)

GLADIEUX STILL HARD TO CATCH

THE BIGGEST NAME IN LOUISVILLE SPORTS HISTORY IS STILL A LITTLE BOY AT HEART.

Bob Gladieux played in the NFL for the Patriots, but the shirt he wears in the autumn says Browns, the team of his youth.

The old man worries about living long enough to see the Cleveland Indians win another World Series (he was 1 the last time they did), and his dream job is still the one Jimmy Dudley used to have, play-by-play announcer for the Tribe.

His wife will ask him when he daydreams behind the wheel, "Why are you driving so slow?" Often enough, it is because his mind has wandered to the leisurely family drives after mass at St. Louis Church, with no particular place to go.

As Gladieux talks of these things, 50 years after scoring Notre Dame's only touchdown in "the game of the century," he lets out a theatrical shriek.

"God!"

Time, he has come to understand, flies much faster than he did, in its peculiar way.

In its way, that is a compliment to time, because Bob Gladieux could fly.

Louisville football was something to behold in the 1940s under head coach Wayne Ashbaugh and later Jim Morgan. It ebbed in the 1950s and did not recover in the first two years of the 1960s, when a Massillon assistant, Gaylord "Hap" Lillick, took over the program.

Fortunes began to turn in 1962, when Gladieux was a sophomore. Across the next five years, the Leopards ran up a 48-1-1 record.

Gladieux was Stark County player of the year, picked by coaches, in 1964, when the Leopards outscored 10 victims by a 420-24 score. In 1965, when he was a freshman at Notre Dame and Louisville went 10-0 behind a combined 427-36 score, the county MVP was Leopard senior Tom Chlebeck.

Louisville's only loss during the run was to Canton South, which had the best football teams in its history. Yet, in 1962, when Frank Dugan scored a county-record 192 points for South, the Wildcats' only loss was to Louisville.

Gladieux broke Dugan's record in 1964 with 196 points.

Much of what made Gladieux a special all-around athlete could not be detected when he walked the halls. He grew to be about 5-foot-11, weighing less than 200 pounds as a young adult.

He was fast, elusive and naturally strong, with lightning reflexes. He worked at it. There was a fire inside.

He was so good at baseball that he started as a Louisville freshman. He made all-county in basketball twice. He was an excellent defensive player in football.

Above all, he was a ball carrier. Everyone who saw him remembers him for that.

"He was very fast," says Greg Parrish, a Louisville coaching icon who grew up watching Gladieux, "and very elusive."

He understood his natural talent and used it to make moves and cuts.

"My mindset was make you miss, don't get hit," he says. "I wasn't a power runner by any means, but I didn't back down. When there was no alternative but to get hit, I'd try to make one last move to put a guy off balance, and then be the guy initiating the contact rather than the other way around."

It worked most of the time.

"I do remember a time when three guys from Hoover got to me simultaneously," he said. "It was the hardest I've ever been hit. The ball went flying."

Otherwise, the Vikings went flying. Louisville was 3-0 and won by a combined 100-20 in Gladieux's games against Hoover.

Gladieux recalls a Louisville in which nobody locked their doors and kids could ride their bicycles anywhere. He remembers Dale "Nubby" McKimm from the Little Leopards program that has helped so many Louisville kids become good football players. He rattles off names of teammates from the top of his head as if reading from a list.

Bob's parents and three brothers lived near the center of town, next to the church.

"They used to have a summer festival with rides and games and elephants," he said. "We'd stay up late and watch out our windows."

Woody Hayes watched Gladieux intently for two years. The Ohio State football coach spoke at the Louisville football banquet, attended Louisville basketball games and was in the Gladieux home.

"I loved Woody Hayes," Gladieux said. "He knew from Day 1 that I loved Notre Dame."

Woody Hayes was old school. So was Gladieux's father, Ted.

"Dad was a little guy with big forearms," he says. "He was a sports fan and a big Notre Dame fan."

Ted taught Bob about the Fighting Irish. He taught him about doing the right thing.

"Dad was a carpet layer and linoleum guy," Gladieux said. "He worked six days a week.

"One time I was helping him get ready to lay carpet down in a house, and he said, 'Bobby, clean up that floor while I get the padding.'

"I thought I had it in good shape when he came back, but he looked at it, and said, 'Hey, I thought I asked you to clean this up.'

"I said, 'Dad, you're putting a half inch of padding on top of this.'

"He said, 'Listen. I do every job like it's my home. Now if you want to help me ...' I finished cleaning it up the way he wanted. Dad ... he was something."

Hayes' recruiting pitch was doomed the day Ted Gladieux's favorite team made an official offer. Bob enrolled at Notre Dame.

He was less than two years removed from graduation day at Louisville when he found himself in "the game of the century." Defending national champ Michigan State was 9-0 heading into a game against unbeaten and No. 1 ranked Notre Dame, coached by Ara Parseghian.

Michigan State surged to a 10-0 lead and seemed in great shape when starting Notre Dame quarterback Terry Hanratty got knocked out of the game by Bubba Smith.

The Fighting Irish, though, got a 34-yard touchdown catch from Gladieux and added a field goal.

The game finished in a 10-all tie, enough to allow Notre Dame to win the national championship with a 51-0 wipeout of USC a week later.

Had Gladieux gone to Ohio State, he would have been part of a team that won a national championship by beating USC in the Rose Bowl.

As it was, USC's last game before the Rose Bowl was a 21-all tie with Notre Dame. Gladieux had a big game and finished a 7-2-1 year as the rushing and scoring leader for the Fighting Irish.

In the 1969 NFL Draft, USC's O.J. Simpson was the No. 1 overall pick. Gladieux was drafted by the Patriots (Round 8, 188th overall), with whom he played for three years before a brief stint as Simpson's teammate in Buffalo.

Gladieux's attitude never much changed. He aimed to be in better shape than the next guy, play without fear, and let it all hang out on the field.

"I tried to play with heart," he said. "I saw people with more talent. I relied on the inner competitiveness. I had to win."

> **"I TRIED TO PLAY WITH HEART. I SAW PEOPLE WITH MORE TALENT. I RELIED ON THE INNER COMPETITIVENESS. I HAD TO WIN."**
>
> **—BOB GLADIEUX**

He still loves to follow sports. He is partial to athletes who give all they have.

"I admire the kids from the service academies," he said. "They might be down 35-6, but they're still stinging you, and stinging you. I love watching the Army-Navy game."

Gladieux was in his 30s when he went back to Notre Dame to get a master's degree and try his hand at coaching. He was in his 40s when he met a world traveler, a native of Germany who spoke five languages. He and Inge have been married for 27 years.

For years, Bob and Inge ran a travel agency in South Bend. Now they are "retired" with three daughters and two grandchildren, spending most of the year in Fort Myers, Fla.

Mrs. Gladieux is in demand as a substitute teacher and works virtually every day. Bob does some subbing and some fishing and talks as if he plays pickleball like he means it.

When he thinks of his Louisville, he marvels at the waves of good players and good people with whom he came up. He sounds proud of where he is from.

He doesn't think of himself as old, seeming to wrestle with the number on his birth certificate, Jan. 2, 1947.

"This year (in 2016), we'll have the 50th anniversary of 'the game of the century'," he said. "I remember being at a 25th anniversary of something, and a 50th anniversary team was being recognized at the same time.

"I'm thinking then, 50 years ... I can't imagine that. Now, bingo, here it is for us."

The Louisville legend lost a step decades ago. Yet, in a sense—still—no one can catch him. — *STEVE DOERSCHUK*

STARKEY BUILT DYNASTY AT LOUISVILLE

THE ROAD TO PAUL STARKEY'S LONG RIDE WAS CLEARED BY A SECRET WEAPON.

Starkey had just taken over as head football coach of the Louisville Leopards. He was game planning his debut against a Glenwood team featuring Cleve Bryant and Dan Dierdorf.

"We had an exchange student from Denmark, Peter Neilsen," Starkey recalls. "He was a soccer player who was out there with our student managers, kicking footballs.

"I checked to find out if exchange students were eligible to play."

No one in town and certainly not Glenwood knew about Neilsen. Game night arrived. He kicked three field goals and an extra point for 10 points, Starkey's margin of victory in the game.

"Peter asked after the extra point, 'How come I only get one?' " Starkey said. "It was the first time he ever saw a football game."

Starkey was 1-0, on his way to 146-51-3 across 20 seasons.

Louisville football is and was the opposite of a secret. Starkey was 28 years old with a tough act to follow when he took over in 1965.

Not long removed from playing football at Heidelberg, he had been the top assistant on head coach Hap Lillick's team, which was coming off a three-year run of 28-1-1.

Lillick left for Kent State, where his Massillon friend Leo Strang had just become head coach. Starkey proved he belonged by going 10-0 in his first year. After the tense Glenwood win, Louisville faced three other Stark County opponents (Canton South, North Canton, Minerva) and beat them 141-8.

After 10-0 years in 1965 and '66, he hit a 3-7 speed bump in 1967, after which the Leopards joined the Federal League and did no better than 8-2 in their first three years.

"At Louisville," Starkey says, "they expect you to do better than maybe 8-2."

One of his best talent groups arrived at a good time, and he went 10-0 in 1971 with what he regards as perhaps his best team. Those Leopards beat Federal League rivals Oakwood, Jackson, Canton South, North Canton, Marlington, Glenwood and Perry by a combined 236-38.

Louisville could be a tough place to coach because of expectations, but it was the place in his heart. It remains his home. It always was.

Starkey grew up on a 120-acre dairy farm in Paris, near the edge of the Louisville and Minerva school districts. He joined the Louisville football team with a real feel for the season-ending Minerva rivalry.

He was a thorn in the Lions' paws. His first season ended with a 62-0 rout of Minerva. During a great era of Minerva football, his Leopards shut out the Lions four times from 1965-71.

In 1973, Minerva entered the game having outscored nine teams by a combined 501-16. Starkey's team beat the Lions 28-9. In 1974, Minerva was 9-0 and had outscored nine victims 319-18. Louisville beat the Lions 26-20.

Later, North Canton became the big rival. The Vikings had Starkey's number for a while, but his last two Federal League champions, in 1978 and '81, went a combined 18-1-1 with wins over Hoover.

Starkey made and kept many friends through the years and remains grateful to those who helped him and the community. He rattles off names of his old players by the dozens.

He cites Dennis Biery as an example of a Louisville kid who gave back to the community. The namesake of Biery Cheese was Louisville's first state wrestling qualifier and has been a benefactor to assorted projects.

"Without him," Starkey said, "we wouldn't have a new stadium."

Starkey coached four Stark County players of the year—Bob Gladieux in 1964, Tom Chlebeck in 1965, Ken Kuhn in 1971 and Jeff Kuhn in 1977. He was an assistant when Gladieux played and a first-year head coach the next year with Chlebeck as a senior.

"Gladieux was Mr. Everything," Starkey says. "The coach at East Palestine said Bob's leg would go one way, his arm would go the other way, and he would run a third way.

"Chlebeck had a different style. He would run over people. In the last game of the season, Tom scored 50 points and broke Gladieux's season scoring record."

The memories run together, melting into a theme. It was about the famous Little Leopards youth program, the big crowds under the Friday lights. It was about a good community.

He thinks back to when he was a young coach and math teacher. A metaphorical memory happens by.

Football season is far away. The seven-man sled is stored on a grade-school field.

"Mark Stier, who was as good as they come, is out there hitting the seven-man," Paul Starkey says. —*STEVE DOERSCHUK*

LOUISVILLE TOP TEN ICONS

1 **BOB GLADIEUX** Charter member of Stark County High School Football Hall of Fame in 2002. Broke Stark County football scoring record with 196 points on a 10-0 team in 1964. All-Ohio back who led '64 Leopards to 10-0 season in which they outscored foes 420-24. Averaged 18.9 points for 1964-65 basketball team that went 17-1. Also starred in baseball.

2 **PAUL STARKEY** Worked under head coach Hap Lillick on teams that began to win big in 1960s. Went 10-0 in his first year after succeeding Lillick, in 1965, at age 28. Went 10-0 in three of his first seven seasons as head coach. Was head coach for 20 years, with a record of 146-51-3. Grew up in Paris and was Louisville athlete. Elected to Stark County High School Football Hall of Fame in 2004.

<<< 3 **MARK STIER** Football standout on offense and defense. All-Ohio end on 1965 team that went 10-0 and outscored opponents 427-36. Key man on 1964-65 Louisville basketball team that went 19-2. Linebacker named MVP on Ohio State's 1968 national championship team. In Rose Bowl game that clinched Buckeyes' crown, main defender controlling USC All-American O.J. Simpson.

4 **JON ALJANCIC** All-Ohio in football, basketball and baseball in the early 1990s. All-county quarterback, defensive standout and kicker on 1992 team that went 12-1. Led Dartmouth's 10-0 Ivy League championship team in 1996. Member of athletic family whose patriarch was longtime city recreation director and is namesake of Andy Aljancic Park.

5 **TOM CHLEBECK** Stark County football MVP and pile-driving ball carrier on 1965 team. Had big roles on offense and defense for 1964 team that went 10-0. Scholarship football and baseball player at Cincinnati, where he was MVP of baseball team in 1970. Returned to Louisville to teach and was head coach of baseball and softball teams.

<<< 6 **KEN KUHN** Most valuable player on 1971 All-Stark County team. Played offense and was a load at linebacker for team that went 10-0 and won Federal League in final year before Ohio introduced postseason playoffs. Two-time All-Federal League first-teamer in basketball. Four-year letter winner at Ohio State. Captain of 1975 Buckeyes team along with Archie Griffin, Tim Fox and Brian Baschnagel.

7 **BRIAN BEATTY** Two-way starter and Stark County MVP on unbeaten 1992 football team. Long-time Leopards saw him as all-around athlete in tradition of Ed Mathie and Paul Metzger. Lettered three years in basketball and four years in baseball. Played college football career for a familiar name: Louisville.

8 **GREG PARRISH** Posted 808-258 record in 31 years of coaching both boys and girls tennis programs, winning 18 league titles. Head girls basketball coach for three years and athletic director for 14 years. Represents strong girls sports tradition at Louisville. Coached charter Louisville Athletic Hall of Fame members Kerri Strobelt in basketball and Nicole Catalano Groves in tennis.

9 **RICK CRISLIP** Key starter for football teams that went 17-3 across 1973 and '74 seasons, then a four-year letterman at Ohio University. State runner-up in wrestling who returned to be head coach of wrestling team for 10 years. Went 77-39 with three playoff seasons in 12 years as head football coach. Father of one of school's top girls athletes, Alyx Crislip.

10 **GREG GRAHAM** Led Stark County basketball in scoring in 1973 with county-best 20.6 scoring average. Four-year letterman for Oregon Ducks before returning to Louisville as head basketball coach. Led 1982 Leopards to share of Federal League championship. Head basketball coach at Boise State from 2002-10 and 2008 Western Athletic Conference Coach of Year.

HONORABLE MENTIONS

DENNIS BIERY
NICOLE CATALANO GROVES
JEFF KUHN
MIKE MALCUIT
DARRYL MICKLEY
BILL SHALOSKY
KERRI STROBELT

WITTE LEFT LASTING IMPACT ON AND OFF COURT

MOMENTS OF DEEP PERSONAL TRAUMA CAN BE HARD TO TALK ABOUT. FEW ARE WILLING TO DISCUSS THEM. EVEN FEWER WOULD BE WILLING TO SHOW VIDEO CLIPS OF THE INCIDENT AND USE IT AS A TEACHABLE MOMENT. THERE JUST ARE NOT MANY PEOPLE LIKE FORMER MARLINGTON HIGH SCHOOL STANDOUT LUKE WITTE IN THE WORLD. THE UNIVERSE IS POORER FOR IT.

The date is January 25, 1972. Witte is a few years removed from being one Stark County's all-time great high school players with the Dukes. An NBA career is on his horizon.

On this day, though, he is a 7-foot junior center on the Ohio State men's basketball team. The Buckeyes lead Minnesota late in a game on the road. Witte drives into the lane where he is fouled hard and knocked to the floor.

A Minnesota player comes over to help Witte to his feet. Witte is violently pulled to his feet and then, out of nowhere, kneed in the groin. The incident touches off a brawl between the teams at midcourt. While cameras focus on the brawl in the middle of the court, they swing back to catch Witte being stomped by Minnesota players while down on the court. One Golden Gopher puts his foot on the top of Witte's crown and slams his face directly into the floor twice. Officials wave off the game as they prepare to take Witte to a medical facility. He is unable to leave the court under his own power as Minnesota fans boo and shower the court with debris.

It's a moment that Witte does not run from when he returns to the area for his annual basketball camp at the Chapel in Marlboro.

"I've been here during the camp,"

"EVERYBODY IN THE COMMUNITY WAS ALWAYS REALLY ENCOURAGING. I HAD A LOT OF GREAT TEACHERS, AND I MADE A LOT OF GREAT FRIENDS THROUGH SPORTS. I THINK THOSE EXPERIENCES REALLY HELPED SET ME ON THE PATH TO BECOMING THE MAN I AM TODAY."

—LUKE WITTE

Marlboro Chapel sports pastor Todd Hostetler said. "He sits the kids down and shows them clips of the injury. It's always a tough moment because the kids like him so much and it's hard for them to see him treated like that."

Witte doesn't mince words or leave out any details of the incident. Even ones that don't portray him in a positive light.

"He always admits that he was an instigator," Hostetler said. "He always talks about how he threw an elbow at a Minnesota player on his way back to the locker room at halftime."

The thing that Witte wants the campers to focus on isn't the video itself, though. Or the injury. Or who is to blame. It's the response to this personal moment of trauma he talks about.

"It's ultimately a story of forgiveness," Hostetler said. "I've seen him tell it a few times and it's always powerful. He tells the story of how he forgave everyone involved. He even helped lead one of the gentleman to Christ that stepped on him eventually."

It's fitting that would be the end result considering Witte's profession. Witte is a pastor these days. The director of the Carolinas Division of the Marketplace Chaplains, in fact. A group that trains and provides chaplains to businesses in the state looking for such services.

It was a career move Witte didn't take lightly.

"A lot of people think I went into this because of the Minnesota incident," Witte said. "That's not really the case. I think all of my life experiences were leading me down that path. I felt the calling but at the same time, I had tried to do everything I could to not go down that path."

Nearly a decade after his three-season NBA career with the Cleveland Cavaliers ended, Witte couldn't ignore the signs any longer. In 1985 he decided to return to school and attend the Asbury Theological Seminary. The decision was not easy and had little to do with anything sports related.

"The biggest hang-up for me was, I'd be entering the same profession as my dad," Witte said. "I didn't really want to follow in his footsteps. ... He left my mom. That was the biggest reason why I didn't want those connections."

Witte didn't become a pastor to hide from trauma. He didn't let his negative experiences with his father deter him either. He made the decision on his own, for his own reasons.

"I didn't have a 'born again moment' or anything like that," Witte said. "In my case, it was more a re-dedication. I had been in church most of my life and it just felt like a natural progression to the way things were going."

It's been more than 20 years now. Witte is in his mid-60s, but don't expect him to let that stop him anytime soon. He still loves basketball and conducting camps.

"I don't do a lot of camps anymore," Witte said. "I do the one at the Chapel in Marlboro and there is one I do out in Kansas. It's something I love doing, though. It takes a lot of time and energy,"

The camps cover a multitude of topics. Playing the game is just one part of the experience of being in one of Witte's camps.

"He teaches kids about respect," Hostetler said. "He teaches them about courage and strength. He also covers nutrition. It's about more than just basketball. It's about life as much as it is about sports."

Witte scored 1,531 points in his Marlington career. That figure ranked third in Stark County history at the time and still ranks ninth all-time in the county. His sophomore year at Ohio State, he earned All-Big Ten honors and helped the Buckeyes win a share of the league title. He was a reserve on the Cavs' "Miracle of Richfield" team, which reached the Eastern Conference finals in his final year in 1976.

To him, though, basketball is about more than records or wins and losses. In fact, some of his best memories from his incredible high school career at Marlington weren't wins at all.

"I remember the three tournament games against McKinley the most," Witte said. "We lost all of them but those games were incredible. There was nothing like going head-to-head with Nick Weatherspoon at the Memorial Field House. Those games were always a good challenge for us and I think we held up our end of things quite well."

Witte also remembers the tremendous support he, as well as the rest of the team, received from the Marlington community.

"That was just a great place for me," Witte said. "Everybody in the community was always really encouraging. I had a lot of great teachers and I made a lot of great friends through sports. I think those experiences really helped set me on the path to becoming the man I am today."

—CLIFF HICKMAN

A LOVE OF TRACK AND FIELD HELPED DAGENHARDT MAKE HIS MARK

HE WAS BROUGHT TO MARLINGTON FROM THE STATE OF WISCONSIN TO BE AN ASSISTANT FOOTBALL COACH IN 1972. LUCKILY FOR THE DUKES, THEN-TRACK AND FIELD HEAD COACH HOWARD KITZMILLER REALIZED WHAT BOB DAGENHARDT'S TRUE CALLING WOULD BE.

"I got to Marlington and I talked to Coach Kitzmiller from time to time and he eventually invited me to be an assistant coach for the track and field team," Dagenhardt said. "I had some modest success in track and field in college and really loved the sport, and was willing to help out anywhere he wanted. It was an easy decision to say yes."

Modest success may be underselling what Dagenhardt accomplished in the sport. He was a state qualifier in high school in Wisconsin and had a knack for getting the most out of himself.

A trait that has carried over to Dagenhardt's teams at Marlington for nearly 30 years in both cross country and track and field. Dagenhardt has coached six state champions and had five teams finish in the top 10 in the state in the team standings.

That success doesn't come easy, and Dagenhardt does more than provide motivational words of wisdom. His teams have long displayed a level of technical excellence that can help make the difference at big events.

"I always want my athletes to have the correct fundamentals," Dagenhardt said. "Right now for example, we have junior Lane Knoch. He is ranked fifth in the state in the indoor 110 hurdles right now. I also nitpick him more than anybody else.

"I do that because I want him to do things the right way. If he does that, I think he's going to go on to college and be a darn good hurdler. It's not all about motivation when you are a track and field coach. It's also about getting kids to do things the right way."

It's the type of coaching that makes a good athlete great.

"Our throwers have always been what you might call undersized at Marlington," Dagenhardt said. "Having the correct fundamentals, though, can help you bridge those gaps. We don't cut any corners."

It's all done with an eye toward helping athletes achieve the most. It's also part of a personal goal that Dagenhardt sets for himself before every season: make his athletes better than he was in high school.

"I've always said that if I can get someone to be better than I was at that age then I must not be doing a bad job coaching," Dagenhardt said with a laugh. "It's a job that I still have a lot of fun with. Whatever success I've had, I definitely want to pass that along to the kids. Anything that they feel they have gained from me, I'm definitely proud of." —CLIFF HICKMAN

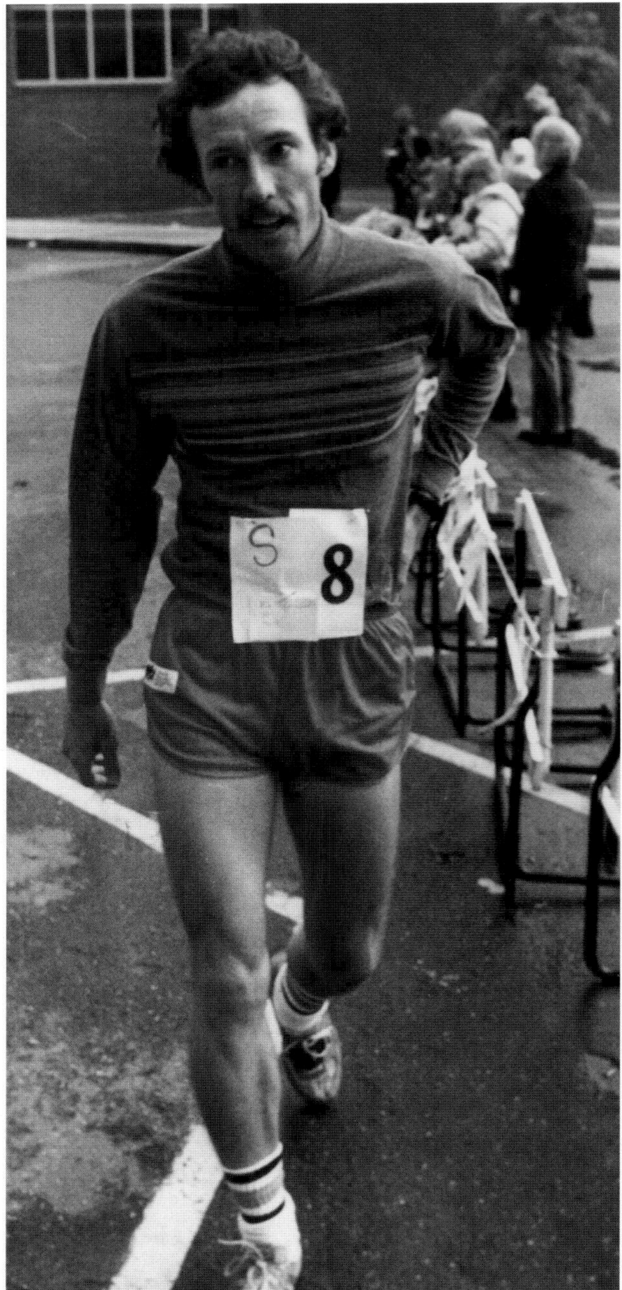

MARLINGTON TOP TEN ICONS

1 LUKE WITTE Witte was one of the most decorated basketball players in the area in the late 1960s. The 7-footer finished his high school career in 1969 with 1,531 points. That is still good for ninth in county history. Witte went on to star for Ohio State and later played for the Cleveland Cavaliers in the NBA.

2 LISA BREIDING One of the great middle distance runners in county history, winning Class AAA state titles in the 800 in 1984 and 1985. Breiding still holds the county record in the 800 (2:11.07), which she set back in 1984. Breiding went on to star in cross country and track and field at Kentucky from 1986-89. Was an NCAA national champion in the 3,000 meters as a freshman with the Wildcats.

3 DYMONTE THOMAS One of several outstanding football players to make his way through the program in the early part of the 2010s under former coach Ed Miley. Thomas combined incredible speed and power to become a nightmare matchup for area teams on both sides of the ball. Thomas ran for more than 3,000 yards during his career and scored 59 total touchdowns. He also had more than 300 tackles while lining up at a variety of positions, earning Repository all-county honors all four years. Currently starts at safety at the University of Michigan.

4 BOB DAGENHARDT Coached championship athletes in a number of events, notably the throws and distance events. Originally brought to Marlington as an assistant football coach, Marlington athletes across five decades continue to be grateful Dagenhardt was recruited to help out with the track and field and cross country programs.

5 MELISSA GRAHAM Won Division II state championships as a freshman (in the 3,200 meters) and as a senior (in the 1,600). She also helped Marlington to a state runner-up finish as a team in the Division II state cross country meet in 1995 where she finished fifth individually.

6 TONY HILEMAN Threw a perfect game in her freshman debut and ended her career by throwing a one-hitter in winning the Division II state championship in 1996. In between, Hileman etched her name among the state's all-time leaders by going 69-18, throwing 12 career no-hitters, recording a 20-strikeout game and striking out 795 batters for her career. She was a first team All-Ohio in 1995 and 1996.

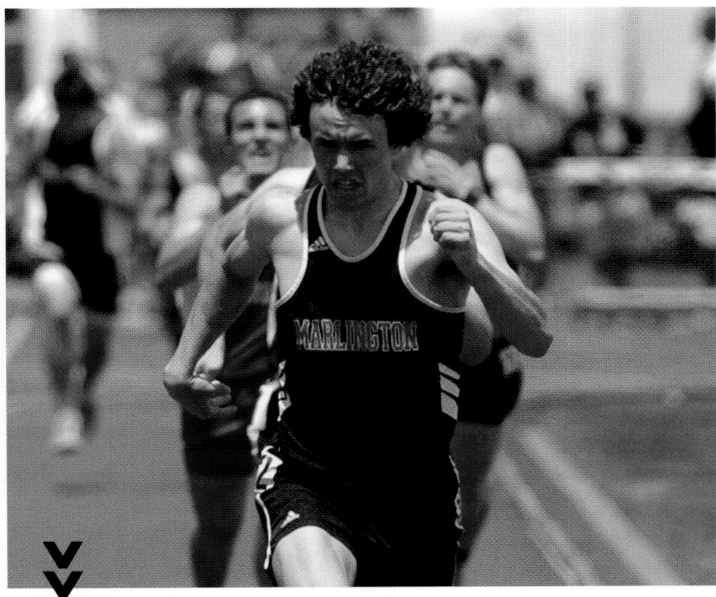

7 JARROD EICK Won state titles in cross country and track as a senior during the 2008-09 school year. He is the only Marlington boy to win a title in cross country and he became the first Marlington male runner to win a championship at the state track and field meet when he won the 1,600. He reached the podium five times overall at the state track and field meet during his career.

8 BILL KOCH Started the Marlington softball program as its first head coach and within eight years delivered the first state softball championship by a Stark County team when the Dukes won the Division II state title in 1996. His teams went 367-189 over his 26 years. He retired in 2013 with seven NBC and three district titles.

9 ALDEN HILL A big, physical, crushing runner, he was the thunder to the lightning that Dymonte Thomas provided. Hill ended his career as Marlington's all-time leading rusher with 4,475 yards. Also holds the single-season mark for rushing yards (2,241) and single-game record for rushing yards (279). Was a first team All Ohio pick as a senior and the AP Division III Offensive Player of the Year as a junior when he was Repository Stark County Player of the Year. He started his college career at Tennessee before transferring to James Madison.

10 LISA EVANICH Won a Division II state title in the discus in 2001and also placed fifth in the shot put that year.

HONORABLE MENTIONS

MARCUS COLDSNOW
MARCY EVANICH
NICK EVANICH
JIM FARRELL
SCOTT GABELT
JACK HAZEN
TRAVIS MIDDLETON
LINDSEY ROYER
LUCAS STROUBLE

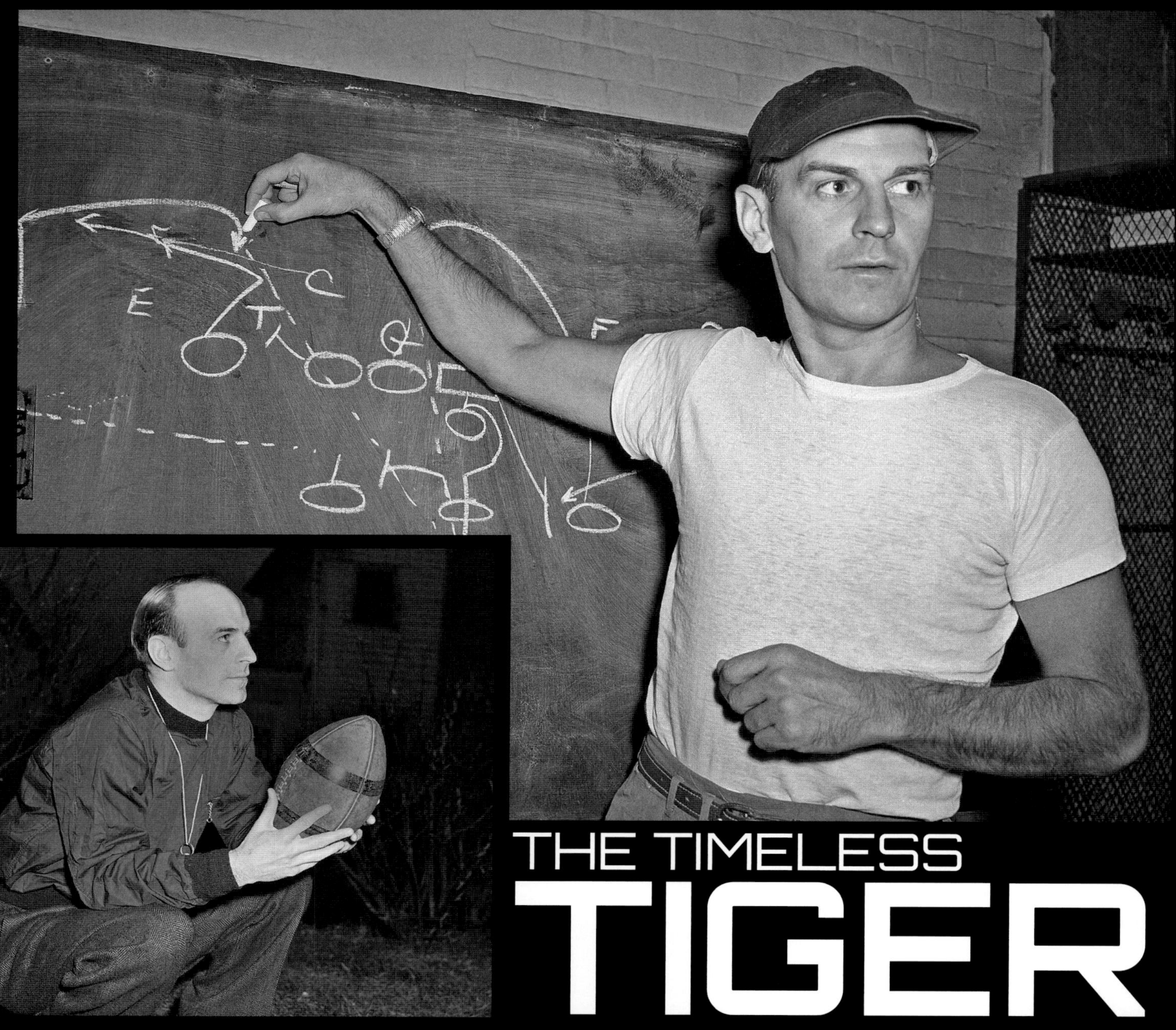

THE TIMELESS TIGER

WHEN SAM RUTIGLIANO WAS HIRED AS THE COACH OF THE CLEVELAND BROWNS IN 1978, THE FIRST THING HE DID WAS GO TO A STORE IN DOWNTOWN CLEVELAND AND BUY A CAMEL HAIR COAT.

The reason? When he was growing up in Brooklyn, he used to go to New York Giants games against the Browns and Paul Brown always wore a camel hair coat.

"I didn't tell (Browns owner) Art Modell," Rutigliano said in a recent phone conversation. "I would have got fired.

"Art Modell went to his grave never knowing what I did."

That's the kind of sway Brown held—and still holds—over coaches. Although he died in 1991 and stopped coaching following the 1975 season, Brown's influence on football can still be seen in everything from equipment (he invented the face mask) to film study (he was the first coach to use it to scout opponents) to playbooks (which he invented as a high school coach in Massillon) to diversity (helping break the pro football's modern color barrier in 1946 when he signed Canton's Marion Motley and Ohio State's Bill Willis) to countless other innovations.

"Everything that he did as a coach, 50 years later, everybody is still basically doing the same thing," Patriots coach Bill Belichick said in the recent NFL Network documentary "Paul Brown: A Football Life." "I really think of him as the father of professional football."

And it all started in the birthplace of professional football.

Although Brown was born in Norwalk, Ohio, he moved to Massillon at age 9 and became part of the school's already storied tradition, going 15-3 as the Tigers' starting quarterback in 1923-1924.

After playing college football at Miami (Ohio), he spent two years coaching at a Maryland prep school (winning a state title in 1930), then was hired as Massillon's head coach in 1932 at age 24. He turned out to be a pretty decent coach, if you're the type of person impressed by an 80-8-2 record, a 35-game winning streak, six state titles and three national titles.

Oh, and there's this: From 1935-40, Massillon outscored its opponents 2,393 to 168.

Ohio State hired him away in 1941 and Brown won the Buckeyes' first national title the following year. He left OSU in 1944 to become a lieutenant in the Navy, spent two years coaching the Great Lakes Bluejackets (which played other service teams and college football teams) and, in 1946, became the coach of the Cleveland Browns, a newly-formed All-America Football Conference team named after him.

During the next 10 years, his Browns played in 10 straight league championship games (the first four in the AAFC, then next six in the NFL) and won seven.

He became the first coach to win titles at the NCAA and NFL levels—Jimmy Johnson, Barry Switzer and Pete Carroll have since done it—and the only one of those four to also win a state high school title.

"When you look at a word like 'icon,' he is THE icon," said Rutigliano, who, as a high school coach in New York, used to get the notes from Brown's coaching clinics in Massillon from another coach because he couldn't afford to attend. "You look at what he accomplished at Massillon High School, then at Ohio State, then with the Cleveland Browns, then the Cincinnati Bengals. Paul Brown changed the face of the NFL.

"I grew up in the same (Brooklyn) neighborhood as (former Penn State coach) Joe Paterno and (former Packers coach) Vince Lombardi. Those guys were great. But nobody is Paul Brown."

Massillon, of course, had plenty of success after Brown, winning 15 more state titles and five more national titles between 1940-1970. But while the Tigers have had famous coaches since then—Chuck Mather (who later coached at Kansas), Lee Tressel (whose son, Jim, won national titles at Youngstown State and OSU), Earle Bruce (who later coached at OSU) and Bob Commings (who went direct to Iowa from Tigertown) to name four—none of them looms as large as Brown, literally (his face is atop the scoreboard in the high school stadium that bears his name) or figuratively.

"It's humbling to know that maybe the greatest football mind ever, maybe the person who's done the most for the game of football ever, was the coach here, played here and this was his home," said Massillon coach Nate Moore, who went 4-6 in his first season coaching the Tigers after winning a state title at Cincinnati La Salle in 2014. "When you look back at everything that's happened since he left, all the success through the '50s, '60s and '70s, you can't talk about it and not think about Paul Brown.

"I look at it as an honor and a duty to add to the tradition that he started here."

Brown died Aug. 5, 1991, at age 82. He has been in the Pro Football Hall of Fame since 1967. His name has adorned the Cincinnati Bengals stadium since 2000. Massillon unveiled a statue of Brown outside its stadium in 2012 and there has been talk of adding a Brown statue outside of Cleveland's FirstEnergy Stadium.

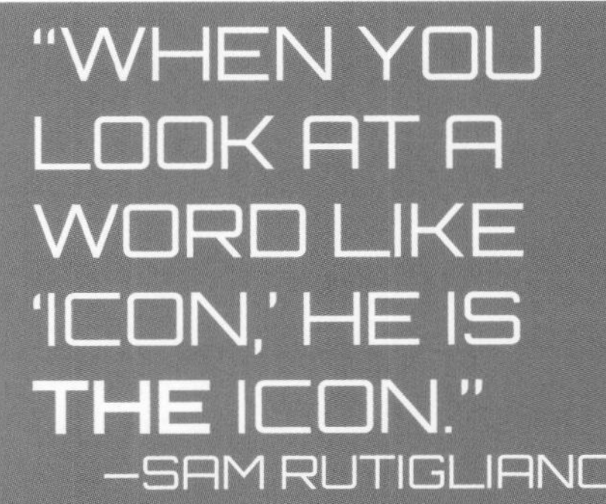
"WHEN YOU LOOK AT A WORD LIKE 'ICON,' HE IS THE ICON."
—SAM RUTIGLIANO

If you formed a "Mount Rushmore" of NFL coaches, Brown would be on it.

"Check the record. Then you tell me who's the greatest coach of all time," said former Bengals receiver Cris Collinsworth, speaking in the NFL Network documentary. "I don't think we'll see anybody have that great an impact. They're not 'The Green Bay Lombardis,' as great as he (Lombardi) was."

Of course, considering the Browns' record since returning to the NFL in 1999, maybe Brown would rather they were named something else.

Since 1999, the Browns have had eight permanent head coaches. From 1946-1995, the Browns had eight permanent head coaches. Rutigliano was the fifth. Quite a change for a franchise Rutigliano liked to call "the flagship of the fleet."

"When I got fired, Paul Brown called me and said, 'Art (Modell) said the same thing to you that he said to me,' " said Rutigliano, who is best known for leading the "Kardiac Kids" to the AFC Central title in 1980. "I said, 'You've got to be kidding me.' Can you imagine comparing himself to me?"

Then, with a laugh, Rutigliano added, "I love talking about Paul Brown. I could talk to you all night." *—JOE SCALZO*

FRANKLIN PAVED WAY FOR FUTURE BLACK QBs

A BLACK QUARTERBACK HAS STARTED EACH OF THE LAST FOUR SUPER BOWLS. THE REIGNING NFL MVP, CAM NEWTON, IS A BLACK QUARTERBACK. OHIO STATE HAS STARTED A BLACK QUARTERBACK EVERY SEASON SINCE 2007. MICHIGAN STARTED A BLACK QUARTERBACK EVERY YEAR FROM 2010 TO '14.

In 2016, that's no longer a big deal. And former Massillon Tiger star Dennis Franklin, who became Michigan's first black quarterback in 1970, feels he's one of the reasons it's no longer a big deal.

"It's much easier to break down barriers in sports than in real life," said Franklin, who spoke recently by phone from California. "In sports, people get along and play for a common goal. It's harder in real life when you don't have that common goal in front of you.

"I think I was absolutely one of those guys that paid his dues so the Russell Wilsons ... of the world could get a chance."

Franklin's race wasn't a big deal at Massillon. He grew up watching another black quarterback, Dave Sheegog, play for the Tigers, and the Massillon coaches were familiar with his talent, considering his older brothers, Walter and Ed, both won state titles there (albeit at different positions).

His senior year, Franklin quarterbacked one of the best teams in school history, piling up more than 1,000 yards rushing and passing as the Tigers outscored opponents 412-29. That 1970 team coached by Bob Commings featured eight Division I recruits.

"That season was pretty cool," he said. "I remember the camaraderie, how well we got along as teammates and how easy it was for us to work together for one common goal. We used to have our own practice sessions and we'd get together and run plays, which was highly unusual in those days. We'd call a few guys, get together and practice and inspire each other. It was fun."

Franklin then headed to Michigan to play for legendary coach Bo Schembechler. As the Wolverines' starting quarterback from 1972 to '74, he went 30-2-1, sharing the Big Ten title with Ohio State all three years. He might have started a year earlier, but the NCAA didn't allow freshmen to play until 1972.

"Not only that, but I had separated my shoulder in an all-star game, so when I got to practice in August, I was injured and had to catch up," he said. "But I eventually beat out the same guys as a sophomore that I was competing against as a freshman, so that tells me I could have beat them out a year earlier."

As a senior in 1974, he earned first team All-Big Ten honors and finished sixth in the Heisman Trophy voting. He was then drafted by the Detroit Lions as a wide receiver in the sixth round of the 1975 draft and appeared in nine games over two seasons, catching six passes for 125 yards. When asked if he misses football, he said, "I miss the competition and the thrill of it all, and I certainly would have liked to make some of that money they're making now."

After retiring, Franklin went to work for King World Productions, which developed TV shows such as "Wheel of Fortune" and Jeopardy!" It allowed him to fly around the world on private planes and attend parties that featured Elton John.

> "ALL I ASK FOR IN LIFE IS A CHANCE. IF I BLOW THAT CHANCE, IT WON'T BE BECAUSE SOMEBODY WAS HOLDING ME BACK OR DIDN'T LIKE WHAT I LOOKED LIKE."
> —DENNIS FRANKLIN

"I can't tell you how exciting and how much fun it was," said Franklin, who now sells real estate in Santa Monica, California. "Again, I think I was a trailblazer in that there weren't a lot of black guys doing what I was doing. But at the same time, people really believed in me and supported me and gave me an opportunity.

"All I ask for in life is a chance. If I blow that chance, it won't be because somebody was holding me back or didn't like what I looked like. Once I got that opportunity, I took advantage of it. I did my job."

— JOE SCALZO

MASSILLON TOP TEN ICONS

1 **PAUL BROWN** Went 15-3 as the Tigers' starting quarterback in 1924-25. Was hired as the team's head coach as a 24-year-old in 1932 and finished 80-8-2 with a 35-game winning streak. Won six state titles and three national titles before being hired at Ohio State, where he won the 1942 national title. Best known for his Hall of Fame coaching career with the Cleveland Browns. Also the founder of the Cincinnati Bengals.

CHRIS SPIELMAN Gained national fame as a high school senior when he became the first high school athlete featured on the cover of Wheaties. Named a USA Today high school All-American. Was a two-time All-American with Ohio State and was inducted in the College Football Hall of Fame in 2009. Made four Pro Bowls with the Detroit Lions from 1988 to '95.

JIM HOUSTON Played end on Massillon's 1953 and 1954 state title teams. Three-year starter at Ohio State and two-time All-American, winning a national title in 1957 and making the College Football Hall of Fame in 2006. Made four Pro Bowls with the Browns from 1960 to '72, winning the 1964 NFL title.

HARRY STUHLDREHER Played quarterback from 1916 to '19 at Massillon, going 8-1 as a senior. Best known as one of Notre Dame's "Four Horsemen," Stuhldreher was a three-time All-American quarterback for the Irish. Coached collegiately at Villanova and Wisconsin. Inducted into the College Football Hall of Fame in 1958.

TOMMY JAMES Played quarterback and halfback for the Tigers from 1938 to '40, going 30-0 with three straight state titles. Helped OSU win the 1942 national title. Played 10 seasons with the Lions (1947), Browns (1948-55) and Colts (1956), winning two AAFC titles and three NFL titles. Made the Pro Bowl in 1953.

DON JAMES Quarterbacked the Tigers from 1947 to '49, winning state titles as a junior and a senior. Set five passing records over a three-year career at Miami (Florida). Was the head coach at Kent State (1971-74) and Washington (1975-92), sharing the 1991 national title with Miami (Florida). Inducted into the College Football Hall of Fame in 1997.

7 **MIKE HERSHBERGER** A two-sport standout for the Tigers, he earned a football scholarship with Cincinnati before signing with the White Sox. Played 11 seasons in the Major Leagues as an outfielder for the Chicago White Sox (1961-64, 1971), Kansas City/Oakland Athletics (1965-69) and Milwaukee Brewers (1970). Batted .252 with 26 homers for his career.

DENNIS FRANKLIN Quarterbacked Massillon's 1970 football team to the state title. Became the first black quarterback to start at Michigan, compiling a 30-2-1 record from 1972-74. Finished sixth in the Heisman voting as a senior. Played briefly as a wide receiver with the Detroit Lions.

CARL "DUCKY" SCHROEDER A Massillon graduate, he taught and coached at his alma mater from 1948-71, helping the Tigers' baseball team make the state finals in 1955 and state semifinals in 1960. Also an assistant football coach, helping Massillon win 13 state championships in 23 years. The school's baseball field bears his name.

10

DEVIN SMITH Was a two-time All-Ohio wideout at Massillon, finishing his career ranked second all-time in receiving yards, receptions and receiving TDs. Won three state track titles and holds Stark County records in the 100 and the long jump. Had a standout career as a wide receiver at Ohio State, helping the Buckeyes win the national title in 2015. Drafted in the second round by the New York Jets last June.

HONORABLE MENTIONS

KELLY BODIFORD
DAVID GRIM
HORACE GILLOM
TOM HANNON
LIN HOUSTON
JIM LETCAVITS
STEVE LUKE
JOHN MCVAY
JOE SPARMA
RICK SPIELMAN
STEVE STUDER
BOB VOGEL

MOTLEY GOES FROM RECORD-SETTING BULLDOG RUNNER TO PRO FOOTBALL PIONEER

OLD BLACK-AND-WHITE HIGHLIGHTS OF HIS GREATEST RUNS—ARGUABLY SOME OF THE GREATEST IN FOOTBALL HISTORY—SERVE AS AN INTRODUCTION OF MARION MOTLEY TO MOST FOOTBALL FANS.

And it's quite an introduction.

The games might not have been televised in hi-def but the man with the football still jumps off the screen.

"He looked bigger than anyone else on the field, bigger than any of the linemen," Packers Hall of Fame linebacker Dave Robinson recently told The Repository. "It was hard to find a 240-pound guard (in those days) let alone a fullback that big. And he was tall."

No facemask. A lineman's number across his chest. Bodies careening off his imposing 6-foot-1, 240-pound figure as he runs the football with stunning power.

Seventy years later, put a young Motley onto a football field against any defense and he still would be equally imposing and exciting. Imagine the fun all of the sports highlight shows would have describing his runs.

Robinson chuckles when asked about watching old films of Motley "running with his helmet off." But Robinson also is quick to point out there was much more to Motley than those grainy clips or the old photos capturing him in a classic football pose.

In fact, to Robinson, they really tell so little about Motley, who died in 1999 at age 79.

"He was a fascinating man," Robinson said.

Motley—nearly a decade after first dazzling football fans as a McKinley Bulldog at a then-new Fawcett Stadium—was one of pro football's pioneers in breaking racial barriers. He was one of the first African-Americans to play pro football during the game's modern era, joining Browns teammate Bill Willis in the AAFC and Kenny Washington and Woody Strode of the NFL's Los Angeles Rams.

That was in 1946. Jackie Robinson broke Major League Baseball's color barrier several months later with the Brooklyn Dodgers in 1947. That date, April 15, is now circled on the MLB calendar each season.

No such celebration exists for Sept. 6, 1946. That's the date

Motley and Willis first played for Cleveland in the All-American Football Conference, which the Browns dominated in its four years of existence before they and several other teams from it were absorbed by the NFL.

Talk of Motley, or the others, being racial pioneers did not dominate their careers. It was not mentioned in 1968 when Motley was enshrined into the Pro Football Hall of Fame in his hometown. Willis, his presenter, did call Motley "the greatest all-around player in professional history."

Motley ran for 4,720 yards and 31 touchdowns during his pro career, which consisted of 106 games—including 99 with the Browns. He never averaged more than 11.7 carries per game in a season. So he made the most of his touches, averaging 5.7 yards per carry for his career.

Motley led the AAFC in rushing in 1948 (964 yards) and then led the NFL in rushing in 1950 (810 yards) during the Browns' first season in the league, which ended in a title. He was at his best in Cleveland's four AAFC title games, averaging 113.3 yards per game in the four wins by the Browns.

His numbers hold up well in the McKinley record book, too, where marks of 264 yards in a game, 1,228 yards in a season and 2,178 for a career still rank among the all-time leaders. His 17.2 yards per carry for his career doesn't seem possible, to which late McKinley football historian Charlie Bowersox used to say, "Well, you never saw him play."

Robinson never got to see Motley play in person. He wishes he had. But he wouldn't trade what he did get to experience—getting to

know Motley in person.

"He and Jackie Robinson were two of my heroes as a young kid," Robinson said. "I was in awe the first time I met him. When I was a little boy, growing up in New Jersey in the African-American community, you had to be a Brooklyn Dodgers fan and a Cleveland Browns fan because of Jackie and Marion."

Once he evolved from a fan to a friend, Dave Robinson learned plenty from Motley.

"The stories he could tell all the old-timers," Robinson said. "He told me the way it happened and gave insight of what it was like in the early days."

Robinson's own playing days in the NFL were from 1963-74, as he spent the first 10 years in Green Bay before two final years in Washington. He dealt with plenty of racism, and that was nearly 20 years after Motley started his career.

"The Civil Rights Act was signed in '64 and it didn't take effect until '68. So it wasn't like you could do things like just go rent an apartment ... and that was anywhere in the country, not just the South, where people said, 'We don't rent to you,'" Robinson said of his own experiences. "I've got a son who's 52 and lot of young people I talk to don't seem to understand what the older guys in those times went through, what even we went through."

Robinson learned Motley "got in situations where he had to bite his tongue."

"He'd know when it was a lose-lose situation, where you'd bite your tongue and take it."

Robinson would have loved having Motley as a mentor during his own career.

"I managed the situation myself, but it would've been nice to have someone to talk to then that had done it before," Robinson said.

Motley kept a sense of humor about it in some of the stories he told.

Robinson remembers one well because Motley loved to tell it. It was a game early in his career where a racist opponent kept heaping abusive language on Motley and took cheap shots at him. Motley kept his cool, so much so the other guy finally lost his.

"Marion says the guy hauls off and hits him right in the mouth. The flag comes in. Marion said 'finally.'"

Then came Motley's punchline: "It's on you for fighting," the ref tells him.

Robinson laughs at the memory of Motley sharing that story.

"Don't know if it's true or not, but he told it a thousand times," Robinson said.

Robinson and Motley spent a lot of time together at various charity golf events. Motley generally absorbed his own expenses because he felt it was the right thing to do and because he had an obligation to give back. They would drive together as far as Chicago or State College, Pa. (Robinson starred in college at Penn State.)

"And every year at the Hall of Fame, he served a barbecue at his house," Robinson said.

Regardless of the setting, the stories flowed.

Robinson learned how Motley and Otto Graham developed the first screen pass together.

When Robinson told Motley about things Vince Lombardi did as a coach, Motley often used a familiar refrain: "He got that from Paul Brown; he got that from Paul Brown."

Coaching full-time at the pro level is the one accomplishment that eluded Motley in his life. Robinson knows that hurt Motley.

"In my mind, he never forgave the Browns for not making him a coach," Robinson said. "For some reason they thought it wasn't a very popular thing to do to have an African-American coach in those days. That bothered him you could tell when he talked about it. ... He was very disappointed.

"I think he would've been very good, just the way he was and the different things he knew and things he said. He could've been a very good coach."

To most, Motley kept any frustrations or disappointments internal. In an interview with The Repository a year before his death, Motley was content with his place in history.

"I can understand why Jackie got all the publicity, and why Larry Doby got it with the Indians," he said in August 1998. "Baseball was the darling of all sports back then. It never really bothered me that I never got the same publicity. I used to talk to Jackie once in a while. We all knew what Bill and I did."

—CHRIS BEAVEN

REARICK HELPED SET WINNING STANDARD IN TWO SPORTS

CONSIDERING McKINLEY HIGH SCHOOL HAS A SPORTS TRADITION STRETCHING BACK MORE THAN 100 YEARS, AN INCLUSIVE ATHLETIC ICON LIST LIMITED TO ONLY 10 IS IMPOSSIBLE. SELECTING EVEN JUST 10 COACHES COULDN'T BE DONE WITHOUT LEAVING OFF WORTHY MEN AND WOMEN WHO MOLDED MCKINLEY'S ATHLETIC PROGRAMS SINCE THE END OF THE 19TH CENTURY.

One McKinley coach, though, managed to do a double duty few could have imagined much less performed successfully to earn his way onto any icon list.

LEGENDARY MCKINLEY HIGH SCHOOL FOOTBALL AND BASKETBALL COACH HERMAN "BUP" REARICK (MIDDLE) POSES FOR AN UNDATED PHOTO WITH JIM THORPE (LEFT) AND PETE CALAC.

Herman "Bup" Rearick won two state titles during an eight-year run as McKinley's head football coach, while also serving as the boys basketball head coach and guiding the Bulldogs to two state tournaments in that same eight-year window—part of his longer tenure as the basketball coach.

Along the way, he also helped provide the Bulldogs with their iconic nickname, the Pups, shortened from its original form ... "Bup's Pups."

His teams, though, were anything but Pups. There was plenty of bite to them, and he made sure of it.

"It's not the size of the dog in the fight, it's the size of the fight in the dog," he liked to say.

Rearick spent the bulk of his McKinley coaching career as the head basketball coach. He manned that post from 1938-49 and from 1953-61. His teams compiled a record of 253-66. Six times they went to the state tournament, finishing as the state runner-up in the big-school division in 1940, 1943 and 1956 (losing to the legendary Jerry Lucas and Middletown).

His eight-year run as head football coach produced a record of 67-8-6, with the two state titles. The first title came in 1942, his first season, when the Bulldogs capped their year by snapping Massillon's streak of 52 games without a loss, the longest in the nation at the time. It was also McKinley's first win over Massillon since 1934.

Rearick got a memorable ride off the field at Massillon following that game on Nov. 21, 1942. He was carried away on the shoulders of his players and fans. His football Bulldogs won another state title in 1944.

Throw in his time coaching football and basketball at Dover in the 1930s, and he put together a high school record of 619-149-10.

At McKinley, he set a coaching standard for all who followed him in both sports—icons to many, such as Bob Rupert, Ken Newlon, Mike Riley, Dave Cady and Dave Hoover in basketball, and Wade Watts, Don Nehlen, Ron Chismar, John Brideweser, Terry Forbes and Thom McDaniels in football.

He also coached a roll call of McKinley greats between the two sports: Joe Bandy, John Colceri, Jack Crider, Wendell Earley, Dale Haverstock, Ray Hamilton, Herm Jackson, Charley Jones, Dick Kempthorn, Elijah Lipkins, Lou Mariano, Jim Mathews, Sam Parks, Ralph Pucci, Joe Pujazon, Hank Smith and Perry Thompson.

The admiration of those who played for him continued long after their days on the basketball court or football field. It lasted into the 2000s with the former "Bup's Pups" still coming together for reunions of the "Rearick Men." —*CHRIS BEAVEN*

McKINLEY TOP TEN ICONS

1

MARION MOTLEY Before he was a pro football pioneer with the Cleveland Browns—one of four men to break pro football's color barrier in 1946 and regarded as one of the finest all-around players ever on his way to the Pro Football Hall of Fame in the Class of 1968—he was star for the Bulldogs in the 1930s.

>>> 5

GARY GRANT Led McKinley to an elusive first state basketball title in 1984 as a dynamic point guard. "The General" went on to set assist and steals records at Michigan where he was selected the Big Ten Player of the Year in 1988. And he played 13 seasons in the NBA.

6

HERMAN "BUP" REARICK Legendary football and boys basketball coach at McKinley, coaching both sports during one eight-season stretch. His football teams won two state titles in that period, while the basketball team reached two state tournaments. Overall, he was 67-8-6 as the football coach from 1942-49 and 253-66 as the basketball coach from 1938-49 and 1953-61. Guided basketball team to six state tournaments in all, with three state runner-up finishes.

^^^ 2

NICK WEATHERSPOON Smooth, high-scoring forward set the standard for basketball in the area in the 1960s, leading Bulldogs to a state tournament and setting scoring records. Earned All-American honors at Illinois, where his number is retired, and played seven seasons in the NBA.

7

ERIC SNOW Following in the footsteps of his football star older brother Percy, Eric chose a different athletic path and became an All-Ohio guard in basketball for the Bulldogs, helping them reach a state final four his junior year. He later was Big Ten Defensive Player of the Year at Michigan State before playing in the NBA Finals three times in his 13-year pro career. He also was honored off the floor in the NBA for his community work, which extends to his hometown and the 2014 opening of the Eric Snow YMCA in downtown.

<<< 3

PHIL HUBBARD By the time he was 20, he had won an Olympic gold medal and played in an NCAA Final Four at Michigan. At McKinley, he was a sensational scorer and rebounder. Enjoyed a 10-year NBA career, most of it with the Cavs.

<<< 8

AMERYST ALSTON Rewrote McKinley and Stark County scoring records (2,032 points), won a state title and was a two-time Ohio Ms. Basketball winner. Followed that up by being a four-year star at Ohio State, becoming the sixth Buckeye to score 2,000 career points and the first Stark County woman drafted by the WNBA.

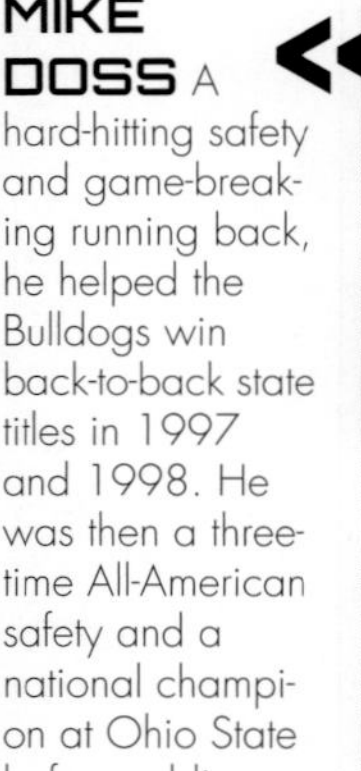

<<< 4

MIKE DOSS A hard-hitting safety and game-breaking running back, he helped the Bulldogs win back-to-back state titles in 1997 and 1998. He was then a three-time All-American safety and a national champion at Ohio State before adding a Super Bowl ring with the Colts.

9

RAYMAR MORGAN Set school's career scoring record (1,553 points) in earning Parade All-American honors and leading Bulldogs to back-to-back state titles in 2005 and 2006. Later started in two Final Fours at Michigan State and spent six seasons playing overseas.

>>> 10

MARTY MULL Starred in the pool under legendary coach Ted Branin, leading the Bulldogs to four straight state titles (1957-60) in a stretch where they won six in a row. He set national records and at one time was regarded as the world's fastest swimmer. He later two won NCAA titles in the 200 IM at Ohio State, helped the Buckeyes win a team title and is a member of the Varsity "O" Hall of Fame.

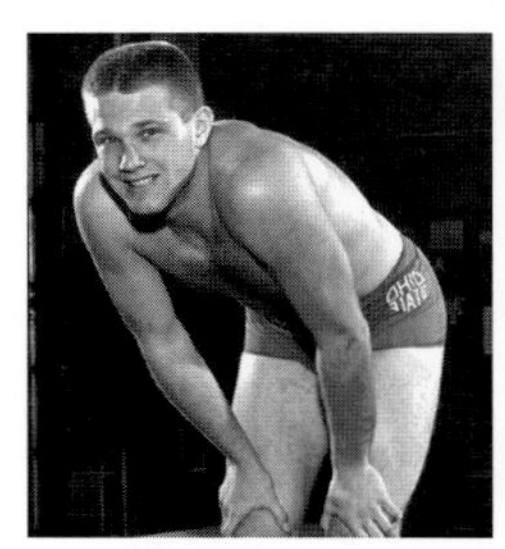

HONORABLE MENTIONS

TED BRANIN
RYAN BRINSON
SUE DAVIS
WAYNE FONTES
RONNIE HARRIS
JOHN GRIMSLEY
ROCH HONTAS
DAVE HOOVER
DICK KEMPTHORN
JOSH MCDANIELS
THOM MCDANIELS
DON SCOTT
PERCY SNOW
HARRY STEEL
RONNIE STOKES
TROY TAYLOR

'PRICELESS' EXPERIENCES

THE BIG 33 ALL-STAR FOOTBALL GAME. THE NAME SPEAKS VOLUMES TO OHIO AND PENNSYLVANIA HIGH SCHOOL FOOTBALL PLAYERS.

"The biggest thrill you can have coming out of Pennsylvania and Ohio is being named to that game," Pro Football Hall of Famer Joe Montana told ESPN's E:60 six years ago.

Well, Minerva High's Roger Bettis started the Big 33 at quarterback in 1974. Against Joe Montana. Bettis and Ohio lost a hard-fought 14-6 game to Pennsylvania and Super Joe.

"Big crowd back then at Hershey Park," Bettis recalled. "I have no clue (how I did). And I did not outplay Joe Montana, not in my dreams. I just remember he had really quick feet and the ability to always get out of harm's way.

"He was a winner." Oddly enough, the Big 33 was the last varsity football game Roger Bettis ever started. That didn't prevent Bettis from becoming a different type of legend of the game.

In his senior season of 1973, he quarterbacked Minerva to 509 points and the highest-scoring 10 regular-season games in Stark County history to this day. He was the first Lion to throw for more than 1,000 yards in a season.

"You could holler at him and he would say, 'Yes, sir' or 'No, sir,' " Minerva head coach Tom Walters said. "I believed in him so much."

Bettis then went to Ann Arbor to play for legendary Michigan coach Bo Schembechler. And he did start for the undefeated Michigan freshman team that beat Montana's Notre Dame team that fall, only to play backup quarterback to Rick Leach for the next three seasons.

"When I went for my visit to Michigan, Bo told me, 'I want you to know I might bring in seven quarterbacks,' " Bettis said. "I told him, 'I don't care, I'm coming.' Well, I was the only one of the seven (he was looking at) that came. But the next year he did bring in seven, including Rick Leach."

The Wolverines were a combined 38-4-2 in his four seasons under Schembechler. Michigan was ranked No. 1 his senior season and his teams played in two Rose Bowls and an Orange Bowl, the latter against Oklahoma to decide the national championship.

Bettis came out of Michigan, worked a year for Ford and then launched his own trucking business, Green Lines Transportation in Malvern.

Along the way he became treasurer of the Pro Football Hall of Fame's board of trustees, where he has served for two decades and met countless Hall of Famers.

So don't feel bad for Bettis. He considers himself the luckiest man in the world—even after getting Wally Pipped by Leach, who is still a close friend.

"I was recently asked to write a letter of recommendation to the College Football Hall of Fame (concerning Leach's credentials)," said Bettis, now 60. "Here is a trivia question for you: What college quarterback won the most games?" Peyton Manning, 39. Rick Leach won 38."

Bettis said playing at Michigan and backing up Leach proved to be integral to his post-college professional life.

"My experiences there were great," he said. "I can't put a value on how important football has been in my life. The disciplines that you practice as an athlete carry over ... the networking opportunities that you come across, some of them you never come across again. But some they just come about and you have to be ready to take advantage.

"It's like a backup quarterback, you have to be ready to step in. Because I was an athlete, I believed it's helped me become a pretty good leader. Playing in front of 100,000 people helps you (mature), too."

Before Michigan and Bo, there was Minerva and Walters for Bettis.

Walters was a titan of the times. He already had built a 10-0 team in 1969 before Bettis came on in 1971 as a sophomore.

"One thing about Tom Walters—he could humble you in a second," Bettis said of his coach, who went 79-19-2 in 10 years at Minerva.

"Not two seconds, one second."

Running the veer offense in the 1970s was a dream role for a mobile, quick-thinking quarterback like Bettis, a hurdler/440 man in track and a quick forward on the hardwood. On the Stark County landscape, no team ran the veer better than Minerva and Bettis. With Bettis at the helm, the Lions put up points at a historic pace in 1973. Minerva started with a 48-8 win over Central Hower and beat East Canton 48-8 in Week 9. In between they buried foes, including powerful Lake by a 69-0 score in a landslide of seven straight shutout victories for a 9-0 start.

"Lake had beaten us the year before in '72," Bettis said. "That was back when if you won the region, you got to go to state. They finished second.

"We thought we were better than them, and we wanted to show it."

Bettis and John Hahn, a third team All-Ohio guard who went on to win a state wrestling title in the winter, were the team's captains as seniors. Junior running back Jamie Morckel led the county in scoring with 183 points, while Len Phillips was a first team All-Ohio defensive end. They had everything but a win in their swan song.

"We lost our final game to Louisville, in a snowstorm," Bettis said of the 29-8 Week 10 defeat. "And we didn't qualify for the playoffs."

Soon thereafter the endless adventures began. Jeremy Hanlon, a former Central Catholic assistant to John McVay, was a Michigan offensive line coach who recruited Bettis. On his visit to Ann Arbor, he met Don Dufek Jr., who was playing on the Michigan hockey team in addition to the gridiron. Dufek was great in both, drafted for both sports and spent eight seasons with the NFL's Seahawks.

"I didn't know anything about hockey," said Bettis. "Michigan and Michigan State were playing a home-and-away. Dufek got his teeth knocked out at Michigan State (on Friday); I met him Saturday and Bo was humiliating the poor guy, who couldn't talk. I went with him and I got to sit on the end of the bench with the hockey guys."

If it wasn't hockey, it was hoops. "Phil Hubbard lived across the hall from me in the dorm," Bettis said about the former McKinley and Michigan basketball great. Some 21 members of the 1976 team alone went on to play in the NFL. Always different, Leach played 10 years in Major League Baseball, ironically mostly as a backup.

There were the coaches, too.

"I played under great coaches," Bettis said of his Michigan days. "Don Nehlen was the quarterbacks coach. He's a legend. Bo. Gary Moeller was the defensive coach. Jack Harbaugh was the defensive line coach, when Jim and John (Harbaugh) were about 10, 11."

Bettis has literally and figuratively treasured his time with the Pro Football Hall of Fame. His first year giving a report as treasurer conjured up a major case of nerves.

"I'm not a CPA, though I am pretty good at reading a spreadsheet and financial reports," he said. "But the first year I gave a report at the annual meeting, I was sitting next to (Kansas City Chiefs owner) Lamar Hunt. I thought my heart was going to come out of my chest! It must have come out all right, because Lamar gave me a hug afterward."

Everything has worked out just fine for Bettis.

"I always thought I got as much out of (Michigan) as anyone who is in the record books," he said. "Records are made to be broken. What I have is priceless."

—JIM THOMAS

DECADE OF DOMINANCE

MINERVA HIGH SCHOOL HAD NEVER WON A FOOTBALL LEAGUE CHAMPIONSHIP WHEN TOM WALTERS ARRIVED IN 1965 TO COACH THE TEAM. BY THE TIME HE LEFT COACHING AFTER 10 YEARS TO BECOME THE SCHOOL'S ASSISTANT SUPERINTENDENT, THE LIONS HAD SEVEN SHINY TROPHIES TO BEHOLD.

The secret, he said, was start with youth.

"We started with nothing," Walters said by phone from Florida on a sunny March afternoon. "We had to build a program. We put a program in place that started with players in the seventh grade. So they played in the seventh, eighth and ninth grades before finally getting to the varsity.

"The idea was when you were a senior and we were calling '54' that you could run that play without thinking."

Walters also played into the community. He was a McKinley graduate who knew what a winning football team meant to the town.

"On game days, we wore read blazers and red ties," said Walters. "We did a town walk (to the game). I had a firm belief in getting everyone involved.

"We had Mothers Club, and the moms prepared meals on Friday nights. Then you had the moms, dads everyone at the game—you had better play pretty darn hard for them."

Either the Minerva kids were quick learners eager to please their coach and community or Walters was a gifted teacher—and most likely it was a combination of both.

Minerva was a winner almost immediately. In his second year, the Lions went 7-3; the third, they took home the Tri-County League title.

"We'd never won one," said Walters. "Then we won four in a row. They didn't invite us back in. They had already started the Senate League. I remember The Canton Repository was saying we weren't going to win. They picked us for seventh.

"We were undefeated and won every Senate League game."

Walters' boys didn't lose many games in either league in his tenure. In his 10 seasons as head coach, Minerva went 79-19-2 and claimed seven league championships. The highlights were the 10-0 1969 squad and the 1973 and 1974 teams that each went 9-1.The 1969 team outscored its foes 304-14. By far, the highlight was an 18-6 Week 10 triumph over Louisville.

"I told those kids that if we won I'd walk down the streets of Louisville barefooted," Walters said. "Well, we won the game, and on the way back, we're in town and the bus stopped. I said 'What's going on?' The kids remembered.

"I took my shoes off, and I walked down the street. I did. I had to."

The 1973 team was nearly as good. Walters just didn't get the chance to make a return walk through Louisville. Minerva won its first nine games by stunning scores on its way to piling up 509 points in the season. It is a Stark County record that still stands 42 years later.

It could not beat the Leopards, though. The Lions were whipped 29-8 in a snowstorm to end their perfect season and playoff bid.

"I remember a guy died, maybe before the game. I was talking to (Louisville head coach) Paul Starkey and he said, 'Something happened.' It was 20 degrees and I said, 'I don't want to be here.' He said, 'I don't want to be here, either.'

"Paul and I had some great battles."

There was really only one battle Walters could not win. The Board of Education came to him and asked him to be director of curriculum and assistant superintendent.

"It came out of nowhere," said Walters. "Teachers didn't make a lot of money. I had a daughter ready to go to college. I couldn't turn it down."

He was more than just football, too. Walters started the wrestling team. By 1974, he had a state champion in John Hahn, who was an All-Ohio guard on the '73 football team.

After Walters retired as superintendent, he moved to Kentucky and taught and coached for five more years. But his heart was in Minerva.

"I can't tell you how much fun we had," said Walters. "The biggest compliments I ever got came from the kids: 'Coach, how I can't tell you how much fun it was.'

"They were just great kids. It was a great town." *—JIM THOMAS*

MINERVA TOP TEN ICONS

1 **ROGER BETTIS** Quarterbacked Minerva to a 9-1 mark and the highest-scoring regular-season point total (509) as a senior in 1973. Was the school's first QB to surpass the 1,000-yard passing plateau with 1,240 in '73. Played at the University of Michigan for four years. Is the treasurer for the Pro Football Hall of Fame's board of directors.

>>> 2 **OSCAR GRIMES** After graduating from Minerva in 1938, played nine-plus years with the Cleveland Indians, New York Yankees and the Philadelphia A's right out of high school. The third baseman batted .256 (469-for-1,832) with 200 RBIs and 243 runs scored. In 1946, Grimes played on the Yankees with Joe DiMaggio, Yogi Berra, Massillon native Tommy Henrich, Phil Rizzuto and Bill Dickey under manager Joe McCarthey.

<<< 3 **WILLIAM POWELL** Before he was a pioneer in golf, he starred on the powerhouse 1932 Minerva football team, which was unbeaten and unscored upon. He was team captain in both football and golf. After returning home from World War II and encountering racial discrimination on the golf course, Powell built his own course and opened it to all—establishing Clearview Golf Club in East Canton in 1946 and opening it to the public two years later. The only course designed, built, owned and operated by an African American, Clearview was named a National Historic Site by the U.S. Department of the Interior in 2001.

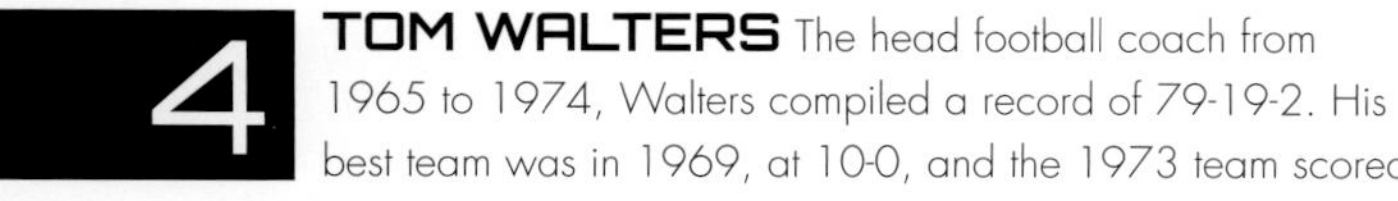

4 **TOM WALTERS** The head football coach from 1965 to 1974, Walters compiled a record of 79-19-2. His best team was in 1969, at 10-0, and the 1973 team scored 509 points, a total that still is the county's highest for 10 games. Walters, who also coached wrestling, was inducted into the Ohio High School Football Coaches Hall of Fame in 1991.

5 **CHRIS HAHN** After finishing sixth at state as a freshman, Hahn won three straight state championships to become the first, with Perry's Steve Luke, to win three times and place in four state meets. Also an all-league football player, Hahn was 24-0 in wrestling as a senior in 2004, had a career mark of 148-11 and set county record for takedowns in a season (259) and career (751).

<<< 6 **LEON POWELL** A running back with power and speed, Powell became the first Stark County player to surpass 2,000 yards rushing in a season, rushing for 2,119 as a junior in 1987 when he was named the Associated Press Running Back of the Year. Powell rushed 4,307 career yards and his 29 touchdowns in '87 are a single-season mark.

7 **LINDSAY SHEARER** Shearer was the NBC Player of the Year in both volleyball and basketball, and an all-leaguer in softball, but she shined brightest on the hardwood. She was first team All-Ohio as a senior in 2002 and finished her career with 1,003 points. Shearer went on to greater heights at Kent State, where she scored 1,799 points, fourth all-time, and was the Mid-American Conference Player of the Year in 2006, when she led the MAC in scoring (20.8).

DALTON HARTSHORN Arguably Minerva's best overall athlete, the 2015 graduate is the wrestling leader in career wins (157) and for a season (46), while setting the rushing yards mark for a game (337) and touchdowns in a career (50) in football. His 1,903 yards in his first team All-Ohio year of 2014 are second only to Powell in school history. He also started four years in baseball.

<<< 8

9 **JEFF WALLACE** Was drafted by the Kansas City Royals in the 25th round right out of high school in 1995. Made his MLB debut in August 1997 with the Pirates and went on to compile a 3-3 record during parts of four seasons and 119 games with a 4.20 ERA for Pittsburgh and Tampa Bay. Wallace was All-NBC in baseball, basketball and football for the Lions.

10 **LYNN MOLEN** The winningest football coach in Minerva history with his 93-30 record spanning two stints and 12 seasons. His Lions were 10-0 in 1987, '88, 89 and 1997. Minerva was the Division II Associated Press state poll champion in '87 and the Division III winner in '97. Molen took them to the state playoffs three times and won four straight league titles at one point, 1986-89.

HONORABLE MENTIONS

JOHN HAHN
GREG KENNEDY
JIM KNUDSEN
KAELE LIGHTFOOT
BRIAN MILLIARD
CHAD NIGRO
CRAIG RODGERS

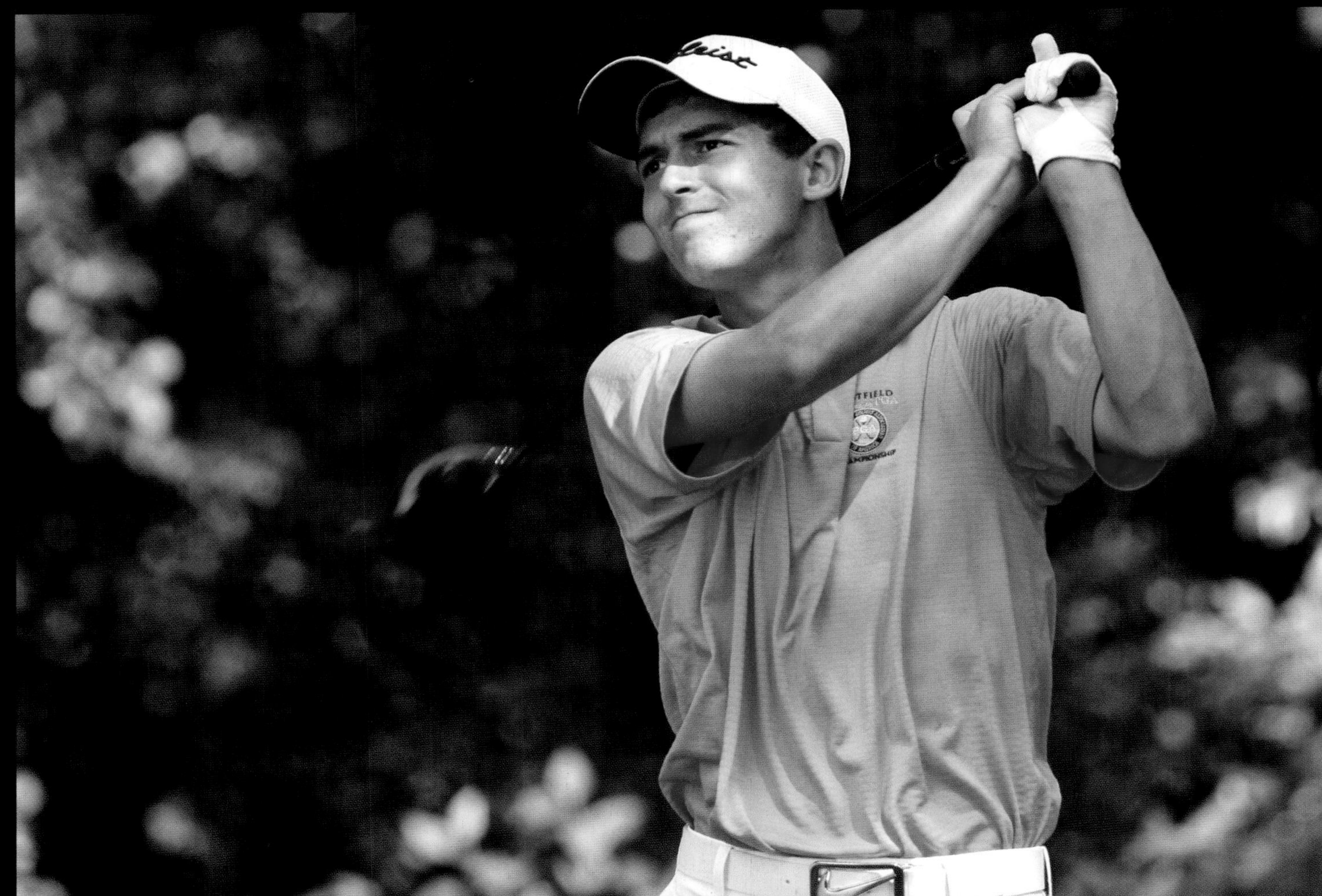

LOWER ACHIEVES EXCELLENCE

FORMER NORTHWEST HIGH SCHOOL GOLFER JUSTIN LOWER CELEBRATES THE 10TH ANNIVERSARY OF HIS DIVISION II STATE CHAMPIONSHIP IN 2016.

"I KNEW IF I COULD GET ON A TEAM, I COULD THRIVE."
—JUSTIN LOWER

He has had quite a journey since then.

Lower won an NAIA national championship at Malone University just over three years later, turned pro and briefly had a taste of life on the PGA Tour. He has been competing on the National Golf Association Pro Golf Tour's Carolina Winter Series, where he won four events and was runner-up twice during a two-month span in 2015.

It's a résumé his father, Tim, and his younger brother, Chris, would be proud of if they were here today.

Lower's father and brother were killed in a single-car crash the year before he won his state title. While he continued to flourish on golf courses, their deaths took a toll on him in school. His grades suffered.

"I didn't have straight A's,

but after that it got really bad," Lower recalled in a 2014 Repository interview. "I remember guidance counselors asking me, 'Justin, what's wrong?' I simply didn't want to be there. I showed up, I took tests, I'd study a little bit, but I just didn't want to do high school any more. I wanted a fresh start and I knew college would give me that start."

It did.

Lower's years at Malone prepared him for life as a pro golfer. He won six events his third season and was named the Jack Nicklaus Player of the Year for the NAIA as a junior.

"I knew if I could get on a team, I could thrive," Lower said.

In 2010, Lower became the second Malone golfer to earn medalist honors at the NAIA tournament. Pioneers head coach Ken Hyland was the first.

"It means a lot more," Lower said then when comparing the two titles he won. "State is just state. It's the furthest you can go in high school. This is as far as I can go in college."

Lower finished third at the national tournament as a senior to become Malone's first four-time NAIA All-American. In addition to winning the Nicklaus Award, he also earned the Arnold Palmer Award for being a medalist at a national championship and the David Toms Award, which goes to the men's golfer on any level who overcomes adversity to achieve excellence. He is the only college player to win all three awards.

Since turning pro in 2011, Lower has competed at different levels.

Lower is a two-time winner at the Ohio Open, the state's biggest non-PGA event. He finished second on the NGA Tour's Pro Series and Carolina Summer Series money lists in 2013. A two-time NGA Tour winner that year, Lower earned an exemption to play in his first PGA event, the Reno-Tahoe Open. He also earned a sponsor's exemption to The Memorial in 2014 and the McGladrey Classic later that year.

In 2014, Lower also played in 13 events on the Web.com Tour, the PGA's developmental tour. He finished in the money in each event and a tour-best ninth-place finish at the BMW Charity Pro-Am.

Lower hopes to earn his PGA Tour card one day and play in the U.S. Open. Barring weather delays, the final round is held on Father's Day. There's no doubt his late father, Tim, would be with him in spirit.

"The U.S. Open would be one of the coolest ones to win," Lower once said. "... For it to be on Father's Day and win that tournament, that would be your storybook ending for me."

—MIKE POPOVICH

CHAMPION COACH

JIM LOWER WENT OUT A CHAMPION 10 YEARS AGO AT NORTHWEST. IT WAS AN APPROPRIATE END FOR ONE OHIO'S MOST SUCCESSFUL BOYS HIGH SCHOOL BASKETBALL COACHES.

Lower won 453 games in 39 seasons, the last 20 with the Indians. His Northwest teams won five Northeastern Buckeye Conference championships, including one in his final season. The Indians finished the regular season 20-0 in 1997-98, won 40 straight regular season games at one point and were Division II state runners-up in 2003-04.

Years earlier, he sometimes learned the hard way what it took to be a success.

Lower began his coaching career at Gnadenhutten High School in the late 1960s and also worked at Western Reserve, Waynedale, Cardington and Garaway. While at Garaway, he coached against another hall of famer, Charlie Huggins.

"A guy like that raises the bar so high," Lower said of Huggins.

Lower's Northwest teams made the district tournament 13 times in 20 years. His 1997-98 team was heartbroken after a first-round loss abruptly ended their perfect season.

The Indians made history and came close to winning it all six years later.

Northwest rallied from a six-point fourth-quarter deficit and beat Orrville to win its first district championship since 1961. For Lower, it was his first trip to the Sweet 16 in 37 years of coaching.

The Indians never slowed down. They beat Warrensville Heights and West Geauga to earn a berth in the state tournament for the first time in program history. A win over Dayton Chaminade Julienne earned them a berth in the Division II state championship game.

Northwest's memorable run ended in disappointment. Ottawa-Glandorf rolled past the Indians 75-42 in the title game.

"It was a shock really," Lower said in 2010. "It's something you look back on and wonder if it really happened. And it happened so fast. It was an unbelievable run.

"It shows what you can do when you have parents, players and coaches all on the same page and pulling in the same direction. We went through some tough times, but we somehow made it through. Kids went at each other. We had tough games, but we kept working our way through it and kept jelling."

Lower coached his five sons—Brian, Steven Mike, Kevin and Jon—during his 20 seasons at Northwest. Two sons followed in their father's footsteps in Stark County.

Mike Lower replaced his father after he retired and recently completed his 10th season as the Indians' head coach. Kevin Lower just wrapped his fifth season as Tuslaw's head coach. It was a memorable year which saw the Mustangs become the first county to finish the regular season 22-0. —*MIKE POPOVICH*

NORTHWEST TOP TEN ICONS

JUSTIN LOWER

Lower became the first Northwest golfer to win an outright state title in 2006 when he won the Division II tournament by three strokes. Four-time All-American at Malone who won the 2010 national championship by six strokes. Turned pro in 2011 and spent time on the NGA Tour and Web.com Tour. Qualified for his first PGA event in 2013 at the Reno-Tahoe Open.

JOE CONCHECK Concheck still holds the team's career scoring record with 1,585 points. Averaged 31.3 points a game and was voted Ohio's Class AA Player of the Year as a senior in 1980-81.

JIM LOWER Lower led the Indians to five Northeastern Buckeye Conference titles, a 20-0 regular season in 1997-98 and a Division II state runner-up finish in 2003-04. Coached for 39 years, including 18 at Northwest. Was inducted into the Ohio High School Basketball Coaches Hall of Fame in 2010.

BRIAN SLATES Slates became Northwest's first state wrestling champion in 1989. Won the Division II state title at 112 pounds. Three-time state qualifier who also finished sixth at 98 pounds as a sophomore and third at 112 as a junior.

SCOTT WEBER

Weber is the Stark County career touchdown leader with 74. Ranks sixth all-time in the county in rushing with 4,891 yards. One of eight running backs in the county to rush for at least 2,000 yards in a season (2,007 in 2004). Helped lead the Indians to their only regional championship in 2004.

6

SHAWN LAZARUS Lazarus earned All-Ohio honors in football, wrestling and track. Played guard, running back, defensive tackle and linebacker on the football team. Went on to play defensive tackle at Michigan for four seasons.

7

ALYSON LINDIC Lindic became Northwest's first state track and field champion in 2012. Cleared 5 feet, 5 inches to win a Division II state title in the high jump. Finished in the top two in the state in her only two seasons as a high school high jumper. Was state runner-up her junior year.

8

KEVIN LOWER Lower was first team All-Ohio guard as a senior. Ranks second behind Joe Concheck on Northwest's career scoring list with 1,172 points. Helped lead the Indians to a 20-0 regular season and a No. 1 ranking in the final Associated Press Division II state poll in 1997-98.

9

RACHEL GREEN Four-year letter winner in basketball and three-year letter winner in volleyball. Finished her basketball career with 958 points, 690 rebounds and 130 assists. Voted Northeastern Buckeye Conference Player of the Year and second team All-Ohio in basketball as a senior when she averaged 16.5 points and 8.1 rebounds.

10

GARY DIAL Longtime Northwest Local Schools coach, teacher and administrator. Compiled a 48-21-1 record in seven seasons as Northwest's head football coach from 1981-83 and 1986-89. Led the Indians to a 9-1 record in 1982, their final season in the Senate League, and a 9-0-1 record in 1983, their first year in the All-Ohio League. Returned to coaching while serving as assistant principal. Coached powerful offensive lines which helped Northwest make a Stark County-record nine straight playoff appearances.

HONORABLE MENTIONS

BRIAN ARMSTRONG
VINCE BAIERA
DAVID HOWARD
KELLI LITTEN
JAMIE NILES
JOHN RAFAILEDES
DAWN REINHARDT

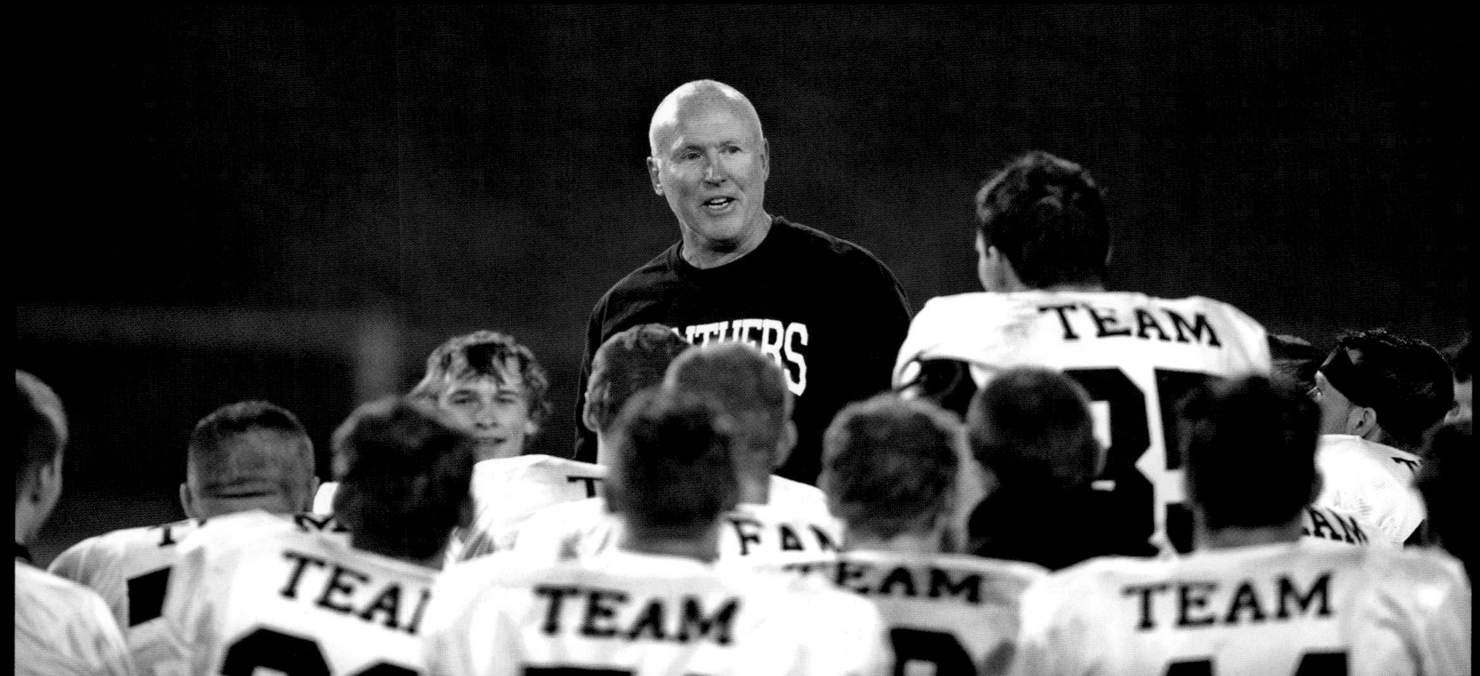

ATTITUDE & EFFORT

THOM MCDANIELS POSTED A PHOTO ON FACEBOOK OF A GROUP OF FRIENDS GATHERED AROUND HIS KITCHEN TABLE IN 1967, HIS SENIOR YEAR AT ORRVILLE HIGH SCHOOL. IN THE LEFT CORNER, WEARING BLACK-RIMMED GLASSES AND A WRY SMILE, IS A KID NAMED KEITH WAKEFIELD.

"Oh, God," Wakefield groaned, when told about the photo. "Thom McDaniels has nothing better to do now than post that stuff, huh?"

Back then, Wakefield was an undersized offensive guard/defensive lineman with a competition addiction, the kind of guy who made up for his small stature with a big heart. The kind of guy who would one day expect his players to do the same.

LONGTIME McKINLEY FOOTBALL COACH THOM McDANIELS POSTED THIS PHOTO ON FACEBOOK SHOWING (FROM LEFT) KEITH WAKEFIELD, TIM MASTRINE, JIM MACRINO, FRED DEHART, TIM MCGUIRE AND DWIGHT BARNETT IN ORRVILLE IN 1967. **COURTESY THOM McDANIELS**

"He was very competitive and he was very committed, whether it was in baseball or football or wrestling," said McDaniels, the longtime McKinley football coach who also had stints with Warren Harding and Jackson. "And he was a tough guy. He was by no means the biggest guard or the biggest defensive lineman, but he played with great effort.

"Much of what you hear Keith espouse today, about the culture he wants to have exist at Perry, that's a culture he was very familiar with early in his life. He was a product of his mom and dad at Orrville High School, and I think he very much reflects that experience he had growing up."

For Wakefield—then and now—success comes down to two things: attitude and effort. Those two qualities are the keys to the Wing-T—an offensive system that already was falling out of favor by 1967 but remains timeless—and the backbone of a program that has won 12 Federal League titles under Wakefield, including in 2015.

The latest championship may have been Wakefield's most impressive since it came two years after the Panthers went winless (in Wakefield's first year back at Perry after an eight-year absence) and was part of a season that saw them advance to the state championship game for the first time in school history.

"When I came back, I didn't know if we could bring it (the program) back," Wakefield said. "If you coach with a tough attitude, a demanding attitude, were the kids going to buy into that? But they did. If you look at the results from three years ago to this past year, they were buying what we were selling."

Part of that comes down to fit. Wakefield believes his old-school style can work with kids anywhere, not just a blue-collar township like Perry.

Parents are a different story.

"Some places just aren't a good fit," said Wakefield, who sometimes butted heads with parents at St. Vincent-St. Mary during his two-year stint from 2004-05. "Perry was a pretty good fit for us. My wife taught in the school system there. My daughter got a good education there. It worked out for us.

"But there's a perception that certain communities have certain kinds of kids, that those kids could never play hard or be tough. And I disagree with that. I don't think that's true at all."

Wakefield went 4-6 in 1982, his first season with the Panthers, then went 2-8. But Perry went 8-2 in his third year, winning its first league title since 1970, and didn't post another losing season until 2004. The Panthers made the playoffs four times during that span (1992, 1999, 2000 and 2002). During his nine-year absence, they made the postseason just once and posted six losing seasons.

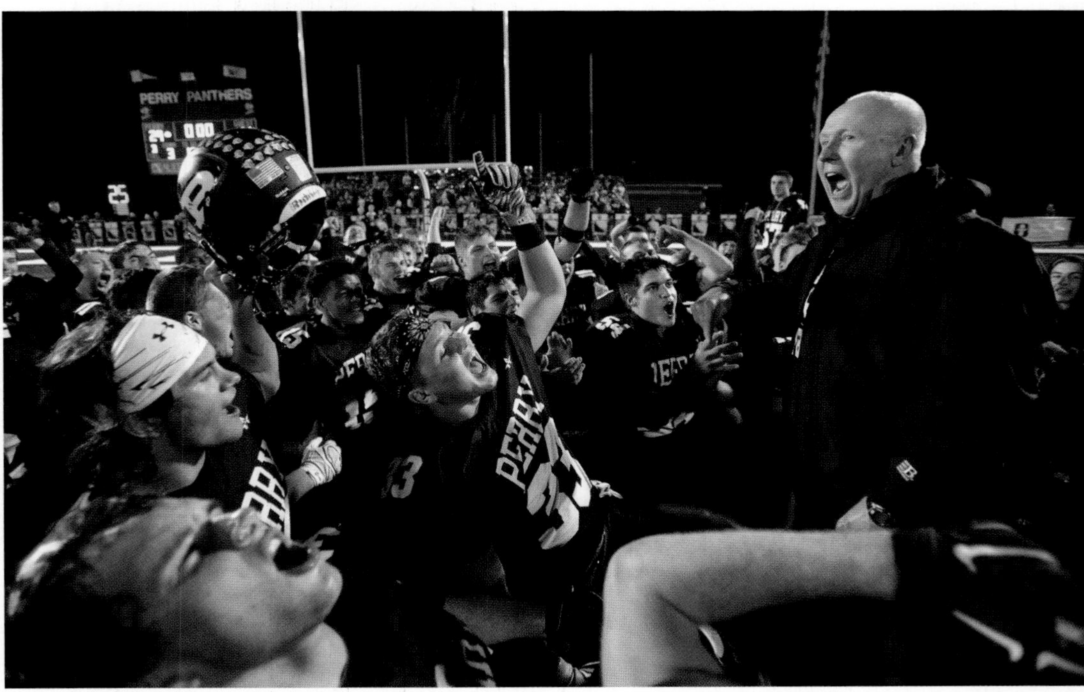

"TO SEE WHAT HAPPENED AFTER COACH WAKEFIELD LEFT—AND I'M NOT DEGRADING ANYONE WHO CAME AFTER HIM—BUT THE FOOTBALL PROGRAM WENT THE OPPOSITE WAY. NOW YOU SEE THE EXCITEMENT IS BACK IN THE SCHOOL DISTRICT, AND HE'S BROUGHT BACK THAT MENTALITY AND THE DISCIPLINE AND THE TOUGHNESS."

—MATT CAMPBELL, IOWA STATE COACH AND FORMER PLAYER

"As a player growing up, I couldn't wait for Friday nights and to be a part of his program," said Iowa State coach Matt Campbell, who played for Wakefield from 1995-97. "To see what happened after Coach Wakefield left—and I'm not degrading anyone who came after him—but the football program went the opposite way. Now you see the excitement is back in the school district, and he's brought back that mentality and the discipline and the toughness."

He's done what he's done with lesser overall talent than some other schools, but with great discipline and effort and attitude. It's really special to see. When I think of Perry High School and Perry football, it's Keith Wakefield."

Wakefield's 175 wins at Perry (against 45 losses) are almost as many as every other coach in school history combined (185). He isn't sure how much longer he will coach, but he doesn't think it will be much longer.

"But I don't really know," he said. "I think, 'What else would I do?' " For now, he's focused on the offseason. Despite the 2015 success, he isn't convinced Perry is all the way back. Sure, the Panthers have made the playoffs each of the last two years, but he can't forget that they went 0-10 in 2013, too.

"Not slighting what we did last year (2015); that was great for the program," he said. "But when we're consistently playing for Federal League championships and have the opportunity to go to the playoffs every year, that's when I'll know we're where we need to be."

Wakefield's hair is gone now. Most days in the fall, his voice is gone, too.

But 49 years later, Wakefield still is pretty much the same guy now that he was back in that picture. And if you look close, you'll see he's wearing the same thing he wore throughout last fall's playoff run, rain or shine, snow or sun, winter or fall.

Shorts.

"With Keith, what you see is what you get," McDaniels said. "It's always been that way."

—*JOE SCALZO*

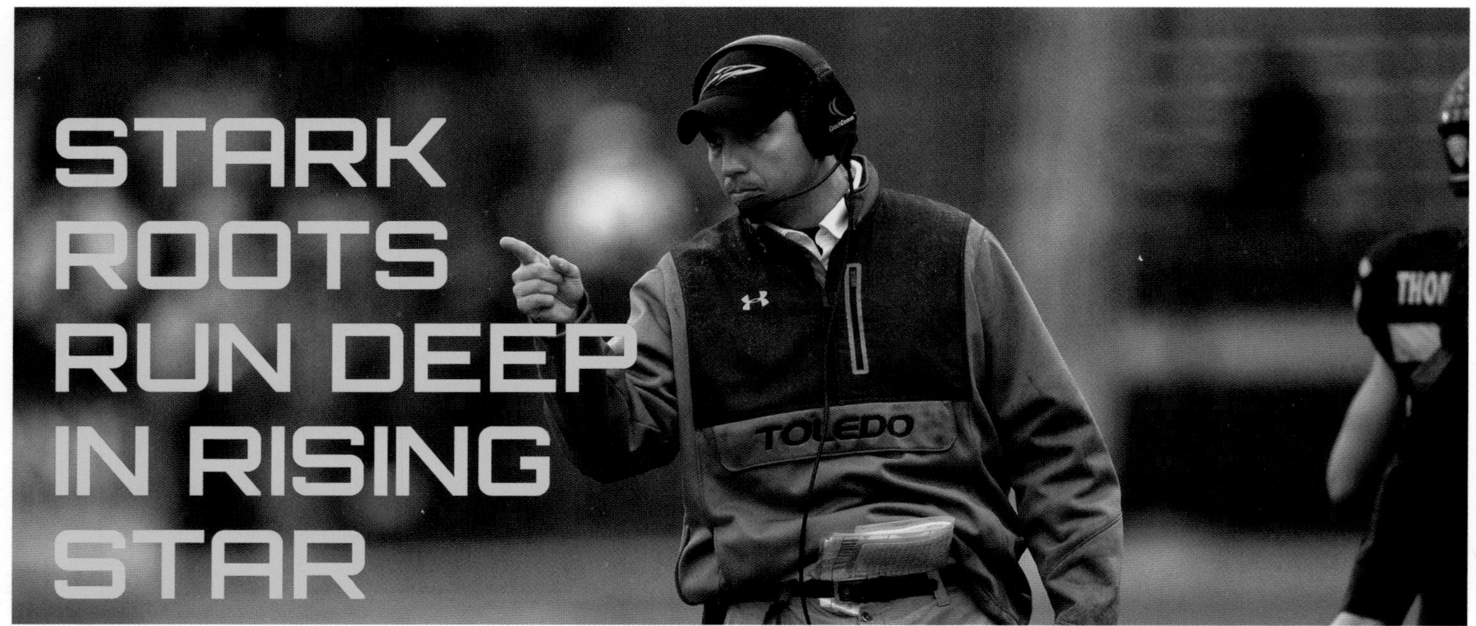

STARK ROOTS RUN DEEP IN RISING STAR

DURING A THREE-YEAR VARSITY CAREER AT PERRY HIGH, A HARD-NOSED OVERACHIEVER NAMED MATT CAMPBELL IMMERSED HIMSELF IN THE CULTURE OF A SUCCESSFUL FOOTBALL PROGRAM, ONE THAT WENT 21-9 WITH FEDERAL LEAGUE TITLES IN 1995 AND 1997.

Then he spent a year at Pitt.

"Even though I was going to have the opportunity to have some success on the football field, the culture of the (Pitt) program was horrific," said Campbell, now the head coach at Iowa State. "I never want a kid in my football program to feel like I felt during that year at Pitt."

After the Panthers' 2-9 finish in 1998, Campbell transferred to Mount Union, where he won three straight Division III national titles and was twice named the Ohio Athletic Conference Defensive lineman of the year.

"I think it changed my life; I'll be honest with you," Campbell said of the decision. "I was blessed to be at Perry High School and play for somebody like Keith Wakefield, with the intangibles and the discipline and seeing how he cared for us as players. Then I had a chance to go to Mount Union and be around Larry Kehres. Even though Larry and Keith are different as people, their cultures are very similar."I know if I had stayed at Pitt, I definitely wouldn't be where I am today."

Wakefield agrees, believing Campbell's story is a classic example of why it's more important where you finish than where you start.

"It's the kind of point I make with kids today," Wakefield said. "You have guys going to a school like Pitt to be on TV or be on a big-time D-I program, and it's just not right for them. Then they go to a smaller school and end up playing and being successful and they're happy as hell.

"I don't know if, in high school, he wanted to become a coach and if he stayed at Pitt, I don't know if that would have happened. But he got that liberal arts education and a lot of coaches come out of Larry's program. He ended up being ultra successful."

Campbell started his coaching career as a graduate assistant at Bowling Green in 2003-04, then spent two years as Mount Union's offensive coordinator, winning national titles both years. He returned to Bowling Green for two years, moved on to Toledo in 2009 and was elevated to the head coach after Tim Beckman left for Illinois after the 2011 season. During the next four years, the Rockets went 35-15, sharing Mid-American Conference West titles in 2014 and 2015.

Campbell was hired by Iowa State in December of 2015, choosing the Cyclones over a higher-profile job with SEC-member Missouri.

"For me, it's always been about people," said Campbell, 36, whose wife just had their fourth child, a son, in mid-February, 2016. "I had to learn that the hard way, through the recruiting process and all those things. I had an opportunity to do different things, but I was never looking for a new job or considering leaving Toledo, but seeing the culture and the passion and the environment out here, it was phenomenal."

Campbell isn't a system coach. He's a culture coach. He believes in Wakefield's philosophy that attitude and effort are more important than talent, because those things don't require talent.

"When you create that mentality in any organization, let alone a football program, you're going to have great success," Campbell said.

And while he may have left Stark County a decade ago to further his coaching career, it's clear Stark County hasn't left him.

"Growing up there had a profound impact on my life," said Campbell, whose father, Rick, was Jackson's head coach when it won its first Federal League title in 1986. "I saw the fabric that football played in that community and continues to play. It's really special. My time at Perry and playing for Coach Wakefield provided the baseline for how I treat football, how I coach the game of football, how I approach it. It's been a great journey and experience since then."

—JOE SCALZO

PERRY TOP TEN ICONS

1

KEITH WAKEFIELD Wakefield holds a 175-90 record over two stints with the Panthers (1982-2003 and 2013-present) with 12 Federal League titles, six playoff appearances, two regional titles (2000 and 2015) and a berth in the 2015 Division II state championship game.

<<< 2

DAVE RIGGS
Riggs coached 30 state wrestling champions, 48 state finalists and 175 state qualifiers while winning both the state dual championship and state tournament championship in 2014. Finished as state runners-up nine times over a 13-year stretch.

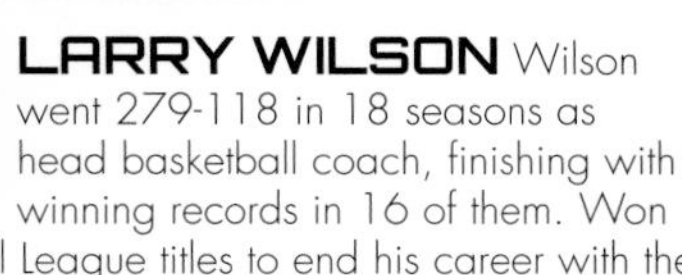

3

LARRY WILSON Wilson went 279-118 in 18 seasons as head basketball coach, finishing with winning records in 16 of them. Won six straight Federal League titles to end his career with the Panthers. Led the 1990-91 team to a 24-2 record before falling to eventual champion Cleveland St. Joseph 68-62 in the state semifinals.

<<< 4

STEVE LUKE
Luke won three state wrestling titles (2002-04) and finished second as a freshman (2001), helping the Panthers to back-to-back runner-up finishes at the state meet. Three-time NCAA All-American at Michigan and three-time Big Ten champion, winning an NCAA 174-pound title in 2009.

5

TIM LAPS A three-year starter at running back, Laps ran for 3,050 yards on 465 attempts, a school record that stood until Keishaun Sims broke the mark last fall. Helped the Panthers to their first 10-0 season in 1969, winning Stark County MVP honors in the process. Inducted into the Stark County High School Football Hall of Fame in 2008.

6

CHIP HARE The 6-foot-9 center was the best player on Perry's only state tournament boys basketball team (1990-91). Holds the Panthers' all-time scoring record (1,420 points) despite missing entire junior season to injury. Averaged 11.8 points per game at Dayton.

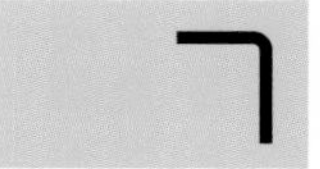

7

MATT CAMPBELL Campbell won conference football championships as a sophomore (1995) and senior (1997). After one season at Pitt, he transferred to Mount Union and was a two-time Ohio Athletic Conference Defensive Lineman of the Year and helped the Purple Raiders win three straight national titles (2000-02). Served as Mount's offensive coordinator in 2003-04, helping the Purple Raiders win national titles both years. Later became head coach at Toledo before moving to Iowa State at the end of last season.

NICOLE MARCELLI
Considered possibly the best all-around female athlete in school history, Marcelli, who also excelled in volleyball, track and softball, earned All-Ohio honors in hoops in 1985 and was a four-year letter winner at Vanderbilt. She was the Federal League and district player of the year in 1985. She also set team records for points, rebounds and assists.

<<< 8

9

STEVE FINK Fink won a state long jump title in 1979. Selected an All-Federal League running back in 1978. Also was a standout in football. Considered by some possibly the best all-around male athlete in school history. Still holds school records in the high jump and long jump.

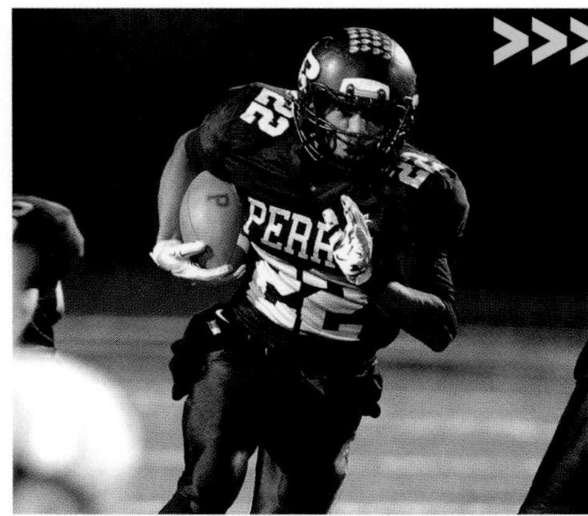

>>> 10

KEISHAUN SIMS Sims set Stark County single-season records for rushing yards (3,224) and touchdowns (43) to help Perry advance to the Division II state championship game last fall. Became just the second Stark County native to win Mr. Football, joining Hoover's Erick Howard (2008-09).

HONORABLE MENTIONS

KIRK BARTON
LANCE BURICK
DENISE CALLAHAN
KENNY FREASE
ERIC HEINZER
ARCHIE HERRING
BRANDON SMITH
DARCY WAKEFIELD
TOM WINKHART

COSTELLO'S NFL JOURNEY STARTED IN MAGNOLIA

AHEAD OF HIS TIME, SURELY. BEHIND THE TIMES, OCCASIONALLY. YET VINCE COSTELLO ALWAYS WAS A MAN WHO LIVED IN THE MOMENT AND WAS ABLE TO RELISH IT AS IT HAPPENED.

There were a lot of precious moments for Costello, an icon from the farm fields of Magnolia to the big cities of Cleveland with the Browns and New York with the Giants.

"If Vince Costello had played (most of his career) for the New York Giants and Sam Huff had played for the Cleveland Browns, Vince Costello would be in the Pro Football Hall of Fame," said Pro Football Hall of Fame Luncheon Club treasurer Dave Seffens, alluding to New York's media influence of the time. "They were the two premier middle linebackers. Costello was pretty awesome."

Costello wound up having a 12-year career at linebacker in the NFL. The first 10 were with the hometown Browns, who took a chance on a then-25-year-old Costello, who was not even drafted after graduating from Ohio University. Costello was a defensive anchor on the 1964 Browns team that won the NFL championship.

> "NO ONE WAS EVER BETTER THAN VINCE WAY BACK THEN. HE WAS GREAT IN FOOTBALL, BASKETBALL AND BASEBALL. HE WAS ONE OF THOSE GUYS WHO COULD DO EVERYTHING."
> —CLIFF FOUST

He played for the iconic Paul Brown and later coached the linebackers under Brown in Cincinnati, as well as for Don

Shula in Miami and ex-Brown Paul Wiggin in Kansas City. However, a young Costello actually coached high school basketball before ever playing a game in the NFL.

But I digress.

Costello was so ahead of his time that he played high school baseball at 13 years old. When he graduated in 1949, at 16, he was the star quarterback for an unbeaten Magnolia High School six-man team that had only been formed the year before at the urgent behest of Costello and his fellow Magnolia students.

"We were going to go strike if they didn't give us football," Costello told The Repository's Todd Porter in 2002 on the eve of Costello's induction into the inaugural Stark County High School Football Hall of Fame class. "And we were serious. The board of education had to give us a football team. There were enough for regular football, but we compromised on a six-man team."

His high school football coach was Cliff Foust. Foust came to Canton to endorse Costello's induction.

"He was a great quarterback and linebacker," Foust told The Repository. "Vince was a great athlete. I was in coaching for 50 years, and I had a lot of great players come through. No one was ever better than Vince way back then. He was great in football, basketball and baseball.

"He was one of those guys who could do everything."

And do it better than almost everyone else, too.

The 6-foot Costello played football and baseball for four years at Ohio University. Ironically, he went to OU on a basketball scholarship and played just one season. Furthering the irony, Costello went on to sign both professional

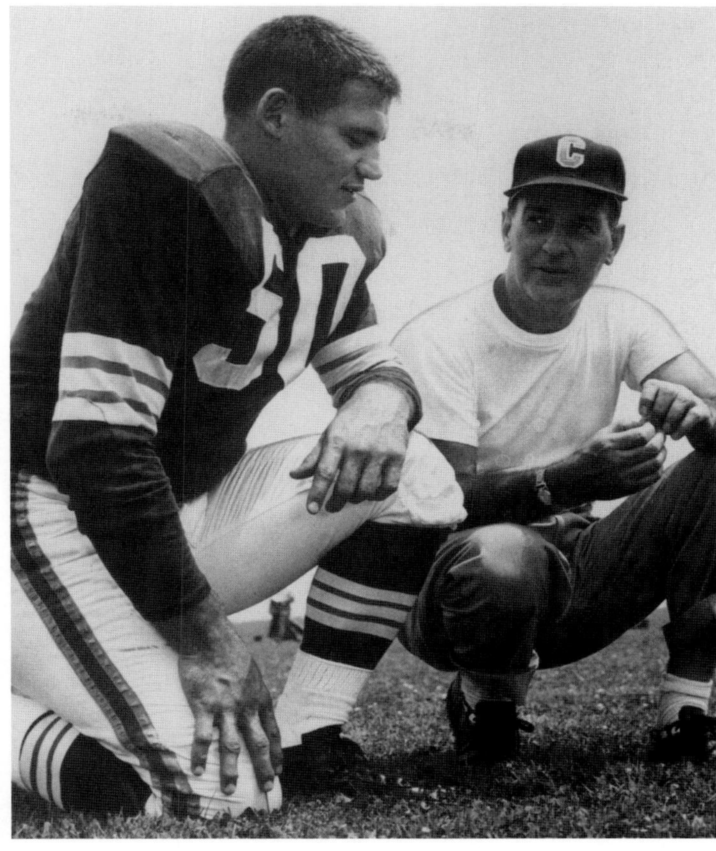

baseball and football contracts.

"I played basketball real well," Costello told the Hall of Fame Luncheon Club on a visit a few years ago. "Basketball is a sport that takes more quickness and moves than football. Football, it's a physical, hard-nosed, stick-it-to-them (sport). The movement in football is not like it is in basketball."

Costello was physical all right. His pro stats give him credit for eight fumble recoveries and 22 interceptions for his career, though he predates stats for tackles and sacks. He was tough, too. He missed just two games in his career in Cleveland.

But his pro football career nearly did not happen at all, and all because of baseball. Fresh out of college, he signed a minor league contract with the Cincinnati Reds in 1953. He had a decent season and went on to post a respectable .267 batting average in 123 games spread over four years. When baseball ended, he went to his birthplace of Delroy and coached the basketball team.

Then Costello was drafted by another organization—the military.

He "played" two years in the Air Force ROTC before being relieved from duty in 1956 and returning to baseball, this time for the Wausau (Wisconsin) Lumberjacks.

A call from an Air Force friend about football led to Costello contacting his former OU assistant coach, Howard Brinker, now with the Browns. Brinker got Costello to sign with the Browns. When he went to audition for the Browns, he ran a slow time because of a pulled muscle he had suffered playing baseball. Paul Brown was told about the injury after the fact and told Costello to heal up and come back the next year.

He did, making the 1957 Browns and intercepting two passes his rookie season. When Brown forged his own team, the AFL's Cincinnati Bengals, in 1968, it was perfect timing. Costello played two games for the Giants in 1968 and then began coaching for Brown in 1969. He coached linebackers for four years, then moved on to Miami as the defensive coordinator for Don Shula for two years.

"Paul Brown was a great coach," Costello told the Hall of Fame Luncheon Club. "I'm indebted to him; he's the guy who put me in football. I worked for him as a coach. I love Paul Brown. Paul Brown is not what people think he is. I always say that he was like a president of a university coaching a football team. He had a lot of dignity. He was good to me. I got along with him."

Coaching agreed with Costello. He was an assistant NFL coach for eight seasons, including defensive coordinator in Kansas City. But when there were no calls coming for a head coaching job after he left the Chiefs, Costello finally hung up his whistle in 1978. He went into the restaurant business in Kansas City and later opened a collectibles business there.

As high as he climbed in the football ranks, he never changed as the boy from Delroy who played six-man football for Magnolia.

"I really like to get back there," Costello told then-Repository sports editor Bob Stewart upon his hire in Miami. "The people are great. It's just a fine place, but I guess I'm a little prejudiced because I grew up there." —*JIM THOMAS*

THOMPSON DAZZLED AT WAYNESBURG, THEN IN COLLEGE WITH BEVO FRANCIS

> "WE THOUGHT WE'D WIN IT ALL. I GUESS WE THOUGHT WE KNEW EVERYTHING BACK THEN."
> —LEROY THOMPSON

WITH THE DEATH OF HIS WIFE OF 61 YEARS, SILVER THOMPSON, LEROY THOMPSON WAS DOING SOME REMINISCING ON A GRAY FRIDAY IN THE LAST WEEK OF FEBRUARY, 2016.

"We had a great life together," LeRoy said. "Our anniversary was Feb. 12, would have been 62 years. We were together 65 years, you know, dating and all."

To tell you how much LeRoy loved Silver, he said he gave up his first love: basketball.

"I played with Bevo Francis at Rio Grande," Thompson said of one of college basketball's most illustrious scorers. "We played in Madison Square Garden. We played down in Florida where they had the big tournament. Bevo scored so many points, everyone wanted to come watch us. He could really shoot. When you got him the ball, that ball was going in.

"I got to see the world. But that was it after one year. I wanted to get home and marry Silver. I wanted to get married."

That was a sacrifice, because LeRoy Thompson was the Bevo Francis of Stark County in the early 1950s.

When Thompson graduated from Waynesburg High School in 1953, before it became part of the Sandy Valley school system, he had scored 1,746 points. His Mohawk teams were County Class B champs every season. With Thompson, Waynesburg averaged well over 20 wins a year and reached the state tournament twice, the finals once.

"I was 6-foot-1, but I could jump," Thompson said. "I could dunk, but they wouldn't allow you to dunk. They would call a foul on you if you did.

"So I shot jump shots from the corner. I made a lot of 2-point baskets that would be 3-pointers today."

He never missed a game from the time he was a freshman. His 1,746 points stood as the Stark County career record until 1995—42 seasons.

"I never sat on the bench," said Thompson. "Walter Headley, he was my junior high coach and then he got the high school job. He gave me a shot. The (starting lineup) was all seniors—they didn't know I was that good."

Thompson said he had good teammates in the likes of John White, Don DelCorso, Ken Estee. With Headley and Thompson on board, they were good from the get-go.

Waynesburg went 21-2 in 1949-50 but lost to Norton in the tournament. In the 50-51 season, the Mohawks won their first 27 to reach the state championship game at the Columbus fairgrounds. There they encountered a huge Grand Rapids team that went 6-7, 6-6 and 6-4 in the frontcourt and lost 52-51.

"We should have won," said Thompson, who scored 21 points. "We didn't shoot very well. But give them credit, they won the game."

Thompson said his team should have won his junior year, when it lost in the state semis to Nelsonville 45-43 despite his 17 points.

"We'd already beaten a team that had beat Nelsonville," Thompson said. "We thought we'd win it all. I guess we thought we knew everything back then."

A loss to Canfield in the regional finals as a senior was so shocking to the victors "that they had a dinner for (the team), and they invited us," Thompson said. "They were so happy they won, I guess."

Thompson gave credit to the Waynesburg players that came before him, particularly Comer Biggums and Bernie Biggums, stars on the 1946 state tournament team.

"There was a big court down there in Waynesburg," Thompson said. "We would play against those guys that graduated. We played all day on Saturdays, played all night.

"They were men. They made us better. We usually beat them. But they would be back there the next day, ready to play.

"Those were the good old days."

—JIM THOMAS

SANDY VALLEY TOP TEN ICONS

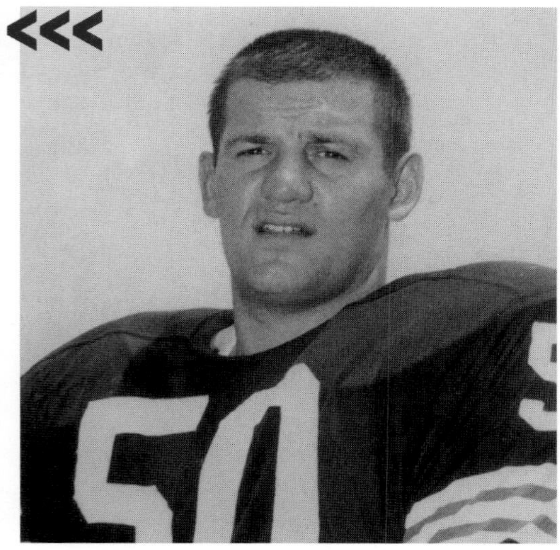

VINCE COSTELLO

The 1949 Magnolia High School graduate played linebacker for 12 seasons in the NFL, the first 10 with the Cleveland Browns. Costello later became a linebackers coach for Paul Brown's Cincinnati team, as well as Don Shula's Dolphins.

LEROY THOMPSON Starred on two Waynesburg teams that reached the state tournament in 1951 and 1952. Thompson's Mohawk teams averaged more than 20 wins a season over his four years. By the time he graduated in 1953 he had scored 1,746 points, the Stark County record until 1995.

3

JOE CRAILLIE It has been more than 20 years, but Craillie's state-winning long jump of 24-3.5 is still the Division II state record. The next year, as a senior in 1995, Craillie set the Division III record in winning again with a 24-1.25 effort. Craillie then was a four-year letterman at Ohio State, with a best of 25-9.25.

JEFF BOALS

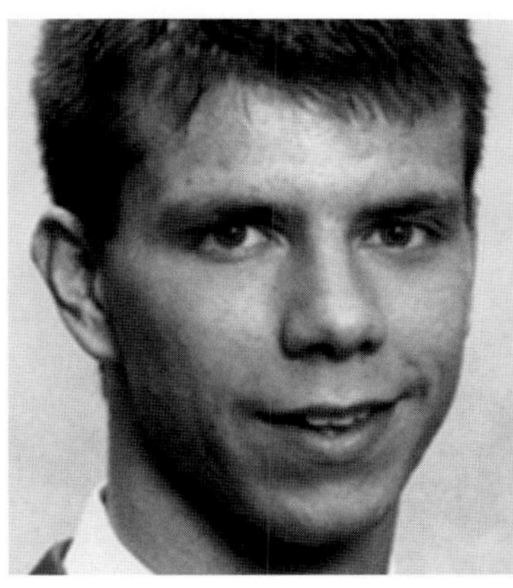

First-team All-Ohioan in basketball in 1990, the 6-6 Boals scored 1,064 points for the Cards. A knee injury forced him to walk on at Ohio University, where he was a four-year letterman. He helped the Bobcats to success in the NCAA Tournament and NIT. Boals then turned to coaching the college game, where he was an assistant coach for the Ohio State men since 2009 until taking over at Stony Brook in 2016.

5

LARRY "LUKE" IZER In 22 seasons as head baseball coach at Sandy Valley, Izer won 312 games and was inducted into the Ohio Baseball Coaches Hall of Fame in 1984. As a junior and a senior in the Sandy Valley system, the 1957 graduate earned All-Ohio football honors and played in the East-West All-Star Game. He was also a four-year starter in baseball and MVP as a senior.

ED LAUDERDALE Coached Sandy Valley track and cross country teams for 39 years, including a state runner-up boys track team in 1995. The 2004 Ohio Cross Country Coach of the Year, Lidderdale coached 74 state qualifiers, 32 state placers and four state champions. He was inducted into the OATCCC Hall of Fame in 2015.

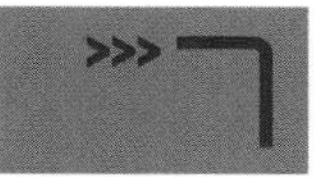

SAM GROFF

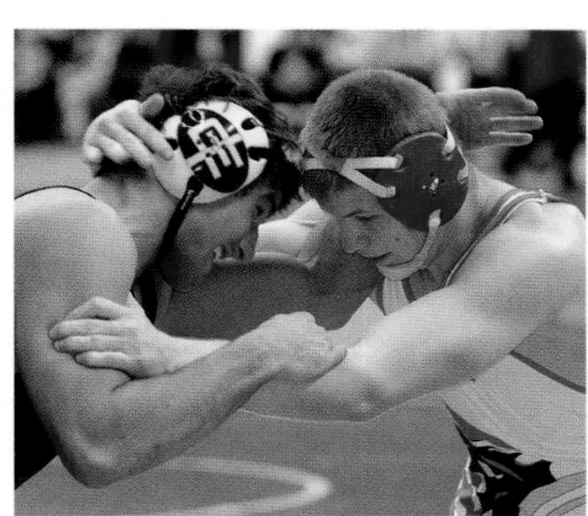

He was Sandy Valley's first four-time state qualifier in wrestling, a two-time placer and runner-up at 182 pounds as a senior in 2012 with a 56-1 record. His 193 victories are the county record. An all-county linebacker/quarterback for the Cardinals, Groff was the leading tackler for Baldwin Wallace in 2015.

8

JOHN BANKERT The 1958 Sandy Valley graduate was a three-sport athlete for the Cardinals (football, basketball, track and field), but Bankert will always be associated with football in Stark County. He started work at the Pro Football Hall of Fame in its library in 1964 and worked his way to executive director of the Hall during his four decades, as he oversaw three major expansions of the Hall.

JOHN GROFF Groff was the Cardinals' head wrestling coach for 36 years had teams that won 397 dual matches, fifth-most in Ohio history. He also was a two-time OAC wrestling champion and the OAC Lineman of the Year for Baldwin-Wallace's football team.

10

ANDRA LEHOTAY She became Sandy Valley's first girls state champ in track and field when she won the 800 meters as a junior at the 2015 Division II state meet. She also won the state indoor 800 earlier her junior season. She was fourth in the 1,600 at state as a sophomore and sixth in the 800 as a freshman. She was the only runner to defeat Aquinas 1,600 state champion Athena Welsh in 2015, when Lehotay won the 1,600 at the Stark County championships.

HONORABLE MENTIONS

MAJOR BARNES
JASON CALKINS
ANDREW MILHOAN
RON MYERS
GARY PROVANCE
JILL WILLIAMS

FORMER AQUINAS STANDOUT NEVER STOPS PUSHING HIMSELF

TONY MIGLIOZZI HAS TRAVELED THOUSANDS OF MILES IN THE AIR AND ON FOOT PURSUING HIS PASSION.

The North Canton native won't be slowing down anytime soon.

The winter of 2015-16 always will be a memorable period in Migliozzi's career as a distance runner. He won the inaugural International Association of Ultrarunners 50K World Championships race in Qatar. He also ran in the United States Olympic Marathon Trials for the first time.

At 26, Migliozzi is still in the early stages of what he hopes is a long, prosperous career.

It began at St. Thomas Aquinas High School, where he helped the Knights cross country team win two state titles. It continued at Malone University, where he was runner-up in the marathon at the NAIA Track and Field Championships.

Malone head distance coach Jack Hazen saw a competitor who pushed himself to eventually become a world champion.

"TONY WAS A GUY WHO I ALWAYS TRIED TO PULL THE REINS ON AND HE WOULD JUST DEFY THE ODDS. HE WOULD DOUBLE UP IN RACES. HE WOULD COME BACK REAL QUICK AFTER A RACE AND RUN ANOTHER RACE. HE'S STILL DOING THAT IN MARATHONS."
—JACK HAZEN

"He was always a hard trainer," Hazen said. "I spent the first couple of years trying to

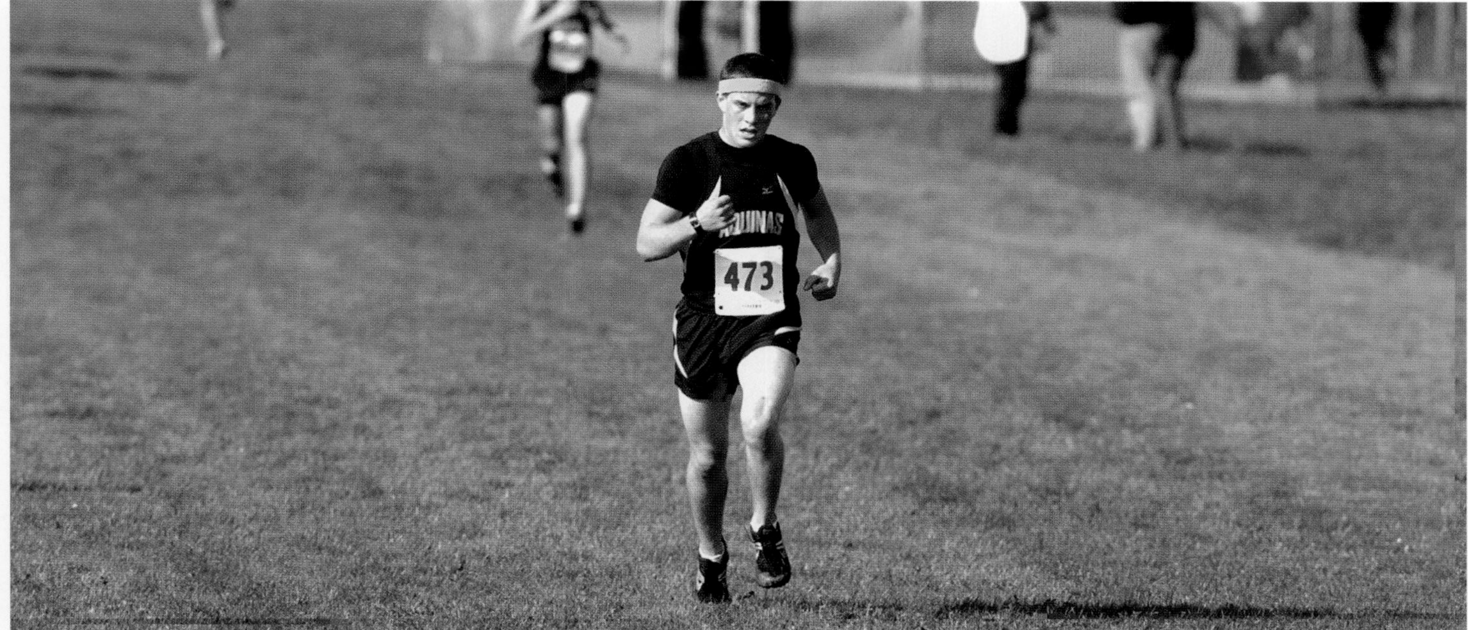

soften him up a little bit and have him step back. I was afraid he was going too fast and was going to get injured.

"Tony was a guy who I always tried to pull the reins on, and he would just defy the odds. He would double up in races. He would come back real quick after a race and run another race. He's still doing that in marathons."

Migliozzi made his marathon debut at the 2011 NAIA national championships. He ran seven marathons from 2014-15. A career-best time of 2:17.27 at the 2015 Chevron Houston Marathon earned him a spot at the Olympic Trials in February.

While training for a marathon in Chicago in 2015, Migliozzi submitted an entry to USA Track & Field for the 50K world championships. He was selected to represent the U.S. and flew to Qatar in December. It was the first time he ever traveled abroad.

Migliozzi overcame the odds on a hot, humid night. He completed the 31.07-mile race in 2:52.09, almost 3 1/2 minutes ahead of the field.

It took awhile for the victory to sink in.

"I didn't really expect to win," Migliozzi said. "That was a huge boost of confidence for me."

The 50K is 8 kilometers longer than a marathon. Migliozzi ran on a hard surface of cobblestone and tiles. The course required runners to complete a 5K loop 10 times. Each loop had four 180-degree turns.

Migliozzi maintained his initial speed and saw the gap between him and the leaders getting smaller. He caught the leaders at the 40K mark. One of the Kenyan runners kept pace, but Migliozzi began to widen the gap and ran uncontested down the stretch.

"At 47K, I had a pretty clear view of the course and realized there really wasn't anyone close to me," Migliozzi said soon after the win. "I was like, 'Oh, my gosh!' I was pretty much trying not to have a heart attack. I had the win wrapped up and was real excited.

"It was a surreal moment. I didn't really think it was going to be possible."

Hazen had no expectation of Migliozzi winning as he watched the race.

"I was just thrilled that he made the team," Hazen said. "I figured with the Kenyans, he probably wouldn't do too well.

"I watched the whole thing, and he kept moving up and moving up. He kept hanging in there, and I thought, 'Wow. He's going to finish in the top 10.' Then pretty soon, 'Wow. He's moving up even with the leaders.'

"When he took a three-minute lead, it was phenomenal. I couldn't believe it."

Migliozzi had just more than two months to recover from the 50K and prepare for the Olympic Trials. He spent time in South Carolina visiting family and training in warmer weather.

A piriformis muscle injury kept Migliozzi at less than 100 percent going into the trials. He made it past the halfway point of the 26.2-mile before he was forced to stop.

The 2016 trials likely won't be Migliozzi's last shot at an Olympic berth.

"I think 2020, maybe 2024 is where I'm going to be at my peak with my body," Migliozzi said. "Those will probably be the big years for me."

Some top marathon runners have competed for many years. At age 41, Meb Keflezighi will compete in his second Olympics this summer. He was the silver medalist in Athens in 2004.

"Tony is quite a ways off from that elite level, but he can keep improving," Hazen said.

Almost 10 years after helping Aquinas' cross country team win the first of back-to-back state titles, Migliozzi is racing among the giants.

"I knew my end game was the marathon," Migliozzi said. "I can do well in a 5K or 10K race, but honestly for me, it's more of a sprint and you just have to hang on the whole way. This, I have a little time to get into my rhythm, get into my zone, and I always was a real strong runner.

"Down the road, I knew the marathon was going to be my best distance." —*MIKE POPOVICH*

WELSH MIGHT HAVE EXCELLED AT ANY SPORT, BUT BECAME DOMINANT DISTANCE RUNNER

SHE COULD HAVE BEEN A CLUTCH CLEANUP HITTER, A DEFENSIVE STOPPER IN THE MIDFIELD OR MAYBE EVEN A SUCCESSFUL FREESTYLIST IN THE POOL.

Instead, Athena Welsh's legacy at St. Thomas Aquinas will be as a great distance runner and one of the most decorated athletes in school and Stark County history.

Welsh entered her final outdoor track and field postseason in the spring of 2016 as an eight-time state champion, including a combined seven state track titles, indoors and outdoors. In 2015, she won her first state championship in cross country.

"Amazing" is one word to describe Welsh's career. Here's something else amazing: She first took up running in eighth grade.

> "IT'S SOMETHING SPECIAL WHEN YOU HAVE SEVEN GIRLS COMPLETELY ON THE SAME PAGE IN THE SAME RACE."
> —ATHENA WELSH

"I swam and played softball for a long time, ever since I was like 6," Welsh said. "I never really ran. I did eighth-grade track, but I wasn't really serious about it at all."

There was no turning back after Welsh ran cross country her freshman year. She did it for the conditioning and to stay in shape for softball. Little did she know she would qualify for the state meet.

"I really fell in love with it," Welsh said. "Freshman year, it was my first time doing it. ... I think when I made it to state, that was really cool, and I was like 'OK, this is kind of like a big thing.'

"I stayed with it, quit softball and ran track my freshman year."

The rest is history.

Welsh won four state championships at the OHSAA Track and Field Championships during the 2014 and 2015 outdoor seasons, helping the Knights win a team title in 2015. Each year, she won the Division III state title in the 1,600 meters and ran on the winning 3,200 relay team. The relay also set a state record of 9:11.66.

Individually, Welsh set Stark County records in the 1,600 and 3,200. The 1,600 record had stood for 16 seasons before Welsh broke it at the 2016 district meet.

A long-awaited state title was claimed in the fall of 2015 when Welsh won the Division III race at the OHSAA Cross Country Championships. Her winning time in her final cross country race was a personal-best 17:58.6.

Welsh learned about a commitment to running from girls cross country head coach Eldon Jones and girls track head coach Randy Crawford. She also was influenced by older teammates Victoria Laubacher, Molly Pusateri and Amanda Vincent.

"They were the three I really looked up to," Welsh said.

Now she set a standard for other runners who are earning championship medals.

Sisters Kalee, Kacee and Hannah Soehnlen ran the 3,200 relay with her. Kalee Soehnlen also won the 800 at the 2015 outdoor state meet.

"We all push each other to do better," Welsh said.

Welsh, who signed with the University of Toledo in 2015, has been a part of three state championship teams.

Aquinas swept the indoor and outdoor track team titles in 2015. The outdoor team became the first Stark County girls team to win a OHSAA track title.

The Knights also won their first cross country state title in 2015, a feat that left Welsh and her teammates very emotional afterward.

"It's takes everyone on the team to win a track title, but it's a little different for cross country," Welsh said. "It's not just everyone on the team, it's everyone on the team doing the same thing, and you all have to be on at the same exact time, same exact race. It's something special when you have seven girls completely on the same page in the same race.

"It also was our first one, and my senior year. That made it more special, too."

—MIKE POPOVICH

ST. THOMAS AQUINAS
TOP TEN ICONS

1 ATHENA WELSH Entered her final outdoor track postseason with eight state championships, including seven in indoor and outdoor track. Broke a 16-year-old county record in the 1,600 meters at the 2016 district meet (4:52.09). Also set the county 3,200 record (10:38.34) during the season. Helped Aquinas become the first Stark County girls track and field team to win a state championship in 2015 when the Knights won the Division III team title. Won her first individual state championship in cross country in 2015. Her win helped lead the Knights to their first team state title in girls cross country, as they won the Division III championship at the meet.

2 TONY MIGLIOZZI Helped lead the Knights cross country team to back-to-back Division III state championships in 2006 and 2007. Was a five-time All-Ohioan. Competed on Malone's NAIA national championship cross country team as a sophomore and was national runner-up in the marathon at the NAIA Track and Field Championships the following year. Won the inaugural International Association of Ultrarunners 50K World Championships race in Qatar and ran in the U.S. Olympic Marathon Trials for the first time in 2016.

3 CHRIS SOEHNLEN Two-way lineman on the Knights' 1984 Division IV state title team. Made 114 tackles and was named All-Ohio the following year as a senior when Aquinas recorded 10 shutouts and was state runner-up. Three-year letterman at Michigan State and a member of the Spartans' 1987 Big Ten championship team.

4 JACK ROSE Guided the Knights to a Division IV state title in football 1984 and a Division IV state runner-up finish in 1985. Compiled a 42-25-1 record in six seasons (1980-85) as head coach. Later coached Massillon and GlenOak to state playoff berths.

5 STEVE BARR First team All-Ohio selection in football in 1974 when he helped lead the Knights to an 8-0-2 record and a state runner-up finish in Class A. Completed 68 of 152 passes for 1,257 yards and 10 touchdowns. Helped turn around a program that finished 1-8-1 prior to his first season. Two-year letterman at Purdue.

6 CELENA (McCOURY) MATTHEWS Won Division II state singles championships as a freshman in 1993 and as a senior in 1996. Holds the Aquinas record for consecutive wins.

7 MIKE RANALLI Knights' all-time leading rusher with 3,337 yards and 49 touchdowns. Averaged 5.7 yards a carry over three seasons. Helped lead Aquinas to a Division IV state championship in 1984 as a junior.

8 EMIL SOEHNLEN Won the Division III state championship at 160 pounds as a senior in 1989. Was state runner-up the previous season.

9 NATALIE BARONE Standout softball player who helped lead the Knights to a Division IV state tournament appearance in 2002 as a senior. Also starred in basketball. Still holds numerous school records set during a four-year softball career at the College of Wooster. Was voted North Coast Athletic Conference Pitcher of the Year in 2005.

10 JAY SPITALE The 1973 Aquinas graduate has served as head golf pro at several area courses. Developed the Spitale Junior Golf Tour in honor of his father, Angelo, for junior golfers in the area. Member of the inaugural class of the Stark County Golf Hall of Fame in 2010. First team All-American at Edinboro University, where he averaged 75.1 strokes during a four-year career.

HONORABLE MENTIONS

LLOYD BAGLEY
CRISSY (DIAMOND) WOODRUFF
TOM DIETRICH
CORY GLINES
CHAD GUIST
ANTHONY MOEGLIN
JACOB PAUL
PAM PIERO
RYAN SHAFFER
GREG SOEHNLEN
DAVE WASEITY

TROJAN PRIDE REMAINS STRONG IN BLACKLEDGE

FINDING TIME TO PLAY ORGANIZED SPORTS NEVER TOOK PRIORITY IN THE LIFE OF RON BLACKLEDGE AS A YOUNG BOY. A MUCH BIGGER PRIORITY WAS HELPING OUT HIS FAMILY BY WORKING WHATEVER JOBS HE COULD FIND AT THE TIME.

That all changed once Blackledge entered Timken High School.

So did the trajectory of his athletics—he continues to enjoy thoroughly.

"Timken gave me so much," Blackledge said.

Giving back to Timken became his priority in retirement, keeping him permanently intertwined with the school which closed in 2015.

"I have the utmost respect for that man," former Timken calls with Blackledge asking "what do you guys need" quickly turning into action.

"I'd say we need pancakes and orange juice for a breakfast and 50 pancakes and 59 cases of orange juice would be there the next day. ... He loved those kids and got to know all of those kids on a very, very personal level, and he made sure stuff done, he got stuff done."

That can-do attitude stems directly from his high school years.

It's why 60 years since graduating from Timken, pride in being a Trojan has never left Blackledge. And the only thing surpassing his pride in his alma mater is his appreciation for the path it sent him on.

belongs to Timken High School."

A star in football at Bowling Green, where he is enshrined in its athletic hall of fame, Blackledge went on to a successful career as a football coach for four decades. Retired since 1997, he now relishes his time with his wife of 57 years ("The beautiful Linda Saccucci from Timken High School," he says) and their three children and 10 grandchildren.

TODD AND RON BLACKLEDGE

It all started with him being a three-sport athlete at Timken, earning the school's top athlete award as a senior.

"He may have been the best all-around athlete to ever come out of Timken," late Timken basketball coach Fred Harold told The Repository in 2002. "And I was there for 39 years."

Blackledge earned nine letters in football, basketball and baseball. He was first team All-Ohio in basketball and baseball as a senior and made the second team in football. He set school records with three interceptions in a game and a 76-yard punt return for a touchdown.

"I'll never be able to repay Timken High School, it was just a blessing to me ... the coaches, the guidance counselors and teachers, the programs and experiences of Timken High School," he said.

Blackledge's love of team sports developed once he arrived at Timken. Before that, he spent a lot of time working jobs such as delivering papers ("I had a couple of paper routes going on, one in the morning, one in the afternoon") and setting pins at a bowling alley.

"Everybody had to work in those days, and we were no different," Blackledge said.

That left him little time for sports. His initial attempt to try out for basketball ended up with him being cut in the seventh grade when the coach just kept the first 12 kids he counted off. ("I never even got to shoot a layup. That was my introduction to athletics.")

A year later, his experience was much better.

"The new coach was Freddy Harold," Blackledge said.

Blackledge made the team at Belden Grade School that year. And Harold made quite an impact on him. Blackledge remembers thinking, "I'd like to be like that guy if I can."

The following year, Harold started coaching at Timken under Ken Kate, and Blackledge was embarking on his life-changing venture into high school athletics.

"When I got there, my coaches said, I think you can do this if you really try," Blackledge said. "They taught me. ... Their attitude was don't say you can't do something until you try it and once you try it don't give up, keep working at it."

Blackledge worked and saw his opportunities to be a Trojan as "a privilege."

"I took that all the way through my NFL career coaching," he said.

When he saw young kids asking his players for autographs, he reminded those players "it's a privilege to sign that little kid's autograph."

Blackledge loved the coaches who influenced him: Harold, Kate, Dan Risaliti, Al Michael. "They were like a father figure to me."

"They taught me the morals ... just teaching me from ground up how to treat your teammates and your peers."

Blackledge looks back almost in awe at being able to play in venues such as Fawcett Stadium, Memorial Field House and Cook Park.

"What an opportunity I had that kids didn't have very often if you didn't grow up in a place like Canton," Blackledge said.

He never forgot those venues, even when he coached for nearly 20 years in the NFL with the Steelers and Colts and entered some of the finest and largest stadiums in the country. He shared his memories with his fellow coaches and the players he coached, explaining why he still called Stark County home.

"I always said I was born and raised in God's country," he said.

He retired from coaching in 1997.

"Once I retired I really did try to make a concentrated effort to support Timken," he said. He hoped to help the coaches in making an impact on the kids like the coaches of his youth impacted him.

"I came from a very, very limited background as far as finances go and I just wanted to let the other people know who went to Timken, yeah you've got a chance," Blackledge said. Hairston loved that Blackledge was there for his players.

"He really got to know our guys, whether it was Darryl Straughter, LePear Toles, Chris Cook," Hairston said. "He got to know them well enough that if they were walking through the mall and saw him, they'd say 'Hey, Mr. Blackledge, how are you doing?' He had a relationship with them. He took the time to get to know them.

"I'm sure that meant a lot to them. And they probably got an understanding of the type of athlete he was. They knew he was pretty good back in his day, and it was pretty cool that 20, 30 and 40 years later, he'd still be there."

Timken's closing a year ago doesn't mean Blackledge has stopped watching or supporting area high school athletics. He has grandchildren competing at Hoover and Jackson. And, of course, his son Todd is the head boys basketball coach at Hoover.

"That's my whole life right now, and I enjoy that," said Blackledge, who turned 78 on April 15.

He remains a big advocate of not just sports, but any school activities.

"It can be a robotics program, a choir program, just let people get involved, find a sense of belonging by doing something."
— *CHRIS BEAVEN*

PONT'S FOOTBALL LIFE STARTED AT TIMKEN BUT LED HIM MANY PLACES

THE FOOTBALL LIFE OF JOHN PONT WAS A LONG AND INTERESTING ONE, TAKING HIM FROM CANTON TO CANADA TO A ROSE BOWL TO ... JAPAN.

He transitioned from being a star player—beginning at Timken High School—to a lengthy coaching career at the college, high school and even international level. He set records as a halfback and helped the Indiana University football team achieve something it had never done before or has done since.

He, in many ways, defined the football lifer.

"To me, the greatest sound in the world is the whistle that starts a football game in which I'm involved," Pont told the Los Angeles Times in the 1980s when he was coaching high school football not too long after being a Big Ten head coach.

At his core, though, his family knew it was more than football that kept him coaching.

"He did have a great love for the game, but one thing that my grandmother says now, too, is he loved teaching," said Pont's grandson, also named John Pont and also a college football coach. "He loved being able to help the athletes just become better football players and better men. And that was so important to him and that's what drove him more than just a love of football. He definitely did love football, but that (love of teaching) was his driving force more than anything."

Pont died July 1, 2008 at the age of 80. At 75, he was still a head football coach.

His coaching legacy lives on with his grandson, who is an assistant at Case Western Reserve University. At 32, the younger John Pont, too, is putting together a diverse resume. He's coached in the Mid-American Conference and had a chance as a young assistant to work at Florida State. "Whether Division I or Division III ... the driving force is to mold them and it's a special profession because of that," he said.

The younger Pont said he was "extremely close" to his grandfather. He does not recall the "specific age" when he realized his grandfather was a respected football coach "because it was always a part of my life as young as I could remember."

His grandfather's football journey began in Canton. As a 145-pound senior at Timken in 1944, he made The Repository All-Stark County First Team. He then entered the military for several years before heading to Miami University on the G.I. Bill.

At Miami, he became a record-setting halfback under two legendary head coaches, Woody Hayes and Ara Parseghian. He was Parseghian's first team captain in 1951.

"As a person, John could identify with everyone he met, from the janitor to the president," Parseghian said in a statement he released when Pont died.

Pont's first college touch of the football resulted in a 98-yard kickoff return for a touchdown in the 1949 opener against Wichita. He led the nation in rushing as a sophomore that year with 977 yards. As a junior, he ran for 67 yards and a TD in Miami's 34-21 win over Arizona State in the Salad Bowl to cap a 9-1 season. Pont ended his career with school records of 2,457 rushing yards and 27 TDs. He earned All-MAC honors all three years and was an honorable mention All-American twice.

Pont became the first Miami athlete to have his number (42) retired by the school in 1951.

After graduation, Pont returned to the military, serving one tour as a Navy submariner, then played one year of football in Canada in the Ontario Rugby Football Association, winning league MVP.

Pont turned to coaching in 1953, joining Parseghian's staff at Miami. When Parseghian left for Northwestern after the 1955 season, Pont became the youngest head coach in the country at 27. Pont's Miami teams won MAC titles in 1957 and 1958, played in the Tangerine Bowl following the 1962 season and went 43-22-2 over seven seasons.

Pont was then off to Yale, going 12-5-1 from 1963-64. Next he spent eight years at Indiana, where he led the Hoosiers to the 1967 Big Ten championship and their only appearance in the Rose Bowl. Pont went from Indiana to Northwestern, serving as head coach from 1973-77 and as athletic director from 1975-80.

Coaching and teaching, though, were still in his blood. He had three-year coaching runs at Hamilton High School in Ohio and College of Mount St. Joseph in Cincinnati. His football journey then took him to Japan, where he coached for 11 seasons. By that point, he had "retired" to Oxford. But even in his final years, he volunteered with the coaches at Talawanda High School.

The younger Pont is a graduate of Miami like his grandfather and got to spend considerable time with him during those years. He lived with his grandparents during his first year there, calling it "a great blessing."

"I got to meet some of his friends (from Canton) and hear their stories growing up from the neighborhood," Pont said. "To me, it was funny, like it came right out of Hollywood with all of their nicknames. There was the skinny guy named Fatty, nicknames that didn't make any sense. It was fun to hear it and meet them and hear their stories. He remained close with several of them."

Today, John Pont loves hearing stories about his grandfather, "and it always chokes me up a little bit." He strives to carry on his grandfather's legacy.

"The most important thing I learned from my grandfather is coaching is all about people, and that was always his legacy, how he lived his life," he said. "He lived his life treating everybody with utmost respect and care. And it wasn't just his players, wasn't just his bosses, it was everybody he came in contact with. That attitude of service and love and care for his fellow man just led to people wanting to play their hearts out for him, as well as just being a great guy to be around.

"It's something I noticed at a young age, and grew to understand more and more and more as I got older and got into coaching. ... I feel like through coaching, I've been able to do that as well. Players enjoy that relationship, and I have the ability to pass along things I have learned to them, especially the things I've learned from such a great man as my grandfather." — *CHRIS BEAVEN*

TIMKEN TOP TEN ICONS

1 **RON BLACKLEDGE** A three-sport athlete at Timken, the 1956 graduate earned first or second team All-Ohio honors in each. He starred in football at Bowling Green and earned a place in its hall of fame. By the early 1960s, Blackledge was starting a four-decade coaching journey, which included various college stops (including being the head coach at Kent State) before a 17-year run in the NFL as a line coach with the Steelers and Colts.

<<< 2 **FRED HAROLD** Earned his nickname "Mr. Timken" by spending much of his life involved with Timken. Among its first students when the school opened in 1939, he graduated from there in 1942. After enlisting in the Coast Guard for three years through the end of World War II and earning his degree at Kent State, Harold returned to Timken as a teacher, coach and administrator for 39 years before spending 14 years on the school board in his retirement. As the head boys basketball coach from 1961-76, his teams won 144 games, and he was known for his loud back-heel kick of the Field House bleachers to show his frustration with a situation.

3 **DON RISALITI** After starring as a quarterback at McKinley High School and Ohio University—and then joining the Army during World War II and fighting in Africa and Italy—returned to Canton to teach and coach at Timken. His 11-year run as head football coach of the Trojans was the program's best, producing a 54-40-6 record from 1952-62.

4 **JOHN NAMCIU** A four-year starter, he remains among Stark County's most prolific scorers, as his 1,633 career points still rank fourth in county history. He led the Trojans to an 18-0 regular season as a senior in 1959-60 when they reached the state semifinals. He also set Greater Canton and Field House records with his 54-point game against Ravenna as a senior. He later earned All-OVC honors at Murray State before starting a coaching career that included a stop at Sandy Valley.

5 **JOHN PONT** A 1945 Timken graduate, he became a star halfback at Miami (Ohio) under Woody Hayes and Ara Parseghian, running for a school-record 2,457 yards from 1949-51. He led the nation in rushing in '49. After a pro career in the CFL, Pont embarked on a long coaching career highlighted by winning more than 65 percent of his games at Miami and Yale before guiding Indiana to its lone Rose Bowl following the 1967 season, when he was AFCA Coach of the Year.

6 **MIKE MIDAY** A dominant 6-foot-8 forward, Miday averaged 23 points and 14 rebounds per game as a senior, breaking Namciu's single-game scoring record when he dropped 57 on Western Reserve Academy in 1976. He was one of the nation's top recruits and went to reigning national champion Indiana, but left after three games because of the rough treatment he received from Bobby Knight. Miday eventually transferred to Bowling Green, where he was a three-year player for the Falcons.

<<< 7 **RICK HAIRSTON** Compiled a record of 214-121 in 15 seasons as Timken's boys basketball coach before the school merged with McKinley for the 2015-16 school year. His final eight teams won 82.9 percent of their games, averaging 19.4 wins a season, winning seven PAC titles and two district championships. The Trojans won 68 straight league games that stretch. Also helped coach football and track at Timken. In his first year as McKinley's coach in 2015-16, the Bulldogs went 21-5, won a district title and reached the regional finals.

8 **HENRY BULLOUGH** An all-county football player, the 1951 Timken graduate went on to great success as a player and coach at Michigan State, as well as the NFL. He was a three-year starter at guard for the Spartans from 1952-54, helping them win a national championship in 1952 and win their first Rose Bowl in 1954. Bullough also played in the NFL and coached in the league for 26 years, helping the Baltimore Colts win a Super Bowl as a defensive assistant and serving as the head coach of the Buffalo Bills.

9 **KEN KATE** Guided the Trojans to three district titles and one state tournament appearance (1960) during 16 seasons as their head coach from 1945-61. His Timken teams went 213-119. Also was an assistant coach on two other district championship teams for the Trojans in the 1940s.

<<< 10 **JIMMAL BALL** A basketball playmaker with a flair, Ball dazzled fans in helping lead the program back to prominence under coach Larry Gerzina, as the Trojans reached the district finals his senior season in 1996 for the first time in 11 years. Ball went on to star for four years at Akron, earning induction into the school's hall of fame in 2016, and played professionally in France for more than a decade.

HONORABLE MENTIONS

ANGIE BONNER	AL MICHAEL	ANGELO SANCHEZ	TUBBY SIRGO
LARRY GERZINA	PERRY REESE JR.	ALAHNA SINGLETON	RON VAN HORN

STAYING POWER

IF IT SEEMS LIKES THERE HAS BEEN A KURZEN IN THE TUSLAW SCHOOL DISTRICT FOREVER, IT'S TRUE. IF IT SEEMS LIKE JIM KURZEN HAS BEEN PLAYING, COACHING AND TEACHING TUSLAW STUDENT-ATHLETES FOR THAT LONG, WELL, THAT'S MOSTLY TRUE, TOO.

"My dad was on the first Tuslaw Board," Jim Kurzen said. "My older brother played on all the sports teams. That's probably where I got the bug to play."

Kurzen was one of Tuslaw's earliest star athletes. He led the basketball team to its first winning season and then its first championship season. Next he became its first to play Division I basketball. Kurzen then became the youngest coach to lead the Mustangs in basketball, a 23-year-old a year out of college. In two stints, he coached a total of 15 seasons, producing some of its best teams. And oh by the way, Kurzen has coached Tuslaw's defensive line in football for three different head coaches during the past 15 seasons despite never having played the sport himself. He also has come back as an assistant for the boys basketball team the past five years. All while teaching for 39 years in the Tuslaw system. But Jim Kurzen may be the most unlikely candidate to have played major college basketball. By his own admission, he graduated Tuslaw in 1972 as a 6-foot, 140-pound guard. Worse, he was slower than his 6-9 college center Paul Griffin, "a point guard that couldn't keep up with the post player," Kurzen said of the future seven-year NBA player.

Yet there he was in Kalamazoo, Mich., barely six months out of Tuslaw, playing in his college debut as a freshman.

"The first game, the backup point guard was (out), I played half the game," Kurzen said. "The next game, against Michigan State, I started. I had to guard (Mike Robinson), the Big Ten scoring leader two years in a row. I held him scoreless the first half. He scored about 20 the second half (in a 76-73 MSU win)."

Robinson averaged 25.3 a game that year. His 24.2 career average is still Michigan State's record. That game was the start of a magical four years at Western Michigan for Kurzen. He played in every game, started them all after his freshman year. It was capped by a senior season that defied logic and branded the Broncos the 10th-best team in the nation by The Associated Press.

"It still seems surreal," Kurzen said of the 25-3 team that won the Mid-American Conference to become the school's first team to reach the NCAA Tournament Round of 32.

"WESTERN MICHIGAN WAS LOOKING AT AN ALL-OHIO KID. THEY WENT TO SEE HIM AND HE DIDN'T HAVE A VERY GOOD GAME. THEY ACTUALLY MADE A STOP AT MY HOUSE. THEY MADE AN OFFER THAT NIGHT."

—JIM KURZEN

That season, Western Michigan did the following: Won its first 19 games; was the subject of a Sports Illustrated article; beat Miami before more than 10,000 fans; lost in overtime at No. 8 Notre Dame and star Adrian Dantley; crushed Bowling Green for the MAC crown; beat Virginia Tech at South Bend for the school's first-ever tourney win; lost to No. 2 Marquette 62-57 in the Sweet 16 round.

"I made a couple big shots that helped us get to overtime at Notre Dame," said Kurzen, a 7.1-points-per-game scorer that season. "(Former Tuslaw coach) Dave Null said (Notre Dame coach) Digger Phelps said I was a below-average shooter, let him shoot. That felt good. Then we went back there two weeks later and beat Virginia Tech in OT.

"Marquette was No. 2. If we had beaten them, we would've played Indiana. That was the year they went undefeated. Just to play at that level, in those packed arenas, it was a dream come true.

"I never felt the stress. It was so enjoyable."

Kurzen had his reason not to worry.

"This might be trite, but it had to be God," he said.

Kurzen explained that he was 16 when he and his girlfriend found God at, of all places, Paul Brown Tiger Stadium. Former Browns defensive lineman Bill Glass spoke about his faith there one day, and it made a tremendous impact on Kurzen. He eventually became a leader of a ministry group at Western Michigan—"That was one of the biggest partying schools in the country," he said. "I still see some close Christian friends from Western Michigan."

Kurzen credits God and local high school coaching greats Null and Ken Newlon for getting him to Western Michigan.

"By my junior year, there was (recruiting) interest," he said. "Dave Null came to Tuslaw my sophomore year. There were about six games I went back between the JV and varsity, then he said I was starting varsity. Dave was a great mentor, a great high school coach.

"After my junior year, I went to Ken Newlon's camp. I had never even heard of a basketball camp. There was a big kid from McKinley there, one of Newlon's (players), and I guess I did pretty well. When Western Michigan was there scouting, Newlon gave me a good recommendation."

And God?

"Western Michigan was looking at an All-Ohio kid," Kurzen said. "They went to see him, and he didn't have a very good game. They actually made a stop at my house. They made an offer that night."

That meant that Dale Brown didn't get his man. The new Louisiana State coach wanted Kurzen, too; Kurzen stayed closer to home so his dad could watch him play some. Ironically, Brown did get to see Kurzen play. His last game was that Sweet 16 loss at LSU's Assembly Hall before 14,150 fans.

In another bit of irony, it was Null who got Kurzen onto the coaching sideline.

"My first year out of college, I was Null's assistant coach," he said. "When he went to take the Massillon job, they asked me (to take over at Tuslaw). I was 23. I wasn't ready. I wanted to coach but I had no great aspirations. No timeline. I just kind of landed.

"My first year, we beat Massillon (and Null) at Massillon in our first game. Then we beat Jackson at Jackson. I thought, 'This is as easy as playing.' Then we lost 40 in a row. Literally."

Kurzen got things going north before long. His 1982 team went 16-5, the '83 team 17-5 behind guard Fred Neil. His coaching highlight was in his second stint, the 1995 season.

"We went 19-5, but we were 6-4 at the midpoint," said Kurzen. "The team averaged 83 points the last 13 games. We lost to Orrville in the district final at Smithville. Orrville won state in Division III. My kids were mainly seniors. Everybody was trying to hold the ball on Orrville. They said, 'We can run with them.'

"We were only down 48-40 at half. We ended up losing by 16 but that was the closest game they had, even at state."

Kurzen is watching and coaching high school basketball again at 62.

"When Kevin (Lower) took over the program five years ago, he said he wanted an old veteran in the building," Kurzen said with a laugh. So there he was on the last Monday of February, scouting Aquinas, looking forward to a possible matchup with the Knights and Stark County's first-ever 22-0 regular-season team, Tuslaw.

Kurzen is still there, teaching eighth-graders at Tuslaw Middle School. Still there coaching basketball, and football.

"I still love what I'm doing," he said. "No regrets." *—JIM THOMAS*

FORMER SOFTBALL STAR WAY AHEAD OF HER TIME

IT HAS BEEN NEARLY 20 YEARS SINCE SHE SLUGGED HER LAST HOME RUN IN HAPPY VALLEY. THE 34TH OF HER PENN STATE CAREER WAS A RECORD-SETTER FOR THE NITTANY LIONS THAT STOOD FOR 15 YEARS, AS WAS THE 118TH RBI THAT ACCOMPANIED IT.

Oh how the game of girls softball has changed, said 1994 Tuslaw High School graduate Shannon Salsburg.

"My first three years at Penn State, I used a men's slow-pitch bat," Salsburg said. "It was 30 ounces. It was a K-Mart special, metal, thin, single-walled, not the double-wall of today.

"My kids today go with a 24-ounce bat. They know that lighter is quicker through the (hitting) zone.

"When I left Penn State with 34 home runs, I was in the top 25 (for NCAA Division I) for six years or so, before technology caught up. The bats are better, the ball has a harder core.

"At the end of the day, it's the same game. But the kids are more advanced—bigger, faster, stronger."

Salsburg knows all about today's college softball players. She has been coaching at the collegiate level since graduating from Penn State and helping Akron make the MAC tournament in 1999-2000 as an assistant. Successful stops at Arkansas and Kent State led to Salsburg being named Bowling Green's seventh head coach in 2007. The Falcons went 33-12 her first season. She was named Mid-American Conference Coach of the Year in 2012 when it posted a 36-22 mark. Salsburg's teams are the only ones to have hit more than 30 home runs in a season in school history, with a high of 47 in 2008. She spent nine years at Bowling Green before being hired as the head coach at Monmouth College in New Jersey last fall.

Just back from a spring swing, Salsburg said that coaching was all she ever wanted to do.

"I really did. My dad (Ted) was a coach at Fairless, Tuslaw and Field, coaching wrestling, football and softball," Salsburg said. "I remember in the fifth grade the teacher asked what I wanted to do. I said be a college athlete and coach.

"She said, 'No, that's not a real job.' "

That teacher was seriously wrong. Salsburg first went on to star on four Tuslaw softball teams that each came within an eyelash of the state tournament, as well as four good Mustangs basketball teams. She had an eye for the basket, scoring 1,211 points. "I was a power player," said Salsburg, a muscular 5-10 in her high school days. "A shooter in basketball, a hitter in softball. In basketball my senior year, we got to the first round of regional play. All four years in softball we went to the regional final—all four years we lost to Akron Hoban.

"It was too bad we never made it to state with all the talent we had."

Salsburg said five Mustangs in her tenure went on to play Division I softball. She wasn't surprised because her summer ball team drew some prize eyes.

"I played on a great summer team," she said. "We had Jackie Beavers from Warren Champion. She was one heck of a pitcher. Coaches from Florida State, Michigan, everywhere, wanted to see her. Myself and all nine girls wound up playing Division I. I still will say that Jackie Beavers is the reason I went to Penn State.

"She went on to become the first great pitcher at Tennessee, and the SEC."

Beavers wasn't the only star Salsburg dealt with. When she was an assistant at Akron, she worked with Kelli Metzger, who hit 57 career homers in her All-American career, and helped her to try and make the women's 2000 Olympic softball team.

"That was a dream of mine," Salsburg said. "I helped her train. That was my chance, through someone else, to have a chance to get to the Olympics. Kelli was one of the very last cuts on the Olympic team."

That was the beginning of her coaching career, which Salsburg said turned into the profession she dreamed it would be.

"And I'm going to keep coaching until I retire." —*JIM THOMAS*

TUSLAW TOP TEN ICONS

1

JIM KURZEN The Class of 1972 graduate and basketball star was the Senate League Player of the Year in helping Tuslaw to its first basketball championship and best season at 15-4. He started at point guard for Western Michigan for four years, including a 25-3 senior season in which the Broncos reached the Sweet 16. Kurzen coached Tuslaw's boys basketball team for 15 years during two stints, winning 16 or more games four times. He has also been a defensive line coach for the football team for the past 15 years.

2

TRACI ALCORN Tuslaw's first female star athlete, Alcorn capped her high school career by winning back-to-back Senate League MVP honors in volleyball in 1981-82. She moved on to Akron, where she was a two-time softball All-American on the Zips' 1985 national runner-up team and 1984 Final Four squad. She finished among Akron's career leaders in hits and batting average.

3

RYAN TRAVIS Travis was first team All-Ohio in football, rushing for 1,321 yards and scoring 166 points in winning PAC-7 Player of the Year in his senior season of 2006. He then switched gears as an H-back at West Liberty, where he caught 104 passes in 2010 and an NCAA-leading 126 in 2011 to make NCAA Division II first team All-American both seasons. Travis also scored 966 points on the basketball court at Tuslaw, including 377 (18.0) as a senior.

4

SHANNON SALSBURG A basketball-softball standout, Salsburg scored 329 points (16.5) as a senior in 1994 to finish with 1,211 for her basketball career. She then earned PAC-7 Player of the Year honors in softball. Salsburg went on to become a three-time captain at Penn State, setting school records in home runs (34) and RBIs (118) in earning All-Big Ten honors twice. As a head college softball coach, she earned Mid-American Conference Coach of the Year honors in 2012 at Bowling Green, where she coached for nine seasons.

5

CHASE HORVATH
Horvath won the 146-pound state championship in his senior year of 1996 to earn Stark County Wrestler of the Year in Division II-III and finish with 105 victories. He was the first Tuslaw football player to have 100 receptions; at defensive back he had 10 interceptions. He played football for Malone and is the head coach of Tuslaw's PAC-7 championship wrestling team.

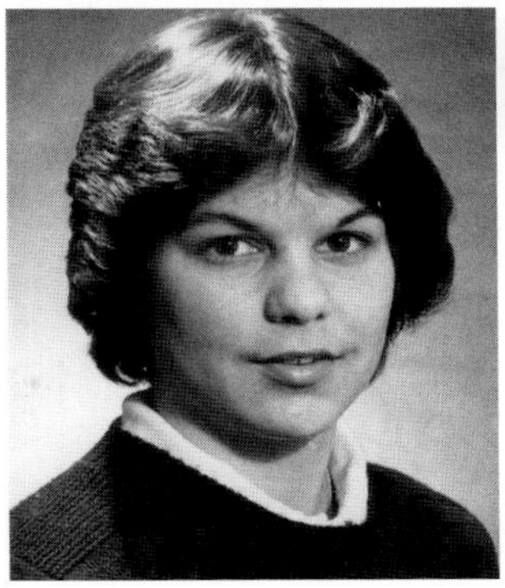

6

DARCY HUFFMAN
Huffman was a three-sport athlete, starring in volleyball, basketball and softball before graduating in 1983. In basketball, she averaged 29.7 points a game as a senior, set the record with 46 in a game and was All-Ohio in 1982 and 1983. Her 1,580 points are the career record and eighth in county history. She scored 1,095 points at Malone and later was the head girls basketball coach for Massillon. In softball, Huffman fired 12 no-hitters for the Mustangs.

7

FRED NEIL Neil was the first Mustang basketball player to score 500 points in a season, averaging 23.5 a game in a 17-5 senior campaign that saw the guard earn third team All-Ohio honors in 1983. He set the school single-game mark with 46 points. Neil, who has enjoyed a long high school coaching career in the county, finished with a Tuslaw record 1,168 career points.

8

BECKY HURD The 1985 graduate placed at the state track meet five times, with three All-Ohio finishes in the long jump. Hurd's 19-9.25 runner-up effort in 1984 stood as the Stark County record for 15 years. Her 5-8 runner-up finish in the high jump in '85 set the county record, too. She then lettered for Ohio State.

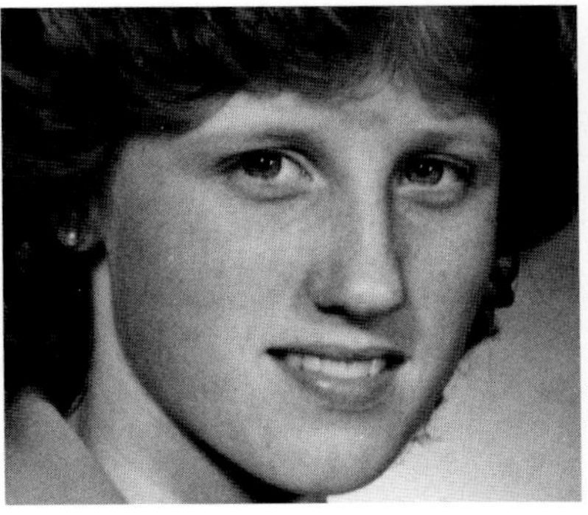

9

ROGER LOAR The school's first state wrestling champion, Loar was perfect in his senior season of 1987. He capped a 33-0 season by winning the 155-pound title to earn Stark County Division II Wrestler of the Year honors. Loar is a member of the Stark County Wrestling Hall of Fame (Class of 1993).

10

DAVE KURZEN The 6-6 Kurzen was All-Ohio in football in 2000 and twice in basketball for the Mustangs, including 2001 when he was the PAC-7 Player of the Year as a senior. Kurzen chose football in college, where he lettered all four years at tight end for Central Michigan.

HONORABLE MENTIONS

JIMMY DOWLING
JEFF MCCLINTOCK
FELICIA NELSON
DAVE NULL
KEN REED
COLLEEN WAGLEY
MELISSA WOHLHETER

CHRISTIAN SCHOOLS

HERITAGE CHRISTIAN
LAKE CENTER CHRISTIAN
MASSILLON CHRISTIAN

1 MATT HACKENBERG of Heritage Christian emerged as one of the county's top point guards and earned first team All-Ohio honors in Division IV as a senior in 2004 when Heritage was ranked as high as No. 7 in the Associated Press state poll for Division IV. He averaged 17.1 points per game and a county-best 8.2 assists, as the Conquerors went 19-1 during the regular season. Followed that up with a successful college career at Kentucky Christian, where he was a four-year starter. Returned to Stark County to coach and has enjoyed unprecedented success as the head coach at St. Thomas Aquinas. The Knights have won district titles the last four years, the first county school to do that since McKinley from 1974-77. They reached the Division IV state finals in 2014. Became head coach at GlenOak in spring of 2016.

>>> 2 SHANE BYLER of Lake Center Christian earned 12 varsity letters in golf, basketball and baseball—reaching districts in golf and earning All-Ohio honors in the latter two. He scored 1,042 career points in basketball. A first team All-Ohio infielder in baseball as a senior in 2009, he led the Tigers to their first district championship that season. After playing baseball in college at Malone he returned to Lake Center, where he is the head baseball and head basketball coach, in addition to being the athletic director. His basketball team won a school-record 19 games in 2014-15.

<<< 3 JENAE LINVILLE of Lake Center Christian, was a five-time All-Ohioan in track and field. Finished as the state runner-up in the discus as a senior in 2013—the only meet she did not win that season. She was a two-time Stark County champ in the shot put and discus, and set the Norwayne district record. Also played basketball and volleyball for the Tigers. Headed to NCAA Division II power Grand Valley State and reached the national meet as a freshman in the hammer.

KEVIN HERSHBERGER of Heritage Christian was four-year guard for the Conquerors, he helped them win their first district title in 1999 and reach the district finals in 1998. He scored 16.2 points per game as a senior, highlighted by 33 points against Zanesville Rosecrans, one of three 30-point games in his career. Scored 1,248 points in his career.

DREW SCHNEIDERS of Heritage Christian, led the Conquerors in scoring (16.5) and 3-pointers (62) when they won their first district title in 1999. Scored a team-high 24 points with eight rebounds in the district finals. Scored 1,088 points over his four-year career, making 112 3s his final two years.

JANA GLICK <<< of Massillon Christian scored more than 1,300 points and grabbed nearly 1,000 rebounds during a four-year career that saw her average a double-double over her career for the Chargers—17.3 points and 12.1 rebounds. Averaged a career-high 13.4 rebounds when the Chargers went 21-0 her sophomore season. She also helped the volleyball team to an unbeaten league season her senior year. Continued her basketball career in college at Kentucky Christian, earning NCCAA Division II All-American and Scholar-Athlete awards as a senior. Averaged 13.2 points and 6.0 rebounds her senior year for the Knights, helping them reach the NCCAA national tournament.

7 KATIE GRIMES of Heritage Christian, became the first Heritage girl to reach the state track and field championships as a junior in 2014 when she qualified in the 400 meters. Returned to state in 2015. The versatile Grimes left Heritage holding every school record in running events, except in the hurdles. Competes at Malone.

JEFF MAST of Heritage Christian The 1996 graduate scored a school-record 1,305 points, including more than 500 as a senior when he averaged 25.8 per game. Eclipsed 30 in a game five times that season, highlighted by 38 against Elyria Open Door.

CODY MILLER of Lake Center Christian set the school's career scoring record at 1,254 points by the time he graduated in 2008. That same year, he became the school's first player to earn first team All-Northeast Inland District honors.

MICHAEL PETERSON of Lake Center Christian helped the Tigers go a school-record 19-6 and become the highest-scoring team in program history in 2014-15 as a senior. He tied the school record by averaging 20.9 points per game, as the Tigers scored 68.4 a game as a team. For his career, scored a record 16.8 a game in tallying 1,075 points.

HONORABLE MENTIONS

RACHELLE BARTON
HERITAGE CHRISTIAN

STEVE DOLVIN
MASSILLON CHRISTIAN

CODY MILLER
LAKE CENTER CHRISTIAN

TRAVIS MULANAX
HERITAGE CHRISTIAN

ASHLEY PHIPPS
LAKE CENTER CHRISTIAN

INDEX